COMMON CORE MATHEMATICS

NEW YORK EDITION

Grade 1, Module 2: Introduction to Place Value Through Addition and Subtraction Within 20

JOSSEY-BASS™
A Wiley Brand

Cover design by Chris Clary

Published by Jossey-Bass
A Wiley Brand
One Montgomery Street, Suite 1200, San Francisco, CA 94104-4594—www.josseybass.com

ISBN: 978-1-118-79336-7

Printed in the United States of America
FIRST EDITION
PB Printing   10 9 8 7 6 5 4 3 2 1

WELCOME

Dear Teacher,

Thank you for your interest in Common Core's curriculum in mathematics. Common Core is a non-profit organization based in Washington, DC dedicated to helping K-12 public schoolteachers use the power of high-quality content to improve instruction.[1] We are led by a board of master teachers, scholars, and current and former school, district, and state education leaders. Common Core has responded to the Common Core State Standards' (CCSS) call for "content-rich curriculum"[2] by creating new, CCSS-based curriculum materials in mathematics, English Language Arts, history, and (soon) the arts. All of our materials are written by teachers who are among the nation's foremost experts on the new standards.

In 2012 Common Core won three contracts from the New York State Education Department to create a PreKindergarten–12th grade mathematics curriculum for the teachers of that state, and to conduct associated professional development. The book you hold contains a portion of that work. In order to respond to demand in New York and elsewhere, modules of the curriculum will continue to be published, on a rolling basis, as they are completed. This curriculum is based on New York's version of the CCSS (the CCLS, or Common Core Learning Standards). Common Core will be releasing an enhanced version of the curriculum this summer on our website, commoncore.org. That version also will be published by Jossey-Bass, a Wiley brand.

Common Core's curriculum materials are not merely aligned to the new standards, they take the CCSS as their very foundation. Our work in math takes its shape from the expectations embedded in the new standards—including the instructional shifts and mathematical progressions, and the new expectations for student fluency, deep conceptual understanding, and application to real-life context. Similarly, our ELA and history curricula are deeply informed by the CCSS's new emphasis on close reading, increased use of informational text, and evidence-based writing.

Our curriculum is distinguished not only by its adherence to the CCSS. The math curriculum is based on a theory of teaching math that is proven to work. That theory posits that mathematical knowledge is most coherently and

---

1. Despite the coincidence of name, Common Core and the Common Core State Standards are not affiliated. Common Core was established in 2007, prior to the start of the Common Core State Standards Initiative, which was led by the National Governors Association and the Council for Chief State School Officers.

2. *Common Core State Standards for English Language Arts & Literacy in History/Social Studies, Science, and Technical Subjects* (Washington, DC: Common Core State Standards Initiative), 6.

effectively conveyed when it is taught in a sequence that follows the "story" of mathematics itself. This is why we call the elementary portion of this curriculum "The Story of Units," to be followed by "The Story of Ratios" in middle school, and "The Story of Functions" in high school. Mathematical concepts flow logically, from one to the next, in this curriculum. The sequencing has been joined with methods of instruction that have been proven to work, in this nation and abroad. These methods drive student understanding beyond process, to deep mastery of mathematical concepts. The goal of the curriculum is to produce students who are not merely literate, but fluent, in mathematics.

It is important to note that, as extensive as these curriculum materials are, they are not meant to be prescriptive. Rather, they are intended to provide a basis for teachers to hone their own craft through study, collaboration, training, and the application of their own expertise as professionals. At Common Core we believe deeply in the ability of teachers and in their central and irreplaceable role in shaping the classroom experience. We strive only to support and facilitate their important work.

The teachers and scholars who wrote these materials are listed beginning on the next page. Their deep knowledge of mathematics, of the CCSS, and of what works in classrooms defined this work in every respect. I would like to thank Louisiana State University professor of mathematics Scott Baldridge for the intellectual leadership he provides to this project. Teacher, trainer, and writer Robin Ramos is the most inspired math educator I've ever encountered. It is Robin and Scott's aspirations for what mathematics education in America *should* look like that is spelled out in these pages.

Finally, this work owes a debt to project director Nell McAnelly that is so deep I'm confident it never can be repaid. Nell, who leads LSU's Gordon A. Cain Center for STEM Literacy, oversees all aspects of our work for NYSED. She has spent days, nights, weekends, and many cancelled vacations toiling in her efforts to make it possible for this talented group of teacher-writers to produce their best work against impossible deadlines. I'm confident that in the years to come Scott, Robin, and Nell will be among those who will deserve to be credited with putting math instruction in our nation back on track.

Thank you for taking an interest in our work. Please join us at www.commoncore.org.

Lynne Munson
President and Executive Director
Common Core
Washington, DC
June 20, 2013

Common Core's K-5 Math Staff

Scott Baldridge, Lead Mathematician and Writer
Robin Ramos, Lead Writer, PreKindergarten-5
Jill Diniz, Lead Writer, 6-12
Ben McCarty, Mathematician

Nell McAnelly, Project Director
Tiah Alphonso, Associate Director
Jennifer Loftin, Associate Director
Catriona Anderson, Curriculum Manager,
  PreKindergarten-5

Sherri Adler, PreKindergarten
Debbie Andorka-Aceves, PreKindergarten

Kate McGill Austin, Kindergarten
Nancy Diorio, Kindergarten
Lacy Endo-Peery, Kindergarten
Melanie Gutierrez, Kindergarten
Nuhad Jamal, Kindergarten
Cecilia Rudzitis, Kindergarten
Shelly Snow, Kindergarten

Beth Barnes, First Grade
Lily Cavanaugh, First Grade
Ana Estela, First Grade
Kelley Isinger, First Grade
Kelly Spinks, First Grade
Marianne Strayton, First Grade
Hae Jung Yang, First Grade

Wendy Keehfus-Jones, Second Grade
Susan Midlarsky, Second Grade
Jenny Petrosino, Second Grade
Colleen Sheeron, Second Grade
Nancy Sommer, Second Grade
Lisa Watts-Lawton, Second Grade
MaryJo Wieland, Second Grade
Jessa Woods, Second Grade

Eric Angel, Third Grade
Greg Gorman, Third Grade
Susan Lee, Third Grade
Cristina Metcalf, Third Grade
Ann Rose Santoro, Third Grade
Kevin Tougher, Third Grade
Victoria Peacock, Third Grade
Saffron VanGalder, Third Grade

Katrina Abdussalaam, Fourth Grade
Kelly Alsup, Fourth Grade
Patti Dieck, Fourth Grade
Mary Jones, Fourth Grade
Soojin Lu, Fourth Grade
Tricia Salerno, Fourth Grade
Gail Smith, Fourth Grade
Eric Welch, Fourth Grade
Sam Wertheim, Fourth Grade
Erin Wheeler, Fourth Grade

Leslie Arceneaux, Fifth Grade
Adam Baker, Fifth Grade
Janice Fan, Fifth Grade
Peggy Golden, Fifth Grade
Halle Kananak, Fifth Grade
Shauntina Kerrison, Fifth Grade
Pat Mohr, Fifth Grade
Chris Sarlo, Fifth Grade

Additional Writers

Bill Davidson, Fluency Specialist
Robin Hecht, UDL Specialist
Simon Pfeil, Mathematician

Document Management Team

Tam Le, Document Manager
Jennifer Merchan, Copy Editor

Table of Contents

GRADE 1 • MODULE 2

Introduction to Place Value Through Addition and Subtraction Within 20

Grade 1 • Module 2

Introduction to Place Value Through Addition and Subtraction Within 20

OVERVIEW

Module 2 serves as a bridge from problem solving within 10 to work within 100 as students begin to solve addition and subtraction problems involving teen numbers (**1.NBT.2ab**). In Module 1, students were encouraged to move beyond the Level 1 strategy of counting all to the more efficient counting on. Now they go beyond Level 2 to learn Level 3 decomposition and composition strategies, informally called make ten or take from ten.[1]

Though many students may continue to count on as their primary means of adding and subtracting, the larger purpose of composing and decomposing ten is to lay the foundation for the role of place value units in addition and subtraction. Meanwhile, from the beginning of the year, fluency activities have focused on the three prerequisite skills for the Level 3 decomposition and composition methods:

1. Partners to ten (**K.OA.4**).
2. Decompositions for all numbers within 10 (**K.OA.3**).
3. Representations of teen numbers as 10 + n (**K.NBT.1** and **1.NBT.2b**). For example, students practice counting the Say Ten way (i.e., ten 1, ten 2, …) from kindergarten on.

To introduce students to the make ten strategy, in Topic A students solve problems with three addends (**1.OA.2**) and realize it is sometimes possible to use the associative and commutative properties to compose ten, e.g., "Maria made 1 snowball. Tony made 5 and their father made 9. How many snowballs did they make in all?" 1 + 5 + 9 = (9 + 1) + 5 = 10 + 5 = 15. Since we can add in any order, we can pair the 1 with the 9 to make a ten first. Having seen how to use partners to ten to simplify addition, students next decompose a second addend in order to compose a ten from 9 or 8, e.g., "Maria has 9 snowballs and Tony has 6. How many do they have in all?" 9 + 6 = 9 + (1 + 5) = (9 + 1) + 5 = 10 + 5 = 15 (**1.OA.3**). Between intensive work with addends of 8 and 9 is a lesson exploring commutativity so that students realize they can compose ten from the larger addend.

---

[1] See Progressions Document "Counting and Cardinality: Operations and Algebraic Thinking," p. 6.

Throughout Topic A, students also count on to add. Students begin by modeling the situations with concrete materials, move to representations of 5-groups and progress to modeling with number bonds. The representations and models make the connection between the two strategies clear. For example, using the 5-groups pictured above, students can simply count on from 9 to 15, tracking the number of counts on their fingers just as they did in Module 1. They repeatedly compare and contrast counting on with making ten, seeing that the latter is a convenient shortcut. Many start to make the important move from counting on, a Level 2 strategy, to make ten, a Level 3 strategy, persuaded by confidence in their increasing skill and the joy of the shortcut. This is a critical step in building flexible part–whole thinking whereby students see numbers as parts and wholes, rather than as discrete counts or one part and some ones. 5-groups will begin to be thought of as ten-frames, focusing on the usefulness of trying to group 10 when possible. This empowers them in later modules and future grade levels to compose and decompose place value units and work adeptly with the four operations. For example, in Grade 1, this will be applied in later modules to solve problems such as $18 + 6$, $27 + 9$, $36 + 6$, $49 + 7$, and others (**1.OA.3**).

To introduce students to the take from ten strategy, Topic B opens with questions such as, "Mary has two plates of cookies, one with 10 and one with 2. At the party, 9 cookies were eaten from the plate with 10 cookies. How many cookies were left after the party?" $10 - 9 = 1$ and $1 + 2 = 3$. Students then reinterpret the story to see its solution can also be written as $12 - 9$.

Level 2: Count on   Level 3: Decompose ten and
                                        compose with the ones

Students relate counting on and subtraction as pictured above. Notice the model is identical but the thinking is very different.

S: To solve $12 - 9$, I count on from 9 to 12, niiiine, 10, 11, 12, three counts. → To solve $12 - 9$, I make 12 into 10 and 2 and subtract 9 from ten. $1 + 2 = 3$.

Students practice a pattern of action, take from ten and add the ones, as they face different contexts in word problems (**MP.8**), e.g., "Maria has 12 snowballs. She threw 8 of them. How many does she have left?" (**1.OA.3**). This is important foundational work for decomposing in the context of subtraction problem solving in Grade 2, e.g., "Hmmm. $32 - 17$, do I take 7 ones from 2 ones or from a ten?" Students will use horizontal linear models of 5-groups, or ten-frames to begin the transition towards a unit of ten, as shown in the above image.

Topic C presents students with opportunities to solve varied *add to with change unknown*, *take from with change unknown*, *put together with addend unknown*, and *take apart with addend unknown* word problems. These situations give ample time for exploring strategies for finding a missing part. The module has focused on counting on and subtracting by decomposing and composing (**1.OA.1**). These lessons open up the possibilities to include other Level 3 strategies, e.g., $12 - 3 = 12 - 2 - 1$.[2] Teachers can include or adjust such strategy use, as they feel the new perspective will enhance understanding or if it will overwhelm or undermine. The topic closes with a lesson to further solidify their understanding of the equal sign as it has been applied throughout the module. Students match equivalent expressions to construct true number sentences and explain their reasoning using words, pictures, and numbers, e.g., $12 - 7 = 3 + 2$, $10 + 5 = 9 + 6$ (**1.OA.7**).

In Topic D, after all their work with 10, the module culminates naming a ten (**1.NBT.2a**). Familiar representations of teen numbers, such as two 5-groups, the Rekenrek, and 10 fingers, are all renamed as a ten and some ones (**1.NBT2b**) rather than 10 ones and some more ones (**K.NBT.1**). The ten is shifting to being one unit, a structure from which they can compose and decompose teen numbers (**1.NBT.2b**, **MP.7**). This significant step forward sets the stage for understanding all the numbers within 100 as composed of a number of units of ten and some ones (**1.NBT.2b**). The horizontal linear 5-groups modeling of 10 will be moved to a vertical representation in preparation for this next stage, in Module 4, as shown in the image on the right. This topic's work is done while solving both abstract equations and contextualized word problems.

a ten
represented
as a 5-group
column

---

[2] See Progressions Document "Counting and Cardinality: Operations and Algebraic Thinking," p. 14.

![COMMON CORE logo] **Module 2:**   Introduction to Place Value Through Addition and Subtraction
                                  Within 20
                     Date: 7/3/13

iv

Distribution of Instructional Minutes

This diagram represents a suggested distribution of instructional minutes based on the emphasis of particular lesson components in different lessons throughout the module.

■ **Fluency Practice**
■ **Concept Development**
■ **Application Problems**
■ **Student Debrief**

MP = Mathematical Practice

Focus Grade Level Standards

Represent and solve problems involving addition and subtraction.

1.OA.1 Use addition and subtraction within 20 to solve word problems involving situations of adding to, taking from, putting together, taking apart, and comparing, with unknowns in all positions, e.g., by using objects, drawings, and equations with a symbol for the unknown number to represent the problem.

1.OA.2 Solve word problems that call for addition of three whole numbers whose sum is less than or equal to 20, e.g., by using objects, drawings, and equations with a symbol for the unknown number to represent the problem.

Understand and apply properties of operations and the relationship between addition and subtraction.

1.OA.3 Apply properties of operations as strategies to add and subtract. (Students need not use formal terms for these properties.) *Examples: If 8 + 3 = 11 is known, then 3 + 8 = 11 is also known. (Commutative property of addition.) To add 2 + 6 + 4, the second two numbers can be added to make a ten, so 2 + 6 + 4 = 2 + 10 = 12. (Associative property of addition.)*

1.OA.4 Understand subtraction as an unknown-addend problem. *For example, subtract 10 – 8 by finding the number that makes 10 when added to 8.*

Add and subtract within 20.[3]

1.OA.6 Add and subtract within 20, demonstrating fluency for addition and subtraction within 10. Use mental strategies such as counting on; making ten (e.g., 8 + 6 = 8 + 2 + 4 = 10 + 4 = 14); decomposing a number leading to a ten (e.g., 13 – 4 = 13 – 3 – 1 = 10 – 1 = 9); using the relationship between addition and subtraction (e.g., knowing that 8 + 4 = 12, one knows 12 – 8 = 4); and creating equivalent but easier or known sums (e.g., adding 6 + 7 by creating the known equivalent 6 + 6 + 1 = 12 + 1 = 13).

Understand place value.[4]

1.NBT.2 Understand that the two digits of a two-digit number represent amounts of tens and ones. Understand the following as special cases:

    a. 10 can be thought of as a bundle of ten ones—called a "ten."

    b. The numbers from 11 to 19 are composed of a ten and one, two, three, four, five, six, seven, eight, or nine ones.

---

[3] The balance of this cluster is addressed in Module 1.

[4] The focus in this module is on numbers to 20. The balance of this cluster is addressed in Modules 4 and 6.

Foundational Standards

K.OA.3 Decompose numbers less than or equal to 10 into pairs in more than one way, e.g., by using objects or drawings, and record each decomposition by a drawing or equation (e.g., $5 = 2 + 3$ and $5 = 4 + 1$).

K.OA.4 For any number from 1 to 9, find the number that makes 10 when added to the given number, e.g., by using objects or drawings, and record the answer with a drawing or equation.

K.NBT.1 Compose and decompose numbers from 11 to 19 into ten ones and some further ones, e.g., by using objects or drawings, and record each composition or decomposition by a drawing or equation (e.g., $18 = 10 + 8$); understand that these numbers are composed of ten ones and one, two, three, four, five, six, seven, eight, or nine ones.

Focus Standards for Mathematical Practice

MP.2 **Reason abstractly and quantitatively.** Students solve *change unknown* problem types such as, "Maria has 8 snowballs. Tony has 15 snowballs. Maria wants to have the same number of snowballs as Tony. How many more snowballs does Maria need to have the same number as Tony?" They write the equation $8 + \_\_ = 15$ to describe the situation, make ten or count on to 15 to find the answer of 7, and reason abstractly to make a connection to subtraction, that the same problem can be solved using $15 - 8 = \_\_$.

MP.4 **Model with mathematics.** Students use 5-groups, number bonds, and equations to represent decompositions when both subtracting from the teens and adding to make teens when crossing the ten.

MP.7 **Look for and make use of structure.** This module introduces students to the unit *ten*. Students use the structure of the ten to add within the teens, to add to the teens, and to subtract from the teens. For example, $14 + 3 = 10 + 4 + 3 = 17$, $8 + 5 = 8 + 2 + 3 = 10 + 3$ and conversely, $13 - 5 = 10 - 5 + 3 = 5 + 3$.

MP.8 **Look for and make use of repeated reasoning.** Students realize that when adding 9 to a number 1–9, they can complete the ten by decomposing the other addend into "1 and __." They internalize the commutative and associative properties, looking for ways to make ten within situations and equations.

Overview of Module Topics and Lesson Objectives

Standards		Topics and Objectives	Days
1.OA.1 **1.OA.2** **1.OA.3** **1.OA.6**	A	**Counting On or Making Ten to Solve *Result Unknown* Problems**	11
		Lesson 1: Solve word problems with three addends, two of which make ten.	
		Lesson 2: Use the associative and commutative properties to make ten with three addends.	
		Lessons 3–4: Make ten when one addend is 9.	
		Lesson 5: Compare efficiency of counting on and making ten when one addend is 9.	
		Lesson 6: Use the commutative property to make ten.	
		Lessons 7–8: Make ten when one addend is 8.	
		Lesson 9: Compare efficiency of counting on and making ten when one addend is 8.	
		Lesson 10: Solve problems with addends of 7, 8, and 9.	
		Lesson 11: Share and critique peer solution strategies for *put together with result unknown* word problems.	
		Mid-Module Assessment: Topic A (assessment 1 day, return 1 day, remediation or further applications 1 day)	3
1.OA.1 **1.OA.3** **1.OA.4** **1.OA.6** 1.OA.5 1.OA.7	B	**Counting On or Taking from Ten to Solve *Result Unknown* Problems**	10
		Lessons 12–13: Solve word problems with subtraction of 9 from 10.	
		Lessons 14–15: Model subtraction of 9 from teen numbers.	
		Lesson 16: Relate counting on to making ten and taking from ten.	
		Lessons 17–18: Model subtraction of 8 from teen numbers.	
		Lesson 19: Compare efficiency of counting on and taking from ten.	
		Lesson 20: Subtract 7, 8, and 9 from teen numbers.	
		Lesson 21: Share and critique peer solution strategies for *take from with result unknown* and *take apart with addend unknown* word problems from the teens.	

Standards		Topics and Objectives	Days
1.OA.1 **1.OA.3** **1.OA.4** **1.OA.6** 1.OA.5 1.OA.7 1.OA.8	C	**Strategies for Solving *Change* or *Addend Unknown* Problems** Lesson 22: Solve *put together/take apart with addend unknown* word problems and relate counting on to the take from ten strategy. Lesson 23: Solve *add to with change unknown* problems, relating varied addition and subtraction strategies. Lesson 24: Strategize to solve *take from with change unknown* problems. Lesson 25: Strategize and apply understanding of the equal sign to solve equivalent expressions.	4
1.OA.1 **1.NBT.2a** **1.NBT.2b** 1.NBT.5	D	**Varied Problems with Decompositions of Teen Numbers as 1 Ten and Some Ones** Lesson 26: Identify 1 ten as a unit by renaming representations of 10. Lesson 27: Solve addition and subtraction problems decomposing and composing teen numbers as 1 ten and some ones. Lesson 28: Solve addition problems using ten as a unit, and write two-step solutions. Lesson 29: Solve subtraction problems using ten as a unit, and write two-step solutions.	4
		End-of-Module Assessment: Topics A–D (assessment 1 day, return 1 day, remediation or further applications 1 day)	3
Total Number of Instructional Days			35

Terminology

New or Recently Introduced Terms

- A ten (Students will focus mainly on *one* ten during this module.)
- Ones (These are individual units, ten of which become a ten.)

Familiar Terms and Symbols[5]

- 5-Groups
- Add
- Equals
- Number bonds

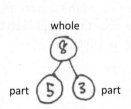

whole

part   part

Number Bond

a ten
represented
as a 5-group
column

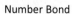

[5] These are terms and symbols students have seen previously.

- Partners to ten
- Subtract
- Teen numbers

Suggested Tools and Representations

- 5-Group formations: 5-groups (and 5-group cards), 5-group rows, 5-group column
- Hide Zero cards
- Number bonds
- Number path
- Rekenrek

Numerals

5-Groups

5-Group Cards

5-Group Rows

$6 + \_ = 9$

$9 - 6 = \_$

Number Path

Rekenrek

5-Group Column

Hide Zero Cards

Scaffolds[6]

The scaffolds integrated into *A Story of Units* give alternatives for how students access information as well as express and demonstrate their learning. Strategically placed margin notes are provided within each lesson elaborating on the use of specific scaffolds at applicable times. They address many needs presented by English language learners, students with disabilities, students performing above grade level, and students performing below grade level. Many of the suggestions are applicable to more than one population. The charts included in Module 1 provide a general overview of the lesson-aligned scaffolds, organized by Universal Design for Learning (UDL) principles. To read more about the approach to differentiated instruction in *A Story of Units*, please refer to "How to Implement *A Story of Units*."

---

[6] Students with disabilities may require Braille, large print, audio, or special digital files. Please visit the website, www.p12.nysed.gov/specialed/aim, for specific information on how to obtain student materials that satisfy the National Instructional Materials Accessibility Standard (NIMAS) format.

Assessment Summary

Type	Administered	Format	Standards Addressed
Mid-Module Assessment Task	After Topic A	Constructed response with rubric	1.OA.1 1.OA.2 1.OA.3 1.OA.6
End-of-Module Assessment Task	After Topic D	Constructed response with rubric	1.OA.1 1.OA.2 1.OA.3 1.OA.4 1.OA.6 1.NBT.2a 1.NBT.2b

Module 2:   Introduction to Place Value Through Addition and Subtraction
Within 20
Date: 7/3/13

xi

Mathematics Curriculum

Topic A

Counting On or Making Ten to Solve *Result Unknown* Problems

1.OA.1, 1.OA.2, 1.OA.3, 1.OA.6

Focus Standard:	1.OA.1	Use addition and subtraction within 20 to solve word problems involving situations of adding to, taking from, putting together, taking apart, and comparing, with unknowns in all positions, e.g., by using objects, drawings, and equations with a symbol for the unknown number to represent the problem.
	1.OA.2	Solve word problems that call for addition of three whole numbers whose sum is less than or equal to 20, e.g., by using objects, drawings, and equations with a symbol for the unknown number to represent the problem.
	1.OA.3	Apply properties of operations as strategies to add and subtract. (Students need not use formal terms for these properties.) *Examples: If 8 + 3 = 11 is known, then 3 + 8 = 11 is also known. (Commutative property of addition.) To add 2 + 6 + 4, the second two numbers can be added to make a ten, so 2 + 6 + 4 = 2 + 10 = 12. (Associative property of addition.)*
	1.OA.6	Add and subtract within 20, demonstrating fluency for addition and subtraction within 10. Use mental strategies such as counting on; making ten (e.g., 8 + 6 = 8 + 2 + 4 = 10 + 4 = 14); decomposing a number leading to a ten (e.g., 13 − 4 = 13 − 3 − 1 = 10 − 1 = 9); using the relationship between addition and subtraction (e.g., knowing that 8 + 4 = 12, one knows 12 − 8 = 4); and creating equivalent but easier or known sums (e.g., adding 6 + 7 by creating the known equivalent 6 + 6 + 1 = 12 + 1 = 13).
Instructional Days:	11	
Coherence -Links from:	GK–M4	Number Pairs, Addition and Subtraction to 10
-Links to:	G2–M3	Place Value, Counting, and Comparison of Numbers to 1000
	G2–M5	Addition and Subtraction Within 1000 with Word Problems to 100

Topic A begins with students solving word problems with three addends (**1.OA.2**) as a way for them to begin to explore the make ten Level 3 strategy in a meaningful context. With problems that always include at least two numbers that yield 10 when added together, Lesson 1 encourages students to use the associative and commutative properties as they set up and read equations in various ways. The story problem on the right, for instance, can be solved by adding 1 + 9 first, then adding the five (see image below story problem).

We had 1 upper grade buddy come visit, with 9 more buddies following him. Soon after that, 5 more buddies came to our classroom. How many buddies came altogether?

$1 + 9 + 5$
$10 + 5 = 15$

$9 + 1 = 10$
$10 + 5 = 15$

This leads into Lesson 2's focus of explicitly using the associative and commutative properties[1] to add three addends without the context of story problems (**1.OA.3**). This lesson is where students practice associating the two addends that make ten (**1.OA.6**), and then adding the third addend; they prove to themselves that this simplification of addition is a viable strategy.

Following this introduction, Lessons 3, 4, and 5 afford students ample practice with adding 9 and another single-digit number as they decompose the second addend to make ten with the 9. Students solve problems such as, "Maria has 9 snowballs and Tony has 6. How many do they have in all?" as follows: 9 + 6 = 9 + (1 + 5) = (9 + 1) + 5 = 10 + 5 = 15. This triad of lessons takes students through a concrete–pictorial–abstract progression as they work with physical 5-groups using objects, 5-group drawings, and finally number bonds.

Lesson 6 reminds students of the commutative property again, by focusing them on when and why they might apply commutativity: to compose ten from the larger addend. Lessons 7, 8, and 9 mirror the earlier set of three lessons, but students decompose one addend to make ten with 8 as they key addend. This extensive practice allows students to internalize both why and how they would compose ten from the larger addend as they come to realize that this is an efficient strategy.

Students use the make ten strategy with 5-group drawings and number bonds to solve a variety of problems involving a mixture of 7, 8, or 9 as addends in Lesson 10. This gives students an opportunity to not only practice their newly discovered strategies, but it also allows them to generalize this make ten strategy to a new number: 7. It is important to note that students can continue to use counting on as a strategy throughout this entire Topic A, although many students will begin to use the make ten strategy more and more as they continually discuss addition strategies and efficiency with one another.

Topic A ends with Lesson 11, where students solve story problems with two addends (**1.OA.1**), using independently selected methods. With students themselves asking each other, "Why did you solve the problem that way? How did we solve these differently?" students are able to engage in rich dialogue about the mathematical strategies and determining which are most useful.

---

[1] Just as the Common Core Standards note, students do not learn or use these formal terms.

A Teaching Sequence Towards Mastery of Counting On or Making Ten to Solve *Result Unknown* Problems

Objective 1: Solve word problems with three addends, two of which make ten.
(Lessons 1)

Objective 2 Use the associative and commutative properties to make ten with three addends.
(Lesson 2)

Objective 3: Make ten when one addend is 9.
(Lessons 3–4)

Objective 4: Compare efficiency of counting on and making ten when one addend is 9.
(Lesson 5)

Objective 5: Use the commutative property to make ten.
(Lesson 6)

Objective 6: Make ten when one addend is 8.
(Lessons 7–8)

Objective 7: Compare efficiency of counting on and making ten when one addend is 8.
(Lesson 9)

Objective 8: Solve problems with parts of 7, 8, and 9.
(Lesson 10)

Objective 9: Share and critique peer solution strategies for *put together with result unknown* word problems.
(Lesson 11)

Lesson 1

Objective: Solve word problems with three addends, two of which make ten.

Suggested Lesson Structure

■ Fluency Practice   (10 minutes)
■ Application Problem   (5 minutes)
▨ Concept Development   (35 minutes)
■ Student Debrief   (10 minutes)
   Total Time   **(60 minutes)**

Fluency Practice (10 minutes)

- Sparkle: The Say Ten and Regular Way **1.NBT.2**   (3 minutes)
- Take Out 1 **1.OA.5**   (2 minutes)
- Equal Number Pairs for Ten **1.OA.6**   (5 minutes)

Sparkle: The Say Ten and Regular Way (3 minutes)

Note: Say Ten counting reinforces place value and prepares students to add ten and some ones.

Count from 10–20, alternating between the regular and the Say Ten way (e.g., 10, ten 1, 12, ten 3, 14, ten 5). If time permits, try counting back, too. (Refer to game directions in G1–M1–Lesson 7.)

Take Out 1 (2 minutes)

Note: This activity supports fluency with decomposing numbers within 10. This skill is critical for using the upcoming Level 3 addition strategy of make ten. Students will need to fluently get 1 out of the second addend when adding 9.

    T: Take out 1 on my signal. For example, if I say 5, you say 1 and 4.

    T: 3 (snap).

    S: 1 and 2.

    T: 10 (snap).

    S: 1 and 9.

Continue with all numbers within 10.

Lesson 1:   Solve word problems with three addends, two of which make ten.
Date: 7/3/13

2.A.4

Equal Number Pairs for Ten (5 minutes)

Materials: (S) 5-group cards (1 "=" card and 2 "+" cards) per set of partners

Note: This activity builds fluency with partners to ten and promotes an understanding of equality. The 5-group cards can be accessed and printed from G1–M1–Lesson 5.

Assign students partners of equal ability. Students arrange 5-group cards from 0 to 10, including the extra 5, and place the "=" card between them. Write 4 numbers on the white board (e.g., 5, 9, 1, or 5). Partners take the 5-group cards that match the numbers written to make two equivalent expressions (e.g., 9 + 1 = 5 + 5).

Suggested sequence: 5, 9, 1, 5; 0, 1, 9, 10; 2, 5, 5, 8; 2, 3, 7, 8; 4, 1, 9, 6; 3, 4, 6, 7.

Application Problem (5 minutes)

John, Emma, and Alice each had 10 raisins. John ate 3 raisins, Emma ate 4 raisins, and Alice ate 5 raisins. How many raisins do they each have now? Write a number bond and a number sentence for each.

Note: This problem was chosen as an application of the culminating subtraction work from Module 1. All three subtraction sentences and number bonds focus on partners to ten, which are foundational to the first lesson of Module 2.

Concept Development (35 minutes)

Materials: (T) Bin, three different kinds of blocks/pattern blocks, string (S) Three different kinds of pattern blocks (10 of each shape, e.g., trapezoid, triangle, and square blocks), personal white boards

Have students sit in a semicircle at the meeting area with their personal white boards.

T: The first grade classrooms each have these special bins with different types of blocks in them. Let's figure out how many we have! (Lay out 9 triangle blocks in a 5-group configuration.) How many triangle blocks do we have?

S: 9 triangle blocks!

T: (Lay out 1 square block and 4 trapezoid blocks. Ask students to state the quantity of each group.) We need to figure out how many there are altogether. Help me write the number sentence.

Lesson 1:   Solve word problems with three addends, two of which make ten.
Date: 7/3/13

2.A.5

S: 9 + 1 + 4 = ____.

T: (Write this on the board.)

T: Talk to your partner. What are some ways we could add these blocks to solve for our unknown?

S: (As students discuss, the teacher circulates and selects students to share.) We could start with the larger number and count on. → We could add the groups together by counting them all.

T: True! Also, I wonder if we can make ten since it is such a friendly number. Talk with your partner.

S: (Discuss.) 9 and 1. → The 9 triangles and the 1 square.

T: Let's check to be sure your idea is true! (Select a student, one who may particularly benefit from proving this to be true, to move the 1 to the 9 in order to make ten.) Did 9 and 1 make ten?

S: Yes!

T: (Place the square block back in its original position.) I'm going to make the 9 and 1 one group, to show this is 10. (Place string around the 9 and 1. Circle 9 and 1 in the equation.) We have 10 (gesture to the 10), and 4 more (gesture to the 4). How many blocks?

S: We have 14 blocks! (Teacher writes 14 to complete the equation.)

T: Talk with your partner. Write the new number sentence explaining what we just did, starting with 10, on your personal white board.

S: (Discuss and write 10 + 4 = 14.)

T: Good! Now it's your turn.

Assign partners and hand out blocks. The following is a suggested sequence of stories to tell as students work with a partner to represent each problem on their personal white boards. Students should put their boards next to one another to make a larger board. Together, they write the expression, circle 10, and solve for the unknown.

- At lunch, Marcus put 2 pepper slices, 8 carrots, and 6 banana pieces on his tray. When he reached the checkout, how many fruits and veggies did he have?

NOTES ON
MULTIPLE MEANS OF
REPRESENTATION:

Facilitate students' discovery of patterns and structure in math by allowing for a variety of responses to questions. For example, some students may use their pictorial representation and see 4 + 1 = 5, and then use the 5 triangles embedded in the 9 to make a ten.

NOTES ON
MULTIPLE MEANS OF
ACTION AND
EXPRESSION:

Having students act out number stories is a great way to provide math-they-can-see. This will help your students who are hearing impaired. It will also provide visual and kinesthetic learners an opportunity to engage in the lesson using their preferred style of learning.

   Lesson 1:   Solve word problems with three addends, two of which make ten.
Date: 7/3/13

2.A.6

- Lina was playing basketball during recess. She made 4 jump shots, 7 layups, and 3 free throws. How many baskets did Lina make?
- We had 5 upper grade buddies come and visit our classroom, with 3 more buddies following them. Soon after that, 5 more buddies came to our classroom. How many total buddies came?

Problem Set (10 minutes)

Students may work individually, in pairs, or in groups when completing Problem Sets. For Problem Sets that include word problems, it may be best to read problems aloud, particularly early in the year. Students should do their personal best to complete the Problem Set within the allotted 10 minutes. Some problems do not specify a method for solving. This is an intentional reduction of scaffolding that invokes MP.5, Use Appropriate Tools Strategically. Students should solve these problems using the RDW approach used for Application Problems.

For some classes, it may be appropriate to modify the assignment by specifying which problems students should work on first. With this option, let the careful sequencing of the problem set guide your selections so that problems continue to be scaffolded. Balance word problems with other problem types to ensure a range of practice. Assign incomplete problems for homework or at another time during the day.

Student Debrief (10 minutes)

Lesson Objective: Solve word problems with three addends, two of which make ten.

The Student Debrief is intended to invite reflection and active processing of the total lesson experience.

Invite students to review their solutions for the Problem Set. They should check work by comparing answers with a partner before going over answers as a class. Look for misconceptions or misunderstandings that can be addressed in the Debrief. Guide students in a conversation to debrief the problem set and process the lesson.

Lesson 1:   Solve word problems with three addends, two of which make ten.
Date: 7/3/13

2.A.7

You may choose to use any combination of the questions below to lead the discussion.

- Earlier, we had 9 triangles, 1 square, and 4 trapezoid blocks on the floor. The teacher next door has 4 triangles and 10 squares in her bin of blocks. Does she have more, less, or the same number of blocks as we have? How do you know? (Re-create the configuration from the concept development if necessary.)
- What similarities do you notice between Problem 3 and Problem 4?
- How did the Application Problem connect to today's lesson?
- What new way or strategy to add did we learn today? Talk with your partner. (Make ten.) Why is 10 such a friendly number?

Exit Ticket (3 minutes)

After the Student Debrief, instruct students to complete the Exit Ticket. A review of their work will help you assess the students' understanding of the concepts that were presented in the lesson today and plan more effectively for future lessons. You may read the questions aloud to the students.

Name _____   Date _____

Read the math story. Make a simple math drawing with labels. (Circle) 10 and solve.

1. Bill went to the store. He bought 1 apple, 9 bananas, and 6 pears. How many pieces
    of fruit did he buy in all?

$$1 + 9 + 6 = 16$$

$$10 + 10 = 16$$

Bill bought __16__ pieces of fruit.

---

2. Maria gets some new toys for her birthday. She gets 4 dolls, 7 balls, and 3 games.
    How many toys did she receive?

$$4 + 7 + 3 = 19$$

$$10 + 4 = 14$$

Maria received __14__ toys.

COMMON CORE   Lesson 1:   Solve word problems with three addends, two of which make ten.
              Date: 7/3/13

© 2013 Common Core, Inc. All rights reserved. commoncore.org

2.A.10

3. Maddy goes to the pond and catches 3 bugs, 2 frogs, and 8 tadpoles. How many
    animals did she catch altogether?

$$\underline{\quad} + \underline{\quad} + \underline{\quad} = \underline{\quad}$$

$$10 + \underline{\quad} = \underline{\quad}$$

Maddy caught _____ animals.

4. Molly arrives at the party first with 4 red balloons. Kenny comes next with 2 green
    balloons. Dara comes last with 6 blue balloons. How many balloons did these
    friends bring?

$$\underline{\quad} + \underline{\quad} + \underline{\quad} = \underline{\quad}$$

$$10 + \underline{\quad} = \underline{\quad}$$

There are _____ balloons.

Name _____   Date _____

Read the math story. Make a simple math drawing with labels. (Circle) 10 and solve.

1. Toby has ice cream money. He has 2 dimes. He finds 4 more dimes in his jacket and 8 more on the table. How many dimes does Toby have?

____ + ____ + ____ = ____

10 + ____ = ____

Toby has _____ dimes.

COMMON CORE™   Lesson 1:   Solve word problems with three addends, two of which make ten.
Date: 7/3/13

2.A.12

Name _____   Date _____

Read the math story. Make a simple math drawing with labels. (Circle) 10 and solve.

1. Chris buys some treats. He buys 5 granola bars, 6 boxes of raisins, and 4 cookies.
    How many treats did Chris buy?

____ + ____ + ____ = ____

10 + ____ = ____

Chris bought _____ treats.

_____

2. Cindy loves pets. She has 5 cats, 7 goldfish, and 5 dogs. How many pets does she
    have in all?

____ + ____ + ____ = ____

10 + ____ = ____

Cindy has _____ pets.

3. Mary gets stickers at school for good work. She got 7 puffy stickers, 6 smelly stickers, and 3 flat stickers. How many stickers did Mary get at school altogether?

$$\underline{\quad} + \underline{\quad} + \underline{\quad} = \underline{\quad}$$

$$10 + \underline{\quad} = \underline{\quad}$$

Mary got _____ stickers at school.

_____

4. Jim went to breakfast at school. He sat at a table with 4 teachers and 9 children. How many people were at the table after Jim sat down?

$$\underline{\quad} + \underline{\quad} + \underline{\quad} = \underline{\quad}$$

$$\underline{\quad} + \underline{\quad} = \underline{\quad}$$

There were _____ people at the table after Jim sat down.

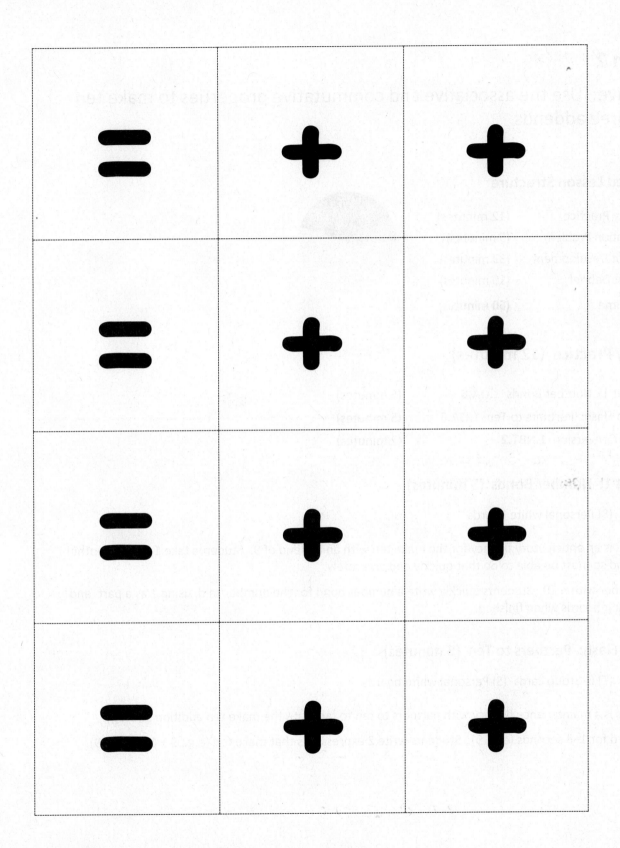

COMMON CORE™ Lesson 1: Solve word problems with three addends, two of which make ten.
Date: 7/3/13

2.A.15

Lesson 2

Objective: Use the associative and commutative properties to make ten with three addends.

Suggested Lesson Structure

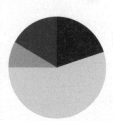

■ Fluency Practice   (12 minutes)
■ Application Problem   (5 minutes)
■ Concept Development   (33 minutes)
■ Student Debrief   (10 minutes)
    Total Time   **(60 minutes)**

Fluency Practice (12 minutes)

- Take Out 1: Number Bonds **1.OA.6**   (5 minutes)
- 5-Group Flash: Partners to Ten **1.OA.6**   (5 minutes)
- Say Ten Conversion **1.NBT.2**   (2 minutes)

Take Out 1: Number Bonds (5 minutes)

Materials: (S) Personal white boards

Note: This is an anticipatory fluency for the make ten with an addend of 9. Students take 1 from the other addend and so must be able to do that quickly and accurately.

Say a number within 10. Students quickly write a number bond for the number said, using 1 as a part, and hold up their boards when finished.

5-Group Flash: Partners to Ten (5 minutes)

Materials: (T) 5-Group cards (S) Personal white boards

Note: This is a maintenance fluency with partners to ten to facilitate the make ten addition strategy.

Flash a card for 1–3 seconds (e.g., 9). Students write 2 expressions that make ten (e.g., 9 + 1 and 1 + 9).

Lesson 2:   Use the associative and commutative properties to make ten with
              three addends.
Date: 7/3/13

2.A.16

Say Ten Conversion (2 minutes)

Note: This activity strengthens students' understanding of the place value system as it relates to counting.

Call out numbers between 10 and 20, alternating between saying the number the regular or the Say Ten way. When you use the Say Ten way, students say the number the regular way. When you use the regular way, students say it the Say Ten way. Play for a minute and then give students a chance to be the caller.

Application Problem (5 minutes)

Lisa was reading a book. She read 6 pages the first night, 5 pages the next night, and 4 pages the following night. How many pages did she read?

Make a drawing to show your thinking. Write a statement to go with your work.

Extension: If she read a total of 20 pages by the fifth night, how many pages could she have read on the fourth night and the fifth night?

Note: This problem applies Lesson 1 objective of adding three addends, two of which make ten. The two addends that make ten are separated within the story, which will be discussed during the Student Debrief in connection with today's lesson.

Concept Development (33 minutes)

Materials: (S) Personal white boards

Have students sit in a semicircle at the meeting area with their materials.

- T: (Write 5 + 3 + 5 = ___ on the board.) Draw to solve for this unknown.
- S: (Draw to solve, as the teacher circulates and notices student strategies.)
- T: Let's see how our friends solved this. (Select a student who added all in a row to show.)
- S: I added 5 + 3 and remembered that was 8. And then counted up 5 more from 8 and got 13! → I drew the groups of 5 together and added those first since I knew they made ten. Then I added 10 and 3 is 13!
- T: Talk with your partner. How were Jo's strategy and Bob's strategy the same and different? Which one was correct?

NOTES ON MULTIPLE MEANS OF REPRESENTATION:

During this lesson it is important for students to articulate the way they chose to solve a problem so that other students can hear how they are thinking. This should help guide students towards the most efficient choice as they benefit from hearing strategies multiple times.

Lesson 2: Use the associative and commutative properties to make ten with three addends.
Date: 7/3/13

2.A.17

S: (Discuss, as the teacher circulates and listens.) They were both correct! → Bob put the fives together and made ten, and Jo added them in order.

T: So, even though they added two different numbers together first, did they get the same total?

S: Yes!

T: Wow! Okay, let's try this again. Let's use Bob's strategy of making ten from two of our addends. (Write 7 + 5 + 3 = ___.) Write the equation. Draw to show the three amounts.

S: (Draw to show the three quantities.)

T: What two numbers make ten?

S: 7 and 3!

T: Good. Show that 7 and 3 make ten in your drawing by circling like we did yesterday with the string.

S: (Circle the 3 and the 7, making a group of 10.)

MP.7

T: Here is a new number sentence that shows what numbers you added first. (Write 7 + 3 + 5 = ___.)

T: I'll make a number bond to show how you made ten from two numbers. (Bond the 7 and 3 to make ten.)

T: You just showed 10 and 5 more, which equals?

S: 15!

T: Good. I'll show how we solved for the unknown. I'll write the new number sentence explaining what we just did, starting with 10 on your personal white board.

S: (Solve 7 + 3 + 5 = ____ while the teacher writes 10 + 5 = 15.)

T: Jo showed us at the beginning of the lesson that she could solve from left to right, without moving the addends around, in order to get the same answer as Bob. Work and talk with your partner to see if this is true again!

Repeat this process, using the following suggested sequence: 9 + 2 + 1, 2 + 4 + 8 (highlighting that students might begin with the 8 rather than the 2), 4 + 3 + 6, and 3 + 8 + 7. Students complete the number sentence, while the teacher completes the drawing for the third example.

NOTES ON
MULTIPLE MEANS OF
ENGAGEMENT:

Addends should be chosen so that students can easily identify the partners to ten, recognizing that they can add these two addends first, regardless of where they are positioned within the number sentence. If students are not fluent with 7 and 3, they may be replaced with 9 and 1, respectively.

Problem Set (10 minutes)

Students should do their personal best to complete the Problem Set within the allotted 10 minutes. For some classes, it may be appropriate to modify the assignment by specifying which problems they work on first. Some problems do not specify a method for solving. Students solve these problems using the RDW approach used for Application Problems.

Note: Look at the example for Problem 1 in the Problem Set. Discuss the importance of making a simple math drawing by drawing three different simple shapes to represent three different numbers in the equation, reminding children about their experience using different concrete materials during previous lessons. Model this drawing if necessary.

Lesson 2:	Use the associative and commutative properties to make ten with three addends.
Date:	7/3/13

2.A.18

Student Debrief (10 minutes)

Lesson Objective: Use the associative and commutative properties to make ten with three addends.

The Student Debrief is intended to invite reflection and active processing of the total lesson experience.

Invite students to review their solutions for the Problem Set. They should check work by comparing answers with a partner before going over answers as a class. Look for misconceptions or misunderstandings that can be addressed in the Debrief. Guide students in a conversation to debrief the Problem Set and process the lesson. You may choose to use any combination of the questions below to lead the discussion.

- Look at your Problem Set. We added amounts in different orders. When we did this, did we get the same amount? Is this always true?

- Talk with your partner. How did you organize your drawings to show the three different amounts? How did you show that you used the make ten strategy in your drawing?

- Look at Problem 1 and Problem 4. What similarities do you notice?

- Are there any problems in the Problem Set that you can solve using your knowledge of doubles?

- Look at Problem 9. How did you show the number bond for making ten? How is it different from some of your other bonds? (Students share strategies of number bond above or below, or rewrite the number sentence below to enable the addends that make ten to be adjacent.)

Exit Ticket (3 minutes)

After the Student Debrief, instruct students to complete the Exit Ticket. A review of their work will help you assess the students' understanding of the concepts that were presented in the lesson today and plan more effectively for future lessons. You may read the questions aloud to the students.

Lesson 2: Use the associative and commutative properties to make ten with three addends.
Date: 7/3/13

2.A.19

Name __Owen__   Date __1-10-20__

Circle the numbers that make ten. Draw a picture. Complete the number sentence.

1. (7) + (3) + 4 = ☐

10
7 + 3 + 4

10 + ____ = ____

2. 9 + 1 + 4 = ☐

10
~~9~~ + ~~1~~ + 4

10 + 4 = 14

3. 5 + 6 + 5 = ☐

10
5 + 5 + 6

10 + 6 = 16

%100

COMMON CORE   Lesson 2:   Use the associative and commutative properties to make ten with three addends.
Date: 7/3/13

2.A.20

4. 4 + 3 + 7 = ☐

10

_7_ + _3_ + _4_   10 + _4_ = _14_

(7+3)

5. 2 + 7 + 8 = ☐

10

____ + ____ + ____   10 + ____ = ____

(Circle) the numbers that make ten, put them into a number bond and solve.

6.   10 + 5 = _15_

10

(9) + (1) + 5 = _15_

7.   (10)   10 + 4 = _14_

8 + 2 + 4 = _14_

8.   10 + 3 = 13

3 + (5) + (5) = ____

9.   3 + 6 + 7 = ____

Name _____Owen_____

Date ___7-11-90___

(Circle) the numbers that make ten.

Draw a picture and complete the number sentences to solve.

a. 8 + 3 + 2 = __13__

__8__ + __3__ + __2__

(10) + __3__ = 13

b. 4 + 7 + 3 = __14__

__4__ + __7__ + __3__

10 + __4__ = 14

COMMON CORE

Lesson 2: Use the associative and commutative properties to make ten with three addends.

Date: 7/3/13

2.A.22

Name _____   Date _____

Circle the numbers that make ten. Draw a picture. Complete the number sentence.

1. ⑥ + 2 + ④ = ☐

___6___ + _____ + __2__ |10| + _____ = _____

---

2. 5 + 3 + 5 = ☐

_____ + _____ + _____   10 + _____ = _____

---

3. 5 + 2 + 8 = ☐

_____ + _____ + _____   _____ + 10 = _____

4. $2 + 7 + 3 =$ ☐

____ + ____ + ____   ___ + 10 = ___

Circle the numbers that make ten. Put them into a number bond and solve. Write the new number bond.

5.

$3 + 5 + 7 =$ ____

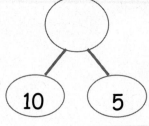

10 + ___ = ___

6.

$4 + 8 + 2 =$ ___

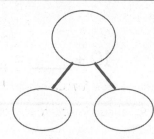

10 + ___ = ___

Challenge: Circle the addends that make ten. Circle the true number sentences.

a. $5 + 5 + 3 = 10 + 3$ c. $3 + 8 + 7 = 10 + 6$

b. $4 + 6 + 6 = 10 + 6$ d. $8 + 9 + 2 = 9 + 10$

Lesson 3

Objective: Make ten when one addend is 9.

Suggested Lesson Structure

■ Fluency Practice   (10 minutes)
■ Application Problem   (5 minutes)
■ Concept Development   (35 minutes)
■ Student Debrief   (10 minutes)

Total Time   **(60 minutes)**

Fluency Practice (10 minutes)

- Take Out 1 **1.OA.6**   (1 minute)
- Break Apart 10 **1.OA.6**   (5 minutes)
- Add Partners of Ten First **1.OA.3**   (4 minutes)

Take Out 1 (1 minute)

Materials: (S) Personal white boards

Note: This is an anticipatory fluency for the make ten addition strategy, as students will need to fluently get 1 out of the second addend when adding 9.

Make the pace quicker now that students have done this for a few days. Celebrate their improvement.

Say a number between 1 and 9. Students say the number decomposed with one part as one.

Break Apart 10 (5 minutes)

Materials: (T) 5-group cards (S) Personal white boards

Students write the numeral 10 on their boards. Flash a 5-group card. Students break apart 10 using the number flashed as a part, without making bubbles or boxes around the numerals.

Add Partners of Ten First (4 minutes)

Note: This activity reviews adding three numbers and prepares students for the make ten addition strategy when one addend is 9.

Build towards three addends. Begin with 9 + 1.

    T: 9 + 1.
    S: 10.
    T: 10 + 5
    S: 15.
    T: 9 + 1 (pause) + 5 is?
    S: 15.

Continue through a few more.

Application Problem (5 minutes)

Tom's mother gave him 4 pennies. His father gave him 9 pennies. His sister gave him enough pennies that he now had a total of 14. How many pennies did his sister give him? Use a drawing, number sentence, and a statement.

Extension: How many more would he need to have 19 pennies?

Note: This application problem challenges students to consider finding an unknown addend within a context with three addends. Students may add 4 and 9 together first, noticing that they need 1 more penny to make 14. Other students may recognize that 14 is made of 10 and 4, and realize that they are looking for the partner for 9 when making ten. During the debrief, students will explore how they could use making ten as a quick strategy to add the sets of pennies that Tom's parents gave him (9 pennies and 4 pennies).

Concept Development (35 minutes)

Materials: (T) 10 red and 10 green linking cubes (S) 10 red and 10 green linking cubes, personal white boards

Have students sit at their seats with materials.

    T: (Project and read aloud.) Maria has 9 snowballs and
         Tony has 3. How many do they have altogether?
    T: What is the expression to solve this problem?
    S: 9 + 3.

**NOTES ON
MULTIPLE MEANS OF
REPRESENTATION:**

While some students are experts at solving **10+** number sentences, others may need pictorial support such as ten-frames (rather than numerals) to help develop mental calculations.

| | Lesson 3: | Make ten when one addend is 9. |
| | Date: | 7/3/13 |

2.A.26

T: Use your green linking cubes to show how many snowballs Maria has.

S: (Lay out 9 green linking cubes.)

T: Using the red cubes, show how many snowballs Tony has. Put them in a separate pile.

S: (Lay out 3 linking cubes.)

T: How would you solve this problem?

S: Count on!

T/S: Niiiine, 10, 11, 12.

T: (Complete the equation 9 + 3 = 12.)

T: Is there a way to make ten with the amounts we have in front of us? Turn and talk to your partner.

S: (Discuss while the teacher circulates.)

T: (Choose a student who used the strategy below.)

S: I made ten by moving 1 green cube to the red pile. I had 9 cubes in that pile but now I have 10.

T: You made ten! Everyone make ten.

S: (Move 1 green cube to the red pile.)

T: Now, we have 10 here. (Gesture to the pile of 10.) What do we have left here? (Point to the other pile.)

S: 2.

T: Look at your new piles. What is our new number sentence?

S: 10 + 2 = 12!

T: (Write 10 + 2 = 12 on the board.) Did we change the *amount* of linking cubes we have?

S: No.

T: So, 9 + 3 is the same as what addition expression?

S: 10 + 2.

T: (Write 9 + 3 = 10 + 2.)

T: What is 10 + 2?

S: 12.

T: What is 9 + 3? Say the number sentence.

S: 9 + 3 = 12.

T: How many snowballs do Maria and Tony have?

S: 12 snowballs.

NOTES ON MULTIPLE MEANS OF REPRESENTATION:

For those students who can fluently solve math facts within 20, cultivate excitement by connecting on-level math to higher math, presenting numbers to 100.

(29 + 3 or 39 + 13)

Repeat the process with snowball situations for 9 + 2 and 9 + 4. Then, change to 5-group drawings instead of cubes and continue to repeat the process with the following suggested sequence: 9 + 5, 9 + 8, 9 + 7. Create different story situations for 9 + 6, 8 + 9, and 9 + 9. Be sure to have students label their pictures, circle 10, and write three number sentences (9 + 6 = 15, 10 + 5 = 15, 9 + 6 = 10 + 5).

Problem Set (10 minutes)

Students should do their personal best to complete the Problem Set within the allotted 10 minutes. For some classes, it may be appropriate to modify the assignment by specifying which problems they work on first. Some problems do not specify a method for solving. Students solve these problems using the RDW approach used for Application Problems.

Note: Students should save the Problem Sets from this lesson through Lesson 6. They will provide comparisons for the students when they begin making ten when one addend is 8. Setting up a portfolio of past Problem Sets and strategies will help students access these readily.

Student Debrief (10 minutes)

Lesson Objective: Make ten when one addend is 9.

The Student Debrief is intended to invite reflection and active processing of the total lesson experience.

Invite students to review their solutions for the Problem Set. They should check work by comparing answers with a partner before going over answers as a class. Look for misconceptions or misunderstandings that can be addressed in the Debrief. Guide students in a conversation to debrief the problem set and process the lesson. You may choose to use any combination of the questions below to lead the discussion.

- Look at Problem 1. What are the two number sentences that show your work?

- Look at Problem 1 and Problem 3 with a partner. How was setting up the problem to complete Problem 1 different from setting up Problem 3? What did you need to be sure to do? Why?

- How can solving Problem 1 help you solve Problem 4?

- After you made ten, what did you notice about the addend you broke apart? (The other addend is left with 1 less!)

- What new strategy did we use today to solve math problems? How is it more efficient than counting on to add?
- Look at your Application Problem. How could you use the make ten strategy to solve the problem?

Exit Ticket (3 minutes)

After the Student Debrief, instruct students to complete the Exit Ticket. A review of their work will help you assess the students' understanding of the concepts that were presented in the lesson today and plan more effectively for future lessons. You may read the questions aloud to the students.

Name _____ Date _____

Draw and (circle) to show how you made ten to help you solve the problem.

1. Maria has 9 snowballs and Tony has 6. How many snowballs do they have in all?

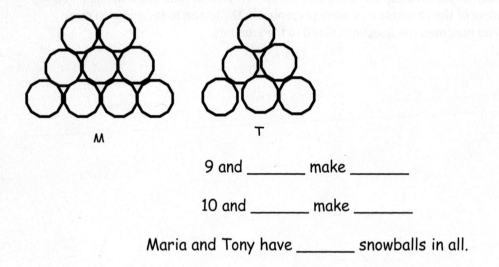

M   T

9 and _____ make _____

10 and _____ make _____

Maria and Tony have _____ snowballs in all.

2. Bob has 9 raisins and Jonny has 4. How many raisins do they have altogether?

9 and _____ make _____

10 and _____ make _____

Bob and Jonny have _____ raisins altogether.

3. There are 3 chairs on the left side of the classroom and 9 on the right side. How many chairs are in the classroom?

9 and _____ make _____

10 and _____ make _____

There are _____ total chairs.

4. There are 7 children sitting on the rug and 9 children standing. How many children are there in all?

9 and _____ make _____

10 and _____ make _____

There are _____ children in all.

Name _____ Date _____

Draw and (circle) to show how to make ten to solve. Complete the number sentences.

1. Tammy has 4 books and John has 9 books. How many books do Tammy and John have altogether?

____ + ____ = ____

____ + ____ = ____   Tammy and John have ____ books.

Name _____   Date _____

Draw, label, and (circle) to show how you made ten to help you solve. Complete the number sentences.

1. Ron has 9 marbles and Sue has 4 marbles. How many marbles do they have in all?

$$9 + 4 = \underline{}$$

$$10 + 3 = \underline{}$$ Ron and Sue have _____ marbles.

---

2. Jim has 5 cars and Tina has 9. How many cars do they have altogether?

$$\underline{} + \underline{} = \underline{}$$

$$10 + \underline{} = \underline{}$$ Jim and Tina have ___ cars.

3. Stan has 6 fish and Meg has 9. How many fish do they have in all?

____ + ____ = ____

____ + ____ = ____   Stan and Meg have ____ fish.

4. Rick made 7 cookies and Mom made 9. How many cookies did Rick and Mom make altogether?

____ + ____ = ____

____ + ____ = ____   Rick and Mom made ____ cookies.

5. Dad has 8 pens and Tony has 9. How many pens do Dad and Tony have in all?

____ + ____ = ____

____ + ____ = ____

Dad and Tony have ____ pens.

Lesson 4

Objective: Make ten when one addend is 9.

Suggested Lesson Structure

■ Fluency Practice   (12 minutes)
■ Application Problem   (5 minutes)
☐ Concept Development   (33 minutes)
■ Student Debrief   (10 minutes)
  Total Time   **(60 minutes)**

Fluency Practice (12 minutes)

- Happy Counting the Say Ten Way **1.NBT.2**   (2 minutes)
- Sprint: Adding Three Numbers **1.OA.3**   (10 minutes)

Happy Counting the Say Ten Way (2 minutes)

Note: Say Ten counting strengthens student understanding of place value.

Tell students to look at your thumb and count up and down between 10 and 120 the Say Ten way. When your thumb points and motions up, the students count up. When your thumb is to the side, students stop. When your thumb points and motions down, the students count down (see example below).

T:

T/S: 4 ten   4 ten 1   4 ten 2   (pause)   4 ten 1   4 ten   (pause)   4 ten 1   4 ten 2   4 ten 3

Choose numbers based on student skill level. If students are very proficient up to 40, start at 40 and quickly go up to 80. If they are proficient between 40 and 80, Happy Count between 80 and 120. Alternate at times between regular and Say Ten counting, too.

Sprint: Adding Three Numbers (10 minutes)

Note: This Sprint provides practice with adding three numbers by making ten first.

Materials: (S) Adding Three Numbers Sprint

Lesson 4:   Make ten when one addend is 9.
Date: 7/3/13

2.A.35

Application Problem (5 minutes)

He has 13 flowrs.

Michael plants 9 flowers in the morning. He then plants 4 flowers in the afternoon. How many flowers did he plant? Make a drawing, number bond, and a statement.

Note: Students can apply the make ten strategy from Lesson 3 as they solve this problem. During the debrief, the teacher will discuss how using rows to show the plants can create a clear and quick visual for identifying the compositions and decompositions needed to apply the make ten strategy.

Concept Development (33 minutes)

Materials: (T) 10 green and 10 red linking cubes, a ten-frame border (S) 10 green and 10 red linking cubes, personal white boards

Have students come to the meeting area with linking cubes and personal white boards.

T: (Project and read aloud.) Maria has 9 green erasers. Tony has 3 red erasers. How many erasers do Maria and Tony have?

T: What is the expression to solve this story problem?

S: 9 + 3.

T: (Show two piles: 9 scattered green erasers and 3 scattered red erasers.)

T: How can you check that I have the correct number of cubes representing Maria's erasers?

S: We can count, one at a time.

T: Okay, but that's not very efficient. Is there a way to organize my green cubes so we can tell there are 9 cubes faster?

S: Put them in a 5-group!

T: Great idea. When we arrange or draw things in a 5-group, we are all going to follow these steps. Just like reading, we'll start with the top row and from the left. (Place 5 green cubes in a row.)

MP.4

T: We start in the next line with 6 and try to match it up to the top as closely as we can. (Place 4 in the bottom row.)

T: Now, can you see we have 9 cubes right away?

S: Yes!

T: (Arrange the 3 red cubes in a 5 group on the other side.) The red cubes are also organized.

T: What do we do to solve 9 + 3?

S: Make ten.

T: (Circle 9 green cubes and 1 red cube.)

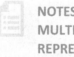

NOTES ON MULTIPLE MEANS OF REPRESENTATION:

It is important to make the connection between concrete math and math models. This helps English language learners and struggling learners understand the math without getting bogged down with language acquisition.

MP.4

T: Here's another way to show ten. (Move 1 red cube to add to 9 green cubes.)

T: (Places a red cube in the tenth slot.) We made ten!

T: I'm going to put a frame around it. (Place the frame around ten.) We are going to call this a **ten-frame**. It looks just like our 5-group drawings but now that we are making ten, we can call it a ten-frame. Whenever we make ten, we make or draw a frame around it. That way, we can see ten right away.

ten-frame

T: Look at the new piles. What new expression do you see?

S: 10 + 2.

T: So, 9 + 3 is the same as?

S: 10 + 2.

T: (Write 9 + 3 = 10 + 2.)

T: What is 10 + 2?

S: 12.

T: What is 9 + 3?

S: 12.

T: How many erasers do Maria and Tony have?

S: 12 erasers.

T: Where are the 9 green erasers? Point to them.

S: (Point to 9.)

T: Where are the 3 red erasers? Point to them.

S: (Point to 1 and 2.)

T: You are pointing to 2 different places. Why?

S: We broke 3 apart to 1 and 2.

T: Let's use a number bond to show how we broke apart 3.

T: Just like we framed the ten in our picture, we'll frame the numbers that make ten. (Circles 9 and 1.)

T: 9 and 1 make?

S: 10.

T: 10 and 2 make?

S: 12.

T: So, 9 plus 3 equals?

S: 12!

> **NOTES ON MULTIPLE MEANS OF REPRESENTATION:**
>
> Be aware of the different learning needs in your class and adjust the lesson as necessary. As some students may need to work at the concrete level for a longer period of time, allow students access to manipulatives.

9 + 2 = 11

Repeat the process by having students work with cubes. Be sure to guide students when organizing their cubes into a ten-frame. The following is a suggested sequence: 9 + 2, 4 + 9, and 5 + 9. In Lesson 4, we are at times putting the smaller addend first. Simply guide students to realize they can still compose ten from the 9 for efficiency during the last two problems.

Next, repeat the process by having students use math drawings to solve the following in this suggested sequence: 9 + 6, 3 + 9, and 7 + 9. The 9 should be drawn with open circles. The other addend should be drawn with filled-in circles. Before students add dark circles to their math drawing, ask them, "How many does 9 need to make ten?" and "How many do you have when you take away 1 from [the other addend]?" to guide how they will decompose the addend. Additionally, encourage students to place the 1 closer to the 9 as they write the number bond below the other addend, making it easier to make ten with 9.

Problem Set (10 minutes)

Students should do their personal best to complete the Problem Set within the allotted 10 minutes. For some classes, it may be appropriate to modify the assignment by specifying which problems they work on first. Some problems do not specify a method for solving. Students solve these problems using the RDW approach used for Application Problems.

Student Debrief (10 minutes)

Lesson Objective: Make ten when one addend is 9.

The Student Debrief is intended to invite reflection and active processing of the total lesson experience.

Invite students to review their solutions for the Problem Set. They should check work by comparing answers with a partner before going over answers as a class. Look for misconceptions or misunderstandings that can be addressed in the Debrief. Guide students in a conversation to debrief the problem set and process the lesson. You may choose to use any combination of the questions below to lead the discussion.

- How did solving Problem 4 help you solve Problem 5?

- What new (or significant) math vocabulary did we use today to make our pictures precise?

- What were some strategies we learned today to solve addition problems efficiently? (Organizing materials and drawings in **ten-frame**, making ten, starting with the 9 to add.)

- Look at your Problem Set. What pattern did you notice when adding 9 to a number? Why is it always a ten and the number that is 1 less than the other addend?

- Look at the Application Problem. Share your drawing with a partner. How could you use the ten-frame to show your work? How does the ten-frame help you see your total amount?

Lesson 4:   Make ten when one addend is 9.
Date: 7/3/13

2.A.38

Exit Ticket (3 minutes)

After the Student Debrief, instruct students to complete the Exit Ticket. A review of their work will help you assess the students' understanding of the concepts that were presented in the lesson today and plan more effectively for future lessons. You may read the questions aloud to the students.

COMMON CORE

Lesson 4:
Date:

Make ten when one addend is 9.
7/3/13

2.A.39

Name _____ Date _____

A *Circle the addends that make ten and add.*

Number correct: _____

1	$9 + 1 + 3 = \square$		16	$6 + 4 + 5 = \square$	
2	$9 + 1 + 5 = \square$		17	$6 + 4 + 6 = \square$	
3	$1 + 9 + 5 = \square$		18	$4 + 6 + 6 = \square$	
4	$1 + 9 + 1 = \square$		19	$4 + 6 + 5 = \square$	
5	$5 + 5 + 4 = \square$		20	$4 + 5 + 6 = \square$	
6	$5 + 5 + 6 = \square$		21	$5 + 3 + 5 = \square$	
7	$5 + 5 + 5 = \square$		22	$6 + 5 + 5 = \square$	
8	$8 + 2 + 1 = \square$		23	$1 + 4 + 9 = \square$	
9	$8 + 2 + 3 = \square$		24	$9 + 1 + \square = 14$	
10	$8 + 2 + 7 = \square$		25	$8 + 2 + \square = 11$	
11	$2 + 8 + 7 = \square$		26	$\square + 3 + 4 = 13$	
12	$7 + 3 + 3 = \square$		27	$2 + \square + 6 = 16$	
13	$7 + 3 + 6 = \square$		28	$1 + 1 + \square = 11$	
14	$7 + 3 + 7 = \square$		29	$19 = 5 + \square + 9$	
15	$3 + 7 + 7 = \square$		30	$18 = \square + 8 + 6$	

COMMON CORE

Lesson 4: Make ten when one addend is 9.
Date: 7/3/13

2.A.40

Name _____　　　Date _____

B* Circle the addends that make ten and add.

1	$5 + 5 + 4 = \square$	16	$6 + 4 + 2 = \square$
2	$5 + 5 + 6 = \square$	17	$6 + 4 + 3 = \square$
3	$5 + 5 + 5 = \square$	18	$4 + 6 + 3 = \square$
4	$9 + 1 + 1 = \square$	19	$4 + 6 + 6 = \square$
5	$9 + 1 + 2 = \square$	20	$4 + 7 + 6 = \square$
6	$9 + 1 + 5 = \square$	21	$5 + 4 + 5 = \square$
7	$1 + 9 + 5 = \square$	22	$8 + 5 + 5 = \square$
8	$1 + 9 + 6 = \square$	23	$1 + 7 + 9 = \square$
9	$8 + 2 + 4 = \square$	24	$9 + 1 + \square = 11$
10	$8 + 2 + 7 = \square$	25	$8 + 2 + \square = 12$
11	$2 + 8 + 7 = \square$	26	$\square + 3 + 4 = 14$
12	$7 + 3 + 7 = \square$	27	$4 + \square + 8 = 18$
13	$7 + 3 + 8 = \square$	28	$7 + 8 + \square = 17$
14	$7 + 3 + 9 = \square$	29	$16 = 3 + \square + 6$
15	$3 + 7 + 9 = \square$	30	$19 = \square + 9 + 3$

Name _____   Date _____

Change the picture to make a ten. Write the easier number sentence and solve.

1. Tom has 9 red pencils and 5 yellow. How many pencils does Tom have in all?

9 + 5 = _____

10 pencils + _____ pencils = _____ pencils

---

10 and solve.

2. 9 + 3

10 + _____ = _____

3. 4 + 9

10 + _____ = _____

Solve. Make math drawings using the ten-frame to show how you made 10 to solve.

4. $9 + 5 =$ ___ \qquad ___ + ___ = _____

5. $6 + 9 =$ ___ \qquad ___ + ___ = ____

6. $8 + 9 =$ ___ \qquad ___ + ___ = _____

Solve. Use a number bond to show how you made a ten.

7. $5 + 9 =$ ____

8. _____ $= 9 + 7$

Name _____   Date _____

Make math drawings using the ten-frame to solve. Rewrite as a 10+ number sentence.

1. 6 + 9 = ___

10 + ___ = ___

2. ___ = 4 + 9

___ + ___ = ___

Name _____ Date _____

Solve. Make math drawings using the ten-frame to show how you <u>made 10 to solve.</u>

9+2 = 11

1. 9 + 3 = ___   ___ + ___ = ___

2. 9 + 6 = ___   ___ + ___ = ___

3.   7 + 9 = ___   ___ + ___ = ___

Match the number sentences to the bonds you used to help you make a ten.

a.   9 + 8 = _____

b.   ___ = 9 + 6

c.   7 + 9 =_____

Make math drawings using ten-frames for the + 9 expressions to find and circle the true number sentences.

d. 5 + 10 = 6 + 9

e. 3 + 10 = 9 + 2

f. 9 + 4 = 10 + 5

Lesson 5

Objective: Compare efficiency of counting on and making ten when one addend is 9.

Suggested Lesson Structure

- ■ Fluency Practice   (13 minutes)
- ■ Application Problem   (5 minutes)
- ■ Concept Development   (32 minutes)
- ■ Student Debrief   (10 minutes)

   Total Time   **(60 minutes)**

Fluency Practice (13 minutes)

- Partners to Ten **1.OA.6**   (5 minutes)
- Add Partners of Ten First **1.OA.6**   (4 minutes)
- Take Out 2 **1.OA.6**   (4 minutes)

Partners to Ten (5 minutes)

Materials: (S) Single-sided 5-group cards and 2 personal white boards per pair

Note: This fluency activity provides maintenance with partners to ten while applying the commutative property.

Students put 5-group cards face down and write 10 on their boards. Each partner takes a 5-group card, then draws a number bond without bubbles using the selected card as one part. Students write two addition sentences for the number bond and check each other's work.

Add Partners of Ten First (4 minutes)

Note: This activity reviews adding three numbers and prepares students for the make ten addition strategy when one addend is 9.

Conduct activity as outlined in G1–M2– Lesson 3.

Take Out 2 (4 minutes)

Note: This is an anticipatory fluency for making ten when one addend is 8 since 8 needs 2 to make ten.

T: Take out 2 on my signal. For example, if I say 5, you say 2 and 3.

T: 3. (Pause. Snap.)

S: 2 and 1.

T: 10. (Pause. Snap.)

S: 2 and 8.

Continue with all numbers within 10 for about a minute. Give about 30 seconds of practice with a partner. Repeat the set as a whole class and celebrate improvement.

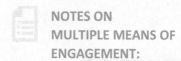

NOTES ON
MULTIPLE MEANS OF
ENGAGEMENT:

Fluency games and activities provide most students the opportunity to gain math confidence by experiencing daily math success. Be sure to highlight students' math successes frequently in order to facilitate continued effort and persistence.

Application Problem (5 minutes)

There are 9 red birds and 6 blue birds in a tree. How many birds are in the tree? Use a ten-frame drawing and a number sentence. Write a number bond to match the story and a number bond to show the matching 10+ fact. Write a statement.

Note: This problem continues to provide contextual practice of solving addition situations where one addend is 9. By drawing a number bond to match the story, and drawing a number bond to match the ten-frame drawing, students will also continue to relate the addition facts of 9 with the addition facts of 10. Students will consider the problem's relationship to today's lesson during the Debrief.

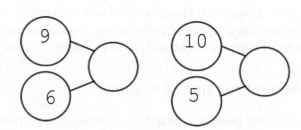

Concept Development (32 minutes)

Materials: (S) Personal white boards

Have students sit at their desks or the meeting area with their materials.

T: (Project or write the two number bonds shown here.) Which number bond is easier to solve?

S: 10 and 5!

T: (Write 10 + 5 = ____.) 10 + 5 = …

S: 15!

T: (Record the solution.) How did you know that so quickly?

S: Because we know our 10+ facts. → Because 10 is a friendly number.

Lesson 5:   Compare efficiency of counting on and making ten when one addend is 9.

Date: 7/3/13

2.A.48

T: (Write 9 + 6 = ____.) Now let's count on to solve 9 + 6.

T/S: Niiiine, 10, 11, 12, 13, 14, 15. 15!

T: (Record the solution.) Wait, 9 + 6 is equal to 10 + 5?

S: Yes!

T: Both number bonds have the same total, but when we had ten to solve, our solution came to us automatically.

T: (Read aloud.) Sergio and Lila were getting ready to go to recess. They both had to solve 9 + 8. The first one to solve it got to go to recess first! Sergio decided he was going to count on to solve it. (Pause.) Was there another way to solve 9 + 8 that Sergio could have used?

S: (Discuss, as the teacher circulates and listens.) Make ten! → Take 1 out from 8 and give it to the 9, in order to make ten.

T: Some of you said that you would make ten. Well, that is just what Lila decided to do. (Assign partners.) Partner A, use your materials to show how Sergio solved 9 + 8 by counting on. Partner B, use your materials to how Lila solved 9 + 8 by making ten.

S: (Use materials to show 9 + 8.)

T: Share the strategy you showed on your white board with you partner. Talk to your partner about what you did.

S: (Discuss and share as the teacher circulates.)

T: Help me make a number bond to show what Sergio did. What were the parts that Sergio used?

S: 9 and 8!

T: (Write the bond.) What was the total?

S: 17.

T: (Complete the bond.) Help me make a number bond to show what Lila did. What were the parts that Lila used?

S: 10 and 7!

T: (Write the bond.)   What was the total?

S: 17.

T: (Complete the bond.) Which number bond will help you solve more efficiently or quickly?

S: 10 and 7.

T: So, based on these number bonds, and the work you and your partner just did, who do you think got to go to recess first?

S: Lila!

T: You're right! By using the make ten strategy, she was able to solve for the unknown quickly or efficiently.

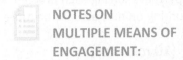

NOTES ON MULTIPLE MEANS OF ENGAGEMENT:

It is important to partner important vocabulary with captions or pictorial representations for all students. It is especially beneficial to English language learners and students with hearing impairments. It may be helpful to have students model or demonstrate their understanding of more difficult vocabulary such as *efficient*.

Continue with partners solving each problem showing how to solve using counting on and making ten: 9 + 6, 9 + 5, 9 + 2 (counting on may actually be more efficient here), 9 + 9.

Problem Set (10 minutes)

Students should do their personal best to complete the Problem Set within the allotted 10 minutes. For some classes, it may be appropriate to modify the assignment by specifying which problems they work on first. Some problems do not specify a method for solving. Students solve these problems using the RDW approach used for Application Problems.

Note: Students should save the Problem Set to provide the opportunity to compare making ten when adding 8.

Student Debrief (10 minutes)

Lesson Objective: Compare efficiency of counting on and making ten when one addend is 9.

The Student Debrief is intended to invite reflection and active processing of the total lesson experience.

Invite students to review their solutions for the Problem Set. They should check work by comparing answers with a partner before going over answers as a class. Look for misconceptions or misunderstandings that can be addressed in the Debrief. Guide students in a conversation to debrief the Problem Set and process the lesson. You may choose to use any combination of the questions below to lead the discussion.

- Which problems could you solve more efficiently by making ten?

- Why was that a more efficient way to solve?

- Were there any problems that you think could have been solved more efficiently using counting on? Why?

- Look at Problems 8–10. What do you notice about the number bonds? How does knowing your 10+ facts help you with your 9 plus facts?

- Look at your Application Problem. What is the related 10+ fact for this problem? How does your drawing show both the 9 plus fact and the related 10+ fact?
- Look at Problems 3–6. Think about these statements: 9 and _____ make _____ and 10 and _____ make _____. (For example, 9 and 2 make 11 and 10 and 1 make 11.) What pattern do you notice?

Exit Ticket (3 minutes)

After the Student Debrief, instruct students to complete the Exit Ticket. A review of their work will help you assess the students' understanding of the concepts that were presented in the lesson today and plan more effectively for future lessons. You may read the questions aloud to the students.

Lesson 5:

Date:

Compare efficiency of counting on and making ten when one addend is 9.

7/3/13

2.A.51

Name _____   Date _____

Make ten to solve. Use the number bond to show how you took the 1 out.

1. Sue had 9 tennis balls and 3 soccer balls. How many balls did she have?

$9 + 3 =$ _____ $10 +$ ___ $=$ _____

Sue has ___ balls.

2.

$9 + 4 =$ _____ $10 +$ ___ $=$ ___

Use number bonds to show your thinking. Write the 10+ fact.

3. $9 + 2 =$ _____   ___ $+$ ___ $=$ _____

4. $9 + 5 =$ _____   ___ $+$ ___ $=$ _____

5. $9 + 4 =$ _____   ___ $+$ ___ $=$ _____

6. 9 + 7 = _____   _____ + _____ = _____

7. 10 + 7 = _____   9 + _____ = _____

Complete the addition sentences.

8. a. 10 + 1 = ___ 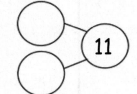   b. 9 + 2 = ___

9. a. 10 + 8 = ___ 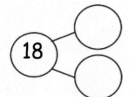   b. 9 + 9 = ___

10. a. 10 + 7 = ___   b. 9 + 8 = ___

11. a. 5 + 10 = ___   b. 6 + 9 = ___

12. a. 6 + 10 = ___   b. 7 + 9 = ___

Name _____   Date _____

Show the most efficient way to solve the number sentences.

   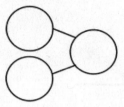

1. $9 + 7 =$ ____   2. ____ $= 9 + 5$ 3. $9 + 2 =$ ____

Name _____   Date _____

Solve the number sentences. Use number bonds to show your thinking. Write the 10+ fact and new number bond.

1. $9 + 6 =$ ___ $10 +$ ___ $=$ ___

2. $9 + 8 =$ ___   ___ $+$ ___ $=$ ___

3. $5 + 9 =$ ___   ___ $+$ ___ $=$ ___

4. $7 + 9 =$ ___   ___ $+$ ___ $=$ ___

Solve and match the number sentence to the 10+ number bond.

9 + 5 = ___   9 + 6 = ___   9 + 8 = ___

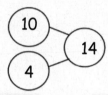

Show the most efficient strategy to solve the number sentences.

1. 9 + 7 = ___   3. 9 + 2 = ___   5. 9 + 1 = ___

2. 8 + 9 = ___   4. 4 + 9 = ___   6. 9 + 9 = ___

Lesson 6

Objective: Use the commutative property to make ten.

Suggested Lesson Structure

- ■ Fluency Practice   (10 minutes)
- ■ Application Problem   (5 minutes)
- ■ Concept Development   (35 minutes)
- ■ Student Debrief   (10 minutes)
- **Total Time**   **(60 minutes)**

Fluency Practice (10 minutes)

- Happy Counting by Twos **1.OA.5**   (2 minutes)
- Take Out 2: Number Bonds **1.OA.6**   (4 minutes)
- Decompose Addition Sentences into Three Parts **1.OA.6**   (4 minutes)

Happy Counting by Twos (2 minutes)

Note: Reviewing counting on allows students to maintain fluency with adding and subtracting 2.

Repeat the Happy Counting activity from G1–M1–Lesson 3, counting by twos from 0 to 20 and back.

Take Out 2: Number Bonds (4 minutes)

Materials: (S) Personal white boards

Note: This is an anticipatory fluency for the make ten addition strategy when one addend is 8.

Say a number within 10. Students quickly write a number bond for the number said, using 2 as a part, and hold up their boards when finished.

Decompose Addition Sentences into Three Parts (4 minutes)

Note: This fluency activity reviews adding three numbers and making ten when one addend is 9.

Lesson 6:   Use the commutative property to make ten.
Date: 7/3/13

2.A.57

Decompose addition sentences into three steps.

 T: (Write 9 + 3.) Say 3 as an addition sentence starting with 1.

 S: 1 + 2.

 T: (Write 1 + 2 below 3.) Say 9 + 3 as a three-part addition sentence.

 S: 9 + 1 + 2 = 12.

Write out the equation for students to see if necessary. Repeat process for other problems.

Application Problem (5 minutes)

There are 6 children on the swings and 9 children playing tag. How many children are playing on the playground? Make ten to solve. Create a drawing, number bond, and number sentence along with your statement.

Note: This problem gives students the chance to apply learning from Lessons 3, 4, and 5 as they solve problems with 9 as an addend. During the Debrief, the teacher can discuss how the commutative property applies to most efficiently solving the problem.

Concept Development (35 minutes)

Materials: (S) Personal white boards

Students sit next to their partner at tables or in the meeting area.

 T: (Write 5 + 9 = ____ on the board.) Turn and talk to your partner. What strategy should we use to solve efficiently?

 S: Make ten.

 T: Should we make ten with 5 or with 9? Let's have each partner try it a different way. Partner A, solve this by making ten with 5. Partner B, solve this by making ten with 9.

 S: (Solve on personal white boards as the teacher circulates.)

 T: Share your solution with your partner. Did you get the same total or a different total? Discuss how you solved it.

 S: (Share solutions and how they broke apart the numbers.)

 T: How much is 5 + 9?

 S: 14!

NOTES ON MULTIPLE MEANS OF ENGAGEMENT:

Some students will be ready for more challenging numbers. Adjust lesson structure as appropriate by providing just right numbers, such as 13 and 9, where students can continue to apply the making ten strategy in a more complex way.

COMMON CORE

Lesson 6: Use the commutative property to make ten.
Date: 7/3/13

2.A.58

T: Did you solve for the total using the same way? How did you and your partner solve this?

S: We used different ways. I broke apart 9 into 5 and 4 so I could make ten with 5 + 5, and my partner broke apart the 5 into 4 and 1 so she could make ten with 9 + 1.

T: (Write the students' solutions on board, including bonds.) So Partner A added 5 + 9 using 5 + 5 + 4. (Point to number bond.) You're saying that this is the same as Partner B's work, where she added 5 + 9 using 9 + 1 + 4. (Point to number bond.) So 5 + 5 + 4 is the same as 9 + 1 + 4? (Point to number bonds.)

S: Yes!

T: Which way did you prefer? Why?

S: I know 9 is made from 5 and 4, so taking apart 9 was fast for me.

S: Making 9 with 10 was fast and easy for me. It's just 1 away from 10. It's easy to take away 1 from a number.

T: Do we always have to start with the first addend when we are adding?

S: No. We can add in any order, as long as we add all of the parts.

T: (Project 3 + 9.) Which number should we start with?

S: 9, because all we have to do is take the 1 out of 3 to make ten.

T: On your board, find the total and show your bonds.

S: (Write 3 + 9 = 12, showing bonds of 2 and 1 under 3.)

T: What is the related 10+ fact to help you solve 3 + 9?

$$3 + 9 = 12$$
$$2 \quad 1$$

S: 10 + 2 = 12.

T: So what is 3 + 9? Say the number sentence.

S: 3 + 9 = 12.

T: (Write 9 + 4 = ___ on the board.) Which number should we make ten with?

S: 9.

$$9 + 4 = 13$$
$$3 \quad 1$$

T: Which number should we break apart?

S: 4.

T/S: (Repeat the process to find the sum.)

Repeat the process using the suggested sequence: 9 + 6, 8 + 9, and 7 + 9. For each problem, have students make ten to solve and alternate writing the related 10+ fact as a number bond and a number sentence.

Problem Set (10 minutes)

Students should do their personal best to complete the Problem Set within the allotted 10 minutes. For some classes, it may be appropriate to modify the assignment by specifying which problems they work on first. Some problems do not specify a method for solving. Students solve these problems using the RDW approach used for Application Problems.

Note: Students should save the Problem Set so it is available as a comparison during debriefs focusing on making ten when one addend is 8.

Student Debrief (10 minutes)

Lesson Objective: Use the commutative property to make ten.

The Student Debrief is intended to invite reflection and active processing of the total lesson experience.

Invite students to review their solutions for the Problem Set. They should check work by comparing answers with a partner before going over answers as a class. Look for misconceptions or misunderstandings that can be addressed in the Debrief. Guide students in a conversation to debrief the Problem Set and process the lesson. You may choose to use any combination of the questions below to lead the discussion.

- Look at Problem 8. Find as many related equal equations as you can.

- Look at Problem 8. In which problem can you use your doubles + 1 fact to help you solve?

- How did we apply the make ten strategy today to solve addition problems efficiently?

- To solve 3 + 9, which addend should we make ten with? Why?

- Look at your Application Problem. Turn and talk to your partner about which addend we should break apart to solve the problem more efficiently.

Exit Ticket (3 minutes)

After the Student Debrief, instruct students to complete the Exit Ticket. A review of their work will help you assess the students' understanding of the concepts that were presented in the lesson today and plan more effectively for future lessons. You may read the questions aloud to the students.

Name _____   Date _____

1. Solve.

Write the bond for
the related 10 fact.

$9 + 2 = 11$ $2 + 9 = 11$

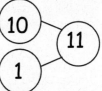

___

2. $9 + 6 =$ ____ $6 + 9 =$ ____

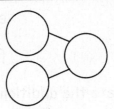

___

3. $7 + 9 =$ ____ $9 + 7 =$ ____

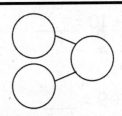

___

Use number bonds to show your thinking.   Write the related 10+ fact.

4. $9 + 4 =$ ____   ____ + ____ = ____

5. $3 + 9 =$ ____   ____ + ____ = ____

6. $9 + 5 =$ ____   ____ + ____ = ____

COMMON CORE | Lesson 6: | Use the commutative property to make ten.
Date: | 7/3/13

2.A.61

7. Match the equal expressions.

a. 9 + 3	10 + 4
b. 5 + 9	10 + 0
c. 9 + 6	10 + 2
d. 8 + 9	10 + 5
e. 9 + 7	10 + 7
f. 9 + 1	10 + 6

8. Complete the addition sentences to make them true.

a. 2 + 10 = ____   f. 7 + 9 = ____   k. __ + 10 = 14

b. 3 + 9 = ____   g. 3 + 10 = ____   l. __ + 9 = 14

c. 10 + 9 = ____   h. 8 + 9 = ____   m. __ + 7 = 17

d. 5 + 9 = ____   i. ___ + 10 = 18   n. __ + 9 = 17

e. 6 + 10 = ____   j. __ + 9 = 16

COMMON CORE™   Lesson 6:   Use the commutative property to make ten.
Date: 7/3/13

© 2013 Common Core, Inc. All rights reserved. commoncore.org

2.A.62

Name _____   Date _____

1. Solve. Use number bonds to show your thinking.

$9 + 5 =$ ____ $5 + 9 =$ ____

Write the bond for the related 10 fact.

(10)

---

2. Solve. Draw a line to match the related facts. Write the related 10+ fact.

$9 + 7 =$ ____   ____ $= 9 + 8$ _____

____ $= 6 + 9$ $7 + 9 =$ ____   _____

$8 + 9 =$ ____ $9 + 6 =$ ____   _____

Name _____ Date _____

1. Solve. Use your number bonds. Draw a line to match the related facts. Write the related 10+ fact.

9 + 6 = ____	____ = 9 + 8
	_____
____ = 3 + 9	____ = 7 + 9
	_____
___ = 9 + 5	6 + 9 = ____
	$10 + 5 = 15$
8 + 9 = ____	9 + 3 = ____
	_____
9 + 7 = ____	5 + 9 = ____
	================

2. Complete the addition sentences to make them true.

a. 3 + 10 = ___

b. 4 + 9 = ___

c. 10 + 5 = ___

d. 9 + 6 = ___

e. 7 + 10 = ___

f. ___ = 7 + 9

g. 10 + ___ = 18

h. 9 + 8 = ___

i. ___ + 9 = 19

j. 5 + 9 = ___

COMMON CORE | Lesson 6:   Use the commutative property to make ten.
Date: 7/3/13

2.A.64

3. Find and color the expression that is equal to the snowman's hat. Write the true number sentence below.

10 + 3 = _____

_____ = _____

_____ = _____

_____ = _____

COMMON CORE™

Lesson 6:   Use the commutative property to make ten.
Date: 7/3/13

2.A.65

Lesson 7

Objective: Make ten when one addend is 8.

Suggested Lesson Structure

■ Fluency Practice   (13 minutes)
▨ Application Problem   (7 minutes)
▢ Concept Development   (30 minutes)
■ Student Debrief   (10 minutes)
  Total Time   **(60 minutes)**

Fluency Practice (13 minutes)

- Add to 9 **1.OA.6**   (5 minutes)
- Friendly Fact Go Around: Make it Equal **1.OA.6**   (5 minutes)
- Take Out 2: Addition Sentences **1.OA.6**   (3 minutes)

Add to 9 (5 minutes)

Materials: (T) 9 + *n* addition cards (S) Personal white boards

Note: This activity supports the make ten addition strategy, as students will need to fluently decompose an addend in order to make ten.

Show an addition flashcard (e.g., 9 + 3). Students write the three-addend expression (9 + 1 + 2 = 12).

Friendly Fact Go Around: Make it Equal (5 minutes)

Materials: (T) Friendly Fact Go Around: Make it Equal

Note: This activity reinforces the make ten adding strategy and promotes an understanding of equality.

Project the Friendly Fact Go Around: Make it Equal (or make and display a poster). Point to a problem and call on a student: 9 + 6 = 10 + ☐. The student answers "five." The class says the number sentence aloud, with the answer, "Nine plus six equals ten plus five." If a student gives an incorrect answer, he then repeats the correct equation that the class gave. The teacher can adapt the problem to individual children, pointing to easier problems for children who are less fluent.

Lesson 7:   Make ten when one addend is 8.
Date: 7/3/13

2.A.66

Take Out 2: Addition Sentences (3 minutes)

Note: This activity supports the make ten addition strategy when one addend is 8, since 8 needs 2 to make ten.

Say a number between 2 and 10 (e.g., 3). Students say an addition sentence beginning with 2 (2 + 1 = 3).

Application Problem (7 minutes)

Stacy made 6 drawings. Matthew made 2 drawings. Tim made 4 drawings. How many drawings did they make altogether? Use a drawing, a number sentence, and a statement to match the story.

Note: Some students may actually create detailed drawings. You may wish to continue discussing how simple shapes, such as squares or circles, can be used to efficiently represent the story's drawings, rather than spending time and thought on elaborate pictures.

Concept Development (30 minutes)

Materials: (T) 10 blue and 10 yellow linking cubes, a ten-frame border (S) 10 blue and 10 yellow linking cubes, personal white boards

Have students sit at their seats with materials.

- T: (Project and read aloud.) Peter has 8 books and Willie has 5. How many books do they have altogether?
- T: What is the expression to solve this problem?
- S: 8 + 5.
- T: Use your blue linking cubes in 5-groups to show how many books Peter has on your personal white board.
- S: (Organize 8 blue linking cubes.)
- T: Use your yellow cubes to show how many books Willie has. Put them in a line of five next to your personal board.
- S: (Organize 5 yellow linking cubes.)
- T: What are the different ways we can solve 8 + 5?
- S: Count on! → Make ten with 5! → Make ten with 8!
- T: (Call on students to demonstrate each of these strategies, saving making 10 with 8 for the end. As a student volunteer makes ten, use the ten-frame border to physically group the ten.)

MP.7

NOTES ON MULTIPLE MEANS OF REPRESENTATION:

When using colors in lessons be sensitive to those students who have difficulty seeing certain colors. If you have these students in your classroom, use primary colors and typically sharp contrast, like green (or red) and yellow that can be distinguished by these students. Be sure to adjust the color names to align when implementing the concept development.

MP.7

T: Let's use the last strategy to solve 8 + 5. Everyone, make ten with 8!

S: (Move 2 yellow cubes to the blue pile.)

T: With your marker, draw a frame around your 10 cubes.

S: (Frame 10 cubes.)

T: We have 10 here. (Gesture to the 10.) What do we have left here? (Point to the other pile.)

S: 3.

T: Look at your new groups. What is our new number sentence?

S: 10 + 3 = 13!

T: (Write 10 + 3 = 13 on the board.) Did we change the *number* of linking cubes we have?

S: No.

T: So, 8 + 5 is the same as what addition expression?

S: 10 + 3.

T: (Write 8 + 5 = 10 + 3.)

T: What is 10 + 3?

S: 13.

T: What is 8 + 5? Say the number sentence.

S: 8 + 5 = 13.

T: How many books do Peter and Willie have?

S: 13 books.

Repeat the process with the following suggested sequence: 8 + 3; 8 + 6; 4 + 8; 8 + 7; 8 + 8. Be sure to have students make ten with 8, reinforcing the concept of commutativity for efficient problem solving. Write both number sentences (8 + 6 = 14, 10 + 4 = 14) and a number sentence equating the equivalent expressions (8 + 6 = 10 + 4).

Problem Set (10 minutes)

Students should do their personal best to complete the Problem Set within the allotted 10 minutes. For some classes, it may be appropriate to modify the assignment by specifying which problems they work on first. Some problems do not specify a method for solving. Students solve these problems using the RDW approach used for Application Problems.

Student Debrief (10 minutes)

Lesson Objective: Make ten when one addend is 8.

Note: Distribute the student Problem Set from Lesson 3 for comparing with today's Problem Set.

The Student Debrief is intended to invite reflection and active processing of the total lesson experience.

Invite students to review their solutions for the Problem Set. They should check work by comparing answers with a partner before going over answers as a class. Look for misconceptions or misunderstandings that can be addressed in the Debrief. Guide students in a conversation to debrief the Problem Set and process the lesson. You may choose to use any combination of the questions below to lead the discussion.

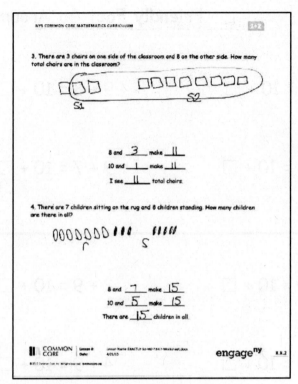

- Look at Problem 1. What are the two number sentences that match the statements? (Repeat with other problems as expeditious and necessary.)

- How can we write a true number sentence with these expressions? (8 + 5 = 10 + 3)

- When you had 8 as an addend, how many objects did you circle from the other addend?

- Look at your Problem Set from a few days ago. How are these problems similar? How are they different? What do you notice about the answers when you have 9 as an addend compared to 8 as an addend? Why do you think this is?

- Look at the Application Problem. What did you add first? Why? (Some students may have added 6 + 4 because it is an efficient way to make ten. Some students may still be adding the numbers in order. If students added 6 + 2 first, ask them to use today's lesson to show making ten to solve.)

Exit Ticket (3 minutes)

After the Student Debrief, instruct students to complete the Exit Ticket. A review of their work will help you assess the students' understanding of the concepts that were presented in the lesson today and plan more effectively for future lessons. You may read the questions aloud to the students.

Friendly Fact Go Around: Make it Equal

$9 + 1 = 10 + \square$ $\qquad$ $9 + 3 = 10 + \square$ $\qquad$ $9 + 5 = 10 + \square$

$9 + 4 = 10 + \square$ $\qquad$ $9 + 7 = 10 + \square$ $\qquad$ $9 + 6 = 10 + \square$

$3 + 9 = 10 + \square$ $\qquad$ $2 + 9 = 10 + \square$ $\qquad$ $8 + 9 = 10 + \square$

$5 + 9 = 10 + \square$ $\qquad$ $4 + 9 = 10 + \square$ $\qquad$ $9 + 9 = 10 + \square$

$9 + 4 = \square + 10$ $\qquad$ $9 + 6 = \square + 10$ $\qquad$ $9 + 5 = \square + 10$

$9 + 2 = \square + 10$ $\qquad$ $9 + 7 = \square + 10$ $\qquad$ $9 + 9 = \square + 10$

$9 + \square = 10 + 5$ $\qquad$ $9 + \square = 10 + 7$ $\qquad$ $9 + \square = 10 + 8$

$9 + \square = 10 + 3$ $\qquad$ $9 + \square = 10 + 4$ $\qquad$ $9 + \square = 10 + 6$

COMMON CORE™
| Lesson 7: | Make ten when one addend is 8. |
| Date: | 7/3/13 |

2.A.70

Name _____   Date _____

Draw and circle to show how you made ten to help you solve.

1. John has 8 tennis balls. Toni has 5. How many tennis balls do they have in all?

J

T

8 and _____ make _____.

10 and _____ make _____.

John and Toni have _____ tennis balls in all.

2. Bob has 8 raisins and Jenny has 4. How many raisins do they have altogether?

8 and _____ make _____.

10 and _____ make _____.

Bob and Jenny have _____ raisins altogether.

3. There are 3 chairs on the right side of the classroom and 8 on the left side. How many total chairs are in the classroom?

8 and _____ make _____.

10 and _____ make _____.

There are _____ total chairs.

4. There are 7 children sitting on the rug and 8 children standing. How many children are there in all?

8 and _____ make _____.

10 and _____ make _____.

There are _____ children in all.

Name _____ Date _____

Draw, label, and (circle) to show how you made ten to help you solve.

Write the number sentences you used to solve.

1. Nick picks some peppers. He picks 5 green peppers and 8 red peppers. How many peppers does he pick in all?

_____ + _____ = _____

_____ + _____ = _____   Nick picks _____ peppers.

Name _____ Date _____

Draw, label, and (circle) to show how you made ten to help you solve.

Write the number sentences you used to solve.

1. Meg gets 8 toy animals and 4 toy cars at a party.
    How many toys does Meg get in all?

8 + 4 = _____

10 + _____ = _____   Meg gets _____ toys.

2. John makes 6 baskets in his first basketball game and 8 baskets in his second.
    How many baskets does he make altogether?

_____ + _____ = _____

_____ + _____ = _____   John makes _____ baskets.

3. May has a party. She invites 7 girls and 8 boys. How many friends does she invite in all?

_____ + _____ = _____

_____ + _____ = _____   May invites _____ friends.

4. Alec collects baseball hats. He has 9 Mets hats and 8 Yankee hats. How many hats are in his collection?

_____ + _____ = _____

_____ + _____ = _____   Alec has _____ hats.

9 + n Addition Cards

Directions: Print on cardstock and cut.

$9 + 2 =$	$3 + 9 =$
$9 + 4 =$	$5 + 9 =$
$9 + 6 =$	$7 + 9 =$
$9 + 8 =$	$9 + 9 =$

Lesson 8

Objective: Make ten when one addend is 8.

Suggested Lesson Structure

■ Fluency Practice	(15 minutes)
■ Application Problem	(5 minutes)
■ Concept Development	(30 minutes)
■ Student Debrief	(10 minutes)
Total Time	**(60 minutes)**

Fluency Practice (15 minutes)

- Sprint: 9 + *n* **1.OA.6**   (10 minutes)
- Happy Counting by Twos **1.OA.5**   (2 minutes)
- Take Out 2: Addition Sentences **1.OA.6**   (3 minutes)

Sprint: 9 + *n* (10 minutes)

Materials: (S) 9 + *n* Sprint

Note: This sprint provides practice with the make ten addition strategy, when one addend is 9.

Happy Counting by Twos (2 minutes)

Note: Reviewing counting on allows students to maintain fluency with adding and subtracting 2.

Repeat the Happy Counting activity from G1–M2–Lesson 4, counting by twos from 0 to 20 and back (this range may be adjusted to meet the needs of students). As students strengthen their skills, start with other numbers such as 1, 7, 11, or 8.

Take Out 2: Addition Sentences (3 minutes)

Note: This activity supports the make ten addition strategy when one addend is 8 since 8 needs 2 to make ten.

Say a number between 2 and 10 (e.g., 3). Students say an addition sentence beginning with 2 (2 + 1 = 3).

COMMON CORE™	Lesson 8: Date:	Make ten when one addend is 8. 7/3/13

2.A.77

Application Problem (5 minutes)

A tree lost 8 leaves one day and 4 leaves the next. How many leaves did the tree lose at the end of the two days? Use a number bond, a number sentence, and a statement to match the story.

Extension: On the third day, the tree lost 6 leaves. How many leaves did it lose by the end of the third day?

Note: This problem revisits the idea of making ten when one addend is 8, which students have been working on since Lesson 7. It also challenges students to use addition though the leaves are being lost.

Concept Development (30 minutes)

Materials: (T) 10 blue and 10 yellow linking cubes, ten-frame border (S) Personal white boards

Have students come to the meeting area with their personal white boards.

T: (Project and read aloud.) Amy wrote 8 letters to her friends. Peter wrote 3 to his friends. How many letters did they write? (Pause.) What is the expression to solve this story?

S: 8 + 3.

T: How many blue cubes do I need to represent the number of letters Amy wrote? How should I arrange it?

S: 8 cubes. Put them in a 5-group.

T: Why should I organize them in 5-group?

S: It's easy for everyone to see that there are 8 instead of counting the cubes.

T: With your partner, figure out how many letters Amy and Peter wrote. Use your personal white board to record how you solved it.

S: (Discuss and solve problem, while teacher circulates and listens.)

T: How many letters did Amy and Peter write?

S: 11!

T: How did you solve the problem?

S: I counted on from 8. Eiiight, 9, 10, 11. → I put 2 cubes with the 8 blue ones and had 1 cube left. That made 11. → I broke apart the 3 into 2 and 1 to make 10 and 1.

T: Let's all try using this last strategy of making ten to solve this problem.

T: (Lay out 8 blue cubes.) How many yellow cubes do I need to represent the number of letters Peter wrote?

S: 3 cubes.

T: (Lay out 3 yellow cubes as a separate pile.) What should we do to add 8 and 3 efficiently?

S: Make ten!

T: How many does 8 need to make ten?

S: 2.

T: (Place 2 yellow cubes into 5-group arrangement.)

T: Now that we have 10 here, we can put a frame around it. (Frame it.) Look at the new piles. What expression is 8 + 3 equal to?

S: 10 + 1.

T: Let's write a true number sentence using these expressions. (Write 8 + 3 = 10 + 1.)

T: What's 10 + 1?

S: 11.

T: (Write 10 + 1 = 11). So, what is 8 + 3? Say the number sentence.

S: 8 + 3 = 11.

T: (Write 8 + 3 = 11.) How many letters did Amy and Peter write?

S: 11 letters.

T: Show me on your personal board how we solved 8 + 3. Remember, it's easy to show how we are solving 8 + 3 if we organize our math drawings just like the way we organized the cubes. Use empty circles to represent 8 and dark circles to represent 3. Don't forget to put a frame around the 10 cubes!

S: (Draw.)

T: Where is the 3 in your picture?

S: (Point to 2 and 1.)

T: You are pointing to two different places. Why?

S: We broke 3 apart to 2 and 1.

T: Let's use a number bond to show how we broke apart 3.

T: Just like we framed the ten in our picture, we'll frame the numbers that make ten. (Ring 8 and 2.)

T: 8 and 2 make?

S: 10.

T: 10 and 1 make?

S: 11.

T: So, 8 plus 3 equals?

S: 11!

NOTES ON MULTIPLE MEANS OF ENGAGEMENT:

Adjust lesson structure to suit specific learning needs remembering that some students may need to keep practicing with their linking cubes as they complete problems.

NOTES ON MULTIPLE MEANS OF ENGAGEMENT:

Offer opportunities for student leadership as "teacher." Have students demonstrate for the class how they are breaking apart and joining their linking cubes. Listen for accurate use of math vocabulary in their description. Words you want to hear them using include *expression, organize, join, broke apart* and *frame*.

Repeat the process adding the numbers 4–9 in order as time allows, alternating 8 as the first and the second addend. Use linking cubes to illustrate what the math drawings should look like for perhaps one more example but move *towards having students draw without the visual aid*.

Before students add dark circles to their math drawing, ask them, "How many does 8 need to make ten?" and "How many do you have when you take away 2 from [the other addend]?" to guide how they will decompose the addend when drawing.

Be sure to have students make ten with 8, reinforcing the concept of commutativity for efficient problem solving, and write two number sentences (8 + 6 = 14, 10 + 4 = 14) and the equivalent expression (8 + 6 = 10 + 4).

Problem Set (10 minutes)

Students should do their personal best to complete the Problem Set within the allotted 10 minutes. For some classes, it may be appropriate to modify the assignment by specifying which problems they work on first. Some problems do not specify a method for solving. Students solve these problems using the RDW approach used for Application Problems.

Student Debrief (10 minutes)

Lesson Objective: Make ten when one addend is 8.

Note: Distribute student Problem Set from Lesson 4 for comparing with today's Problem Set.

The Student Debrief is intended to invite reflection and active processing of the total lesson experience.

Invite students to review their solutions for the Problem Set. They should check work by comparing answers with a partner before going over answers as a class. Look for misconceptions or misunderstandings that can be addressed in the Debrief. Guide students in a conversation to debrief the Problem Set and process the lesson. You may choose to use any combination of the questions below to lead the discussion.

- Look at Problem 1 and Problem 6. How are your drawings different? Which drawing shows how you solved 8 + 5 more easily?
- What did you notice about having 8 as an addend? What happens to the other addend when it gets broken apart?
- How did Problem 6 help you solve Problem 7?
- Look at your Problem Set from a few days ago. What do you notice about the answers when you have 9 as an addend compared to 8 as an addend? Why do you think this is?
- How would you solve 8 + 9? Turn and talk to your partner. Explain your strategy.

- Why is it important to make our math drawings in an organized way?
- Look at your Application Problem. Draw an organized picture to show how you can solve this problem.

Exit Ticket (3 minutes)

After the Student Debrief, instruct students to complete the Exit Ticket. A review of their work will help you assess the students' understanding of the concepts that were presented in the lesson today and plan more effectively for future lessons. You may read the questions aloud to the students.

Name _____   Date _____

A *Write the missing number.

Number correct: ☆

1	$9 + 1 = \square$		16	$9 + 5 = \square$	
2	$10 + 1 = \square$		17	$9 + 6 = \square$	
3	$9 + 2 = \square$		18	$6 + 9 = \square$	
4	$9 + 1 = \square$		19	$9 + 4 = \square$	
5	$10 + 2 = \square$		20	$4 + 9 = \square$	
6	$9 + 3 = \square$		21	$9 + 8 = \square$	
7	$9 + 1 = \square$		22	$9 + 9 = \square$	
8	$10 + 4 = \square$		23	$9 + \square = 18$	
9	$9 + 5 = \square$		24	$\square + 6 = 15$	
10	$9 + 1 = \square$		25	$\square + 6 = 16$	
11	$10 + 6 = \square$		26	$13 = 9 + \square$	
12	$9 + 7 = \square$		27	$17 = 8 + \square$	
13	$9 + 1 = \square$		28	$10 + 2 = 9 + \square$	
14	$10 + 8 = \square$		29	$9 + 5 = 10 + \square$	
15	$9 + 9 = \square$		30	$\square + 7 = 8 + 9$	

Name _____   Date _____

B* Write the missing number.

Number correct:

1	$9 + 1 = \square$		16	$5 + 9 = \square$	
2	$10 + 2 = \square$		17	$6 + 9 = \square$	
3	$9 + 3 = \square$		18	$9 + 6 = \square$	
4	$9 + 1 = \square$		19	$9 + 7 = \square$	
5	$10 + 1 = \square$		20	$7 + 9 = \square$	
6	$9 + 2 = \square$		21	$9 + 8 = \square$	
7	$9 + 1 = \square$		22	$9 + 9 = \square$	
8	$10 + 3 = \square$		23	$9 + \square = 17$	
9	$9 + 4 = \square$		24	$\square + 5 = 14$	
10	$9 + 1 = \square$		25	$\square + 4 = 14$	
11	$10 + 5 = \square$		26	$15 = 9 + \square$	
12	$9 + 6 = \square$		27	$16 = 7 + \square$	
13	$9 + 1 = \square$		28	$10 + 4 = 9 + \square$	
14	$10 + 4 = \square$		29	$9 + 6 = 10 + \square$	
15	$9 + 5 = \square$		30	$\square + 6 = 7 + 9$	

COMMON CORE™   Lesson 8:   Make ten when one addend is 8.
Date: 7/3/13

2.A.83

Name _____　　　Date _____

Circle to make ten. Write the 10+ number sentence and solve.

1.　Tom only has 8 goldfish and 5 angelfish. How many fish does Tom have in all?

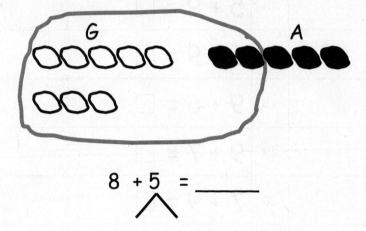

8 + 5 = _____

10 fish + _____ fish = _____ fish

Make ten by circling and solve.

2.　8 + 3 = _____

10 + _____ = _____

3.　4 + 8 = _____

10 + _____ = _____

COMMON CORE　Lesson 8:　Make ten when one addend is 8.
Date:　7/3/13

2.A.84

Solve. Make math drawings using the ten-frame to show how you made ten to solve.

4. 8 + 4 = ____   ____ + ____ = ____

5. 6 + 8 = ____   ____ + ____ = ____

6. 8 + 5 = ____   ____ + ____ = ____

Solve. Use a number bond to show how you made a ten.

7. 5 + 8 = ____

8. ____ = 8 + 7

Name _____ Date _____

Make math drawings using the ten-frame to solve. Rewrite as a 10+ number sentence.

1. 6 + 8 = ____

2. ____ = 4 + 8

10 + ____ = ____

____ + ____ = ____

Name _____   Date _____

Solve. Make math drawings using the ten-frame to show
how you made ten to solve.

1. 8 + 3 = ___   ___ + ___ = _____

2. 8 + 6 = ___   ___ + ___ = _____

3. 7 + 8 = ___   ___ + ___ = _____

Make math drawings using ten-frames to solve. Circle the true number sentences.

Write an X to show number sentences that are not true.

a. $8 + 4 = 10 + 2$

b. $10 + 6 = 8 + 8$

c. $7 + 8 = 10 + 6$

d. $5 + 10 = 5 + 8$

e. $2 + 10 = 8 + 3$

f. $8 + 9 = 10 + 7$

Lesson 9

Objective: Compare efficiency of counting on and making ten when one addend is 8.

Suggested Lesson Structure

■ Fluency Practice   (12 minutes)
■ Application Problem   (8 minutes)
■ Concept Development   (30 minutes)
■ Student Debrief   (10 minutes)

  Total Time   **(60 minutes)**

Fluency Practice (12 minutes)

- Decompose Addition Sentences into Three Parts **1.OA.6**   (5 minutes)
- Cold Call: Break Apart Numbers **1.OA.6**   (2 minutes)
- Make It Equal **1.OA.6**   (5 minutes)

Decompose Addition Sentences into Three Parts (5 minutes)

Note: This fluency activity reviews adding three numbers and making ten when one addend is 8.

Decompose addition sentences into three steps.

    T: (Write 8 + 3.) How many do we need from 3 to make ten?
    S: 2.
    T: Say 3 as an addition expression, starting with 2.
    S: 2 + 1.
    T: (Write 2 + 1 below the 3, showing the decomposition of 3.) Say 8 + 3 as a three-part addition
         sentence.
    S: 8 + 2 + 1 = 12.

Repeat process for other problems.

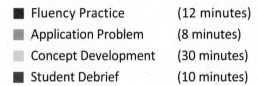

Lesson 9:	Compare efficiency of counting on and making ten when one addend is 8.	2.A.89
Date:	7/3/13	

© 2013 Common Core, Inc. All rights reserved. commoncore.org

Cold Call: Break Apart Numbers (2 minutes)

Note: This is an anticipatory fluency for making ten when one addend is 7 since 7 needs 3 to make ten.

Say a number between 3 and 10. Tell students you will Cold Call them to say the number bond with 3 as a part. Alternate between calling on individual students, the whole class, and groups of students (e.g., only boys, only girls). Use the example below as a reference.

- T: 4 (Pause to provide thinking time.) Everybody.
- S: 3 and 1.
- T: 6. (Pause.) Boys.
- S: (Only boys.) 3 and 3.

Repeat with numbers 3 through 10.

Make It Equal (5 minutes)

Materials: (S) 5-group cards, 1 "=" card, and 2 "+" cards (from G1–M2–Lesson 1) per set of partners

Note: This activity reinforces the make ten addition strategy as students relate $10 + n$ addition sentences to an equivalent sentence with an addend of 8 or 9. Students ready to use the numeral side of the 5-group cards should be encouraged to do so.

Assign students partners of equal ability. Students arrange 5-group cards from 0 to 10, including the extra 5, and place the "=" card between them.

Write four numbers on the white board (e.g., 10, 9, 1, and 2). Partners take the 5-group cards that match the numbers written to make two equivalent expressions (e.g., 10 + 1 = 9 + 2).

Suggested sequence: 10, 9, 1, 2; 10, 3, 9, 2; 10, 4, 5, 9; 10, 8, 1, 3; 10, 8, 4, 2; etc.

Application Problem (8 minutes)

A squirrel found 8 nuts in the morning, 5 nuts in the afternoon, and 2 nuts in the evening. How many nuts did the squirrel collect in all?

Extension: The next day, the squirrel found 3 more nuts in the morning, 1 more in the afternoon, and 1 more in the evening. How many did he collect over the two days?

Note: This problem uses three addends, revisiting the associative and commutative properties from earlier in this topic. During the Debrief, students who used making ten as a strategy to solve will share their work, supporting students' development toward independent use of the strategy.

Concept Development (30 minutes)

Materials: (S) Personal white boards

Have students sit at their desks or the meeting area with their materials.

T: (Project or write the two number bonds shown here.) Which number bond are you able to solve faster?

S: 10 and 4!

T: (Write 10 + 4 = ___.) 10 + 4 = ?

S: 14!

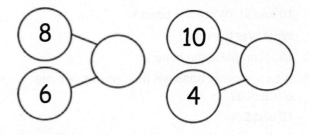

T: (Record the solution.) How did you know that so quickly?

S: Because we know our 10+ facts. → Because 10 is a friendly number.

T: (Write 8 + 6 = ___.) Let's count on to solve 8 + 6.

T/S: Eeeiiiight, 9, 10, 11, 12, 13, 14. 14!

T: (Record the solution.)

T: (On another line, write 8 + 6 = ___.) What expression is equal to 8 + 6?

S: 10 + 4!

T: (Record this to make the true number sentence 8 + 6 = 10 + 4.) Use your personal white board to show how you can solve 8 + 6 by making ten, to be sure that this is a true number sentence.

S: (Solve by making ten with 8, taking apart 6 into 2 and 4, etc.)

T: (Read aloud.) Our friends Sergio and Lila are back again! They were getting ready to go to P.E. They both had to solve 8 + 7. The first one to solve it got to go to P.E. first! Sergio decided he was going to count on to solve it again. (Pause.) Was there another way to solve 8 + 7 that Sergio could have used?

S: (Discuss, as teacher circulates and listens.) Make ten! → Take 2 from 7 to make ten from 8.

T: Some of you said that you would make ten. Well, that is just what Lila decided to do again. (Assign partners.) Partner A, explain to your partner how Sergio solved 8 + 7 by counting on. Partner B, explain to your partner how Lila solved 8 + 7 by making ten. Use your personal white board if it helps you share your thoughts.

S: (Discuss, as teacher circulates and listens.)

NOTES ON
MULTIPLE MEANS FOR
ENGAGEMENT:

Students enjoy the use of interactive technology in the classroom. Do an Internet search of *make ten* or something similar. This provides some websites for use during independent time or if you have the means to use the website with the entire class.

COMMON CORE   Lesson 9:   Compare efficiency of counting on and making ten when one addend is 8.

Date: 7/3/13   2.A.91

T: Help me make a number bond to show what Sergio did. What were the parts that Sergio used?

S: 8 and 7! (Write the bond.)

T: What was the total?

S: 15. (Complete the bond.)

T: Help me make a number bond to show what Lila did. What were the parts that Lila used?

S: 10 and 5! (Write the bond.)

T: What was the total?

S: 15. (Complete the bond.)

T: Which number bond will help you solve more efficiently?

S: 10 and 5.

T: So, based on these number bonds, and the work you and your partner just did, who do you think got to go to P.E. first?

S: Lila!

T: Again, you're right! Since Lila really knows how to use the make ten strategy, she was able to solve for the unknown very quickly or efficiently. Sometimes it takes practice before we can use a strategy quickly. When a strategy is new to us, it can take longer for us to use it until we get better at it. Let's keep practicing.

Continue with partners solving each problem showing how to solve using counting on and making ten. The following is a suggested sequence of problems: 8 + 5; 8 + 4; 8 + 8; 8 + 3 (counting on may actually be more efficient here); 8 + 9.

Problem Set (10 minutes)

Students should do their personal best to complete the Problem Set within the allotted 10 minutes. For some classes, it may be appropriate to modify the assignment by specifying which problems they work on first. Some problems do not specify a method for solving. Students solve these problems using the RDW approach used for Application Problems.

Student Debrief (10 minutes)

Lesson Objective: Compare efficiency of counting on and making ten when one addend is 8.

NOTES ON MULTIPLE MEANS OF ACTION AND EXPRESSION:

While encouraging students to use the most efficient strategy when solving number sentences, some may be able to use different number combinations as efficiently. For example, some might see 7 + 8 as 7 + 7 + 1 or 8 + 8 – 1, and some may already know 7 + 8 but benefit from the strategy discussion. Use this opportunity to show your students how we all think differently and have the students communicate their mathematical thinking to the class.

Note: Distribute student Problem Set from Lesson 5 for comparing with today's Problem Set.

The Student Debrief is intended to invite reflection and active processing of the total lesson experience.

Invite students to review their solutions for the Problem Set. They should check work by comparing answers with a partner before going over answers as a class. Look for misconceptions or misunderstandings that can be addressed in the Debrief. Guide students in a conversation to debrief the Problem Set and process the lesson. You may choose to use any combination of the questions below to lead the discussion.

- Look at Problem 1 and Problem 2. How are your bonds different? How can Problem 1 help you solve Problem 2?

- Look at Problems 8–10. What do you notice about the number bonds? How does knowing your 10+ facts help you with your 8+ facts?

- Look at Problem 5 and Problem 8. Do you think counting on or making ten was more efficient to solve these? Why?

- Look at your Problem Set from a few days ago. What do you notice about the answers when you have 9 as an addend compared to 8 as an addend? Why do you think this is?

- Look at your Application Problem. Would counting on or making ten help you solve this problem most efficiently? If you used making ten to solve this, share your work and explain your thinking.

- One first grader I know makes ten for some of her 8+ facts, some she counts on to solve. Sometimes she just knows the solution. Is that true for any of you? Which 8+ facts do you use a particular strategy to help you solve? Why?

Exit Ticket (3 minutes)

After the Student Debrief, instruct students to complete the Exit Ticket. A review of their work will help you assess the students' understanding of the concepts that were presented in the lesson today and plan more effectively for future lessons. You may read the questions aloud to the students.

Name _____   Date _____

Make ten to solve. Use a number bond to show how you took 2 out to make ten.

1. Ben has 8 green grapes and 3 purple grapes. How many grapes does he have?

$8 + 3 = $ _____ $10 + $ ____ $ = $ _____

Ben has ____ grapes.

2. $8 + 4 = $ _____ $10 + $ ____ $ = $ _____

Use number bonds to show your thinking. Write the 10+ fact.

3. $8 + 5 = $ _____   ____ $ + $ ____ $ = $ ____

4. $8 + 7 = $ _____   ____ $ + $ ____ $ = $ ____

5. $4 + 8 =$ _____   _____ $+$ _____ $=$ _____

6. $7 + 8 =$ _____   _____ $+$ _____ $=$ _____

7. $8 +$ _____ $=$ _____   _____ $+$ _____ $=$ _____

Complete the addition sentences.

8. a. $10 + 1 =$ ___   b. $8 + 3 =$ ___

9. a. $10 + 5 =$ ___   b. $8 + 7 =$ ___

10. a. $10 + 6 =$ ___   b. $8 + 8 =$ ___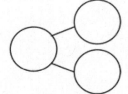

11. a. $2 + 10 =$ ___   b. $4 + 8 =$ ___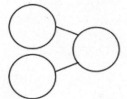

12. a. $4 + 10 =$ ___   b. $6 + 8 =$ ___

Name _____   Date _____

Seyla has 3 stamps in her collection. Her father gives her 8 more stamps. How many stamps does she have now? Show how you make ten and write the 10+ fact.

3 + 8 = _____   10 + _____ = _____

Complete the addition sentences.

a. 8 + 6 = _____   b. 10 + _____ = 14

COMMON CORE | **Lesson 9:**   Compare efficiency of counting on and making ten when one
                   | addend is 8.
                   | **Date:**   7/3/13

2.A.96

© 2013 Common Core, Inc. All rights reserved. commoncore.org

Name _____   Date _____

Use number bonds to show your thinking. Write the 10+ fact.

1. 8 + 3 = _____   10 + _____ = _____

2. 6 + 8 = _____   _____ + 10 = _____

3. _____ = 8 + 8   _____ = 10 + _____

4. _____ = 5 + 8   _____ = 10 + _____

Complete the addition sentences.

5. a. 7 + 8 = _____   b. 10 + 5 = _____

6. a. 16 = _____ + 8   b. 10 + 6 = _____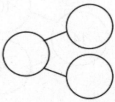

COMMON CORE

Lesson 9:   Compare efficiency of counting on and making ten when one
addend is 8.

Date: 7/3/13

2.A.97

7. a. ____ = 9 + 8   b. 10 + 7 = ____

Draw a line to the matching number sentence. You may use a number bond or 5-group drawing to help you.

8. 11 = 8 + 3

| 8 + 6 = 14 |

9. Lisa had 5 red rocks and 8 white rocks. How many rocks did she have?

| 10 + 1 = 11 |

10.

| 13 = 10 + 3 |

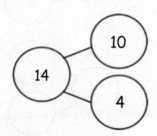

COMMON CORE   Lesson 9:   Compare efficiency of counting on and making ten when one addend is 8.

Date: 7/3/13

2.A.98

Lesson 10

Objective: Solve problems with addends of 7, 8, and 9.

Suggested Lesson Structure

- ■ Fluency Practice   (10 minutes)
- ■ Application Problem   (6 minutes)
- ■ Concept Development   (30 minutes)
- ■ Student Debrief   (14 minutes)
- **Total Time**   **(60 minutes)**

Fluency Practice (10 minutes)

- 1, 2, and 3 Less **1.OA.6**   (3 minutes)
- Decomposing Addition Sentences **1.OA.6**   (5 minutes)
- Happy Counting by Threes **1.OA.5**   (2 minutes)

1, 2, and 3 Less (3 minutes)

Note: This fluency activity prepares students for today's lesson, as students will decompose numbers to make ten with addends of 7, 8, and 9.

- T: On my signal, say the number that is 1 less.
- T: 3 (snap).
- S: 2.

Continue with all numbers within 10. Then repeat with 2 less and 3 less.

Decomposing Addition Sentences (5 minutes)

Note: This activity reviews how to decompose numbers to make ten, creating equivalent but easier number sentences.

Write number sentences on the board to model how to decompose number sentences into three addends.

$$9 + 5 = 14$$
$$9 + 1 + 4 = 14$$

- T: (Write 9 + 5 = ___ on the board.) What does 9 need to make ten?
- S: 1.
- T: (Write 9 + 1 below 9 + 5 = ___.)
- T: (Point to the 5.) If we take 1 from 5 to make ten, what part is left?

COMMON CORE   Lesson 10:   Solve problems with addends of 7, 8, and 9.
                   Date: 7/3/13   2.A.99

S: 4.

T: (Add "+ 4" after 9 + 1.) Say the number sentence with the answer.

S: 9 + 1 + 4 = 14.

T: (Write 14 to complete 9 + 1 + 4 = ___.) 9 + 1 + 4 = 14. 9 + 5 is?

S: 14.

T: (Write 14 to complete 9 + 5 = ___.)

Continue with other 9 + *n* and 8 + *n* addition sentences. If students are ready, give them personal white boards to independently decompose addition sentences into three parts.

Happy Counting by Threes (2 minutes)

Note: Reviewing counting on and back allows students to maintain fluency with adding and subtracting 3.

Repeat the Happy Counting activity from G1–M2–Lesson 4, counting by threes from 0 to 12 and back.

NOTES ON
MULTIPLE MEANS OF
ENGAGEMENT:

Maintain student attention with short fluency games that are energetically presented. You will hear students asking to play many of these games during fluency time as they enjoy this active engagement.

Application Problem (6 minutes)

There were 4 boots by the classroom door, 8 boots in the hallway, and 6 boots by the teacher's desk. How many boots were there altogether?

Extension: How many pairs of boots were there in all?

Note: In this problem, the numbers 4, 8, and 6 are used as addends, allowing students to choose either making ten by adding (4 + 6) + 8, or by decomposing either the 4 or 6 to make ten with 8. During the Debrief, students will have the opportunity to share work and notice how peers are using Level 3 strategies such as making ten to solve.

Concept Development (30 minutes)

Materials: (S) Personal white boards, numeral cards or 5-group cards, 1 "+" card for each student, 1 "=" card
(from G1–M2–Lesson 1) for each pair of students

Have students come to the meeting area with their personal white boards and sit in a semi-circle.

T: (Write 9 + 6 = ____ on the board.) Using an organized math drawing or a number bond, solve 9 + 6.
Think about the equal 10+ fact and write a true number sentence using two expressions.

S: (Solve by drawing or using a number bond as teacher circulates.)

	Lesson 10:	Solve problems with addends of 7, 8, and 9.
	Date:	7/3/13

2.A.100

T: (Choose one student to share the use of counting on and another student to share the use of making ten.) When there is a 9 as an addend, what could you do to the other addend?

S: Get the 1 out! Break apart 6 into 1 and 5 as parts.

Repeat the process with 4 + 8. Begin by asking students which number they should make ten with to solve more efficiently.

T: (Write 7 + 6 = ___ on the board.) Turn and talk to your partner. How might you solve this problem using what you already know about the make ten strategy?

T: Which number should we make ten with? Why?

S: Make ten with 7 because it's only 3 away from 10. → 6 is 4 away from 10. → It's easier for me to get the missing part from 7 than 6.

NOTES ON MULTIPLE MEANS OF ACTION AND EXPRESSION:

Before students share the strategies they used with the class, have them turn and talk with a partner and share strategies as a pair. Hearing how problems were solved more than once will help those students who are still learning the process and your English language learner students.

T: With your partner, use a number bond to solve this problem.

T: Look at your picture. What expression is 7 + 6 the same as?

S: 10 + 3!

T: Write that as true number sentence.

S: (Write 7 + 6 = 10 + 3 or 10 + 3 = 7 + 6.)

T: What is 10 + 3?

S: 13.

T: So what is 7 + 6? Say the number sentence.

S: 7 + 6 = 13.

Repeat the process with 4 + 7, 7 + 5, and 7 + 7.

T: When 7 is the bigger addend, what could you do to the other addend?

S: Get the 3 out! Make 3 as a part.

T: Now we are going to play Simple Strategies! (Assign partners. Instruct each pair to combine their numeral cards and make two piles: digits 1–6 and digits 7–9, placing the 9 card on top of this second pile.) Here's how you play:

1. Partner A picks a card from the first pile (digits 1–6).
2. Using the 9 card from the second pile and the card picked by Partner A, Partner B writes an addition expression (e.g., 6 + 9).
3. Partners use counting on and then use making ten to solve the expression.
4. After using the make ten strategy, Partner A writes down the equal 10 + ___ fact.
5. Partners place the equal sign card between the boards to make a true number sentence.
6. Switch roles. Keep the 9 card up each time you begin a new expression.

Lesson 10:   Solve problems with addends of 7, 8, and 9.
Date: 7/3/13

2.A.101

As students play, the teacher circulates and moves students to replacing the 9 card with the 8 card and then the 7 card, as appropriate.

Problem Set (10 minutes)

Students should do their personal best to complete the Problem Set within the allotted 10 minutes. For some classes, it may be appropriate to modify the assignment by specifying which problems they work on first. Some problems do not specify a method for solving. Students solve these problems using the RDW approach used for Application Problems.

Student Debrief (14 minutes)

Lesson Objective: Solve problems with addends of 7, 8, and 9.

The Student Debrief is intended to invite reflection and active processing of the total lesson experience.

Invite students to review their solutions for the Problem Set. They should check work by comparing answers with a partner before going over answers as a class. Look for misconceptions or misunderstandings that can be addressed in the Debrief. Guide students in a conversation to debrief the Problem Set and process the lesson. You may choose to use any combination of the questions below to lead the discussion.

- Look at Problems 8–10. Can you find number sentences that have the same total? What are the number sentences? How are they related?

- Why is it efficient to start with a larger addend when you add? Give an example.

- Solve $9 + 6 = $ ___, $8 + 6 = $ ___, $7 + 6 = $ ___. What patterns do you notice? Look at how you broke apart the second addend. What patterns do you see there? How did this breaking apart affect your totals? (When you take out 1 more from the second addend, your total is 1 less.)

- Which is easier for you to use? Counting on, making ten, or just knowing? Why?

Exit Ticket (3 minutes)

After the Student Debrief, instruct students to complete the Exit Ticket. A review of their work will help you assess the students' understanding of the concepts that were presented in the lesson today and plan more effectively for future lessons. You may read the questions aloud to the students.

Name _____   Date _____

Solve. If you want to, use drawings or number bonds. Write the equal 10+ fact.

1. $4 + 9 =$ ___

2. $6 + 8 =$ ___

3. $7 + 4 =$ ___

$10 +$ ___ $=$ ___ $10 +$ ___ $=$ ___ $10 +$ ___ $=$ ___

4. Match the equal expressions.

a. $9 + 3$ $10 + 1$

b. $5 + 8$ $10 + 4$

c. $9 + 6$ $10 + 2$

d. $8 + 9$ $10 + 5$

e. $4 + 7$ $10 + 7$

f. $6 + 8$ $10 + 3$

COMMON CORE | Lesson 10:   Solve problems with addends of 7, 8, and 9.
                | Date: 7/3/13

Complete the addition sentences to make them true.

(A)	(B)	(C)
5. $9 + 2 = \underline{\hspace{1cm}}$	$8 + 4 = \underline{\hspace{1cm}}$	$7 + 5 = \underline{\hspace{1cm}}$
6. $9 + 5 = \underline{\hspace{1cm}}$	$8 + 3 = \underline{\hspace{1cm}}$	$7 + 6 = \underline{\hspace{1cm}}$
7. $6 + 9 = \underline{\hspace{1cm}}$	$6 + 8 = \underline{\hspace{1cm}}$	$4 + 7 = \underline{\hspace{1cm}}$
8. $7 + 9 = \underline{\hspace{1cm}}$	$5 + 8 = \underline{\hspace{1cm}}$	$7 + 7 = \underline{\hspace{1cm}}$
9. $9 + \underline{\hspace{1cm}} = 17$	$8 + \underline{\hspace{1cm}} = 16$	$7 + \underline{\hspace{1cm}} = 16$
10. $\underline{\hspace{1cm}} + 9 = 15$	$\underline{\hspace{1cm}} + 8 = 15$	$\underline{\hspace{1cm}} + 7 = 17$

Name _____ Date _____

Solve. Use number bonds or 5-group drawings if needed. Write the equal 10+ number sentence.

9 + 5 = ___

8 + 4 = ___

7 + 6 = ___

10 + ___ = ___

10 + ___ = ___

10 + ___ = ___

Name _____   Date _____

Solve. Match the number sentence to the 10+ number bond that helped you solve the problem. Write the 10+ number sentence.

9 + 3 = 12

10 + 2 = 12

8 + 6 = ___

11 — 10, 1

___ + ___ = ___

7 + 5 = ___

15 — 10, 5

___ + ___ = ___

5 + 8 = ___

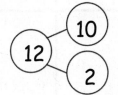

12 — 10, 2

___ + ___ = ___

4 + 7 = ___

14 — 10, 4

___ + ___ = ___

6 + 9 = ___

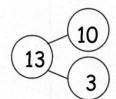

13 — 10, 3

___ + ___ = ___

Complete the number sentences so that they equal the given number bond.

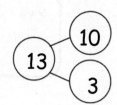

10 / 4 (third bond top)

9 + ___ = 12   9 + ___ = 13   9 + ___ = 14

8 + ___ = 12   8 + ___ = 13   8 + ___ = 14

7 + ___ = 12   7 + ___ = 13   7 + ___ = 14

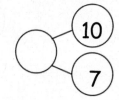

10 / 7 (sixth bond top)

15 = 9 + ___   16 = 9 + ___   ___ = 9 + 8

___ = 8 + ___   ___ = 8 + ___   ___ = 8 + ___

___ = 7 + ___   7 + ___ = ___   ___ = 7 + ___

2.A.108

Lesson 11

Objective: Share and critique peer solution strategies for *put together with result unknown* word problems.

Suggested Lesson Structure

- ■ Fluency Practice   (13 minutes)
- ■ Application Problem   (6 minutes)
- ▢ Concept Development   (31 minutes)
- ■ Student Debrief   (10 minutes)
  - **Total Time**   **(60 minutes)**

Fluency Practice (13 minutes)

- Sprint: Adding Across Ten **1.OA.6**   (10 minutes)
- Rekenrek: Ten Less **1.NBT.5**   (3 minutes)

Sprint: Adding Across Ten (10 minutes)

Materials: (S) Sprint: Adding Across Ten

Note: This sprint reviews the make ten addition strategy.

Rekenrek: Ten Less (3 minutes)

Materials: (T) Rekenrek

Note: This is an anticipatory fluency for the take-from-ten subtraction strategy in Topic B, as students will need to decompose numbers by taking out a ten.

  T: (Show 14 on the Rekenrek). Say the number.

  S: 14.

  T: Say it the Say Ten way.

  S: Ten 4.

  T: What will my number be if I take out ten ones?

  S: 4.

  T: Let's check. (Take out ten.) Yes!

Continue with other teen numbers.

	Lesson 11:	Share and critique peer solution strategies for *put together* with *result unknown* word problems.	
	Date:	7/3/13	**2.A.109**

Application Problem (6 minutes)

Nicholas bought 9 green apples and 7 red apples. Sofia bought 10 red apples and 6 green apples. Sofia thinks she has more apples than Nicholas. Is she right? Choose a strategy you have learned to show your work. Also, write number sentences to show how many apples Nicholas and Sofia each have.

Note: This problem allows students to revisit equivalent expressions, as they work with 9 + 7 and 10 + 6. The teacher can extend this thinking by either showing 9 + 7 = 10 + 6, or having students write the true number sentence themselves, then asking students to explain how they know.

N
9+7=16
6

S
10+6=16

Sophia is rong!

Concept Development (31 minutes)

Materials: (T) Student work samples (S) Personal white boards

Have students come to the meeting area and sit in a semi-circle.

T: (Project and read.) Louie made 7 puppets out of paper bags. Roberto made 6 puppets out of socks. How many puppets did the boys make? (Pause.) Turn and talk to your partner about how you would solve this problem.

S: (Discuss, as teacher circulates and listens.)

T: (Project Student A sample.) How did Student A solve this problem? Explain to your partner what this student was thinking.

S: She counted all the circles starting with 1. → Maybe she used counting on. Seeeven, 8, 9, 10, 11, 12, 13.

T: (Project Student B sample.) How did Student B solve this problem? Can you explain his thinking? Turn and talk to your partner.

S: He drew his shapes in 5-groups. When he made ten starting with 7, he drew a frame around it so you can see 10 and 3. His strategy was to make ten from 7 by breaking 6 into 3 and 3.

T: (Project Student C sample.) How did Student C solve this problem? How is it similar and different from Student B's work?

S: She didn't need to make a picture. She used the make ten strategy. But instead of making ten with 7, she made ten with 6 and broke apart 7 into 4 and 3.

T: (Project Student D sample.) How did Student D solve the problem?

Student A

OOOODOO●●●●●
7 + 6 = 13

Student B

OOOOO
OO xxx | xxx
7 + 6 = 13
3   3

Student C

7 + 6 = 13
3 4

Student D

ooo | xxx
oo o | xxx
7 + 6 = 13

Lesson 11: Share and critique peer solution strategies for *put together* with *result unknown* word problems.

Date: 7/3/13

2.A.110

S: He drew a picture but it's a little hard to count because the shapes are not organized. He probably had to count all of them, starting with 1. Or maybe he counted on from 7. Seeeven, 8, 9, 10, 11, 12, 13.

T: Do these all show ways to solve the problem? Which way seems like it's a better shortcut? Turn and talk to your partner.

S: (Discuss, as teacher circulates and listens.)

T: Oh, I found one more! Actually, I did this one. Ta-dah! Pretend you are my teacher and take a look at my work. What are your thoughts? (Project teacher work.)

S: Your picture is organized. I like the way you drew your circles in a 5-group. But you didn't solve it right. The picture doesn't make sense.

T: What do you mean? With your partner, draw a picture that will help me see how I can make this better.

S: (Discuss, as teacher circulates and listens.)

T: How can you help me get the correct answer? What did I do wrong?

S: You need to make ten by taking apart 3 from 6. You just added 10 and 6 here. Not 10 and 3.

T: Good work! Let's try another problem!

T: (Project and read aloud, "Louie glued on 5 pieces of brown yarn for his puppet's hair. He then glued on 8 pieces of red yarn for more hair. How many pieces of yarn did Louie use?") Solve this problem by showing your work clearly on your personal white board.

S: (Solve.)

Have students swap personal white boards with their partner and discuss the following:

IP.3

- Study what strategy your partner used.
- Did you get the same answer?
- Take turns to explain your partner's strategy.
- Are your strategies similar? How? Are they different? How?
- What did your partner do well?
- Which strategy is more efficient?

If time allows, repeat partner work following the suggested sequence: 9 + 7, 8 + 6, and 7 + 7.

NOTES ON MULTIPLE MEANS OF ENGAGEMENT:

Make sure to validate the different strategies students are using to solve so no one feels they have completed the work incorrectly. Be sensitive to students thinking in different ways and encourage and cultivate healthy competition in your classroom.

NOTES ON MULTIPLE MEANS OF ENGAGEMENT:

As students compare their strategies, be sure to listen to their conversations. By having these discussions with one another, you are facilitating students' reflection and ability to actively process what they are learning.

COMMON CORE

Lesson 11: Share and critique peer solution strategies for *put together* with *result unknown* word problems.

Date: 7/3/13

2.A.111

Problem Set (10 minutes)

Students should do their personal best to complete the Problem Set within the allotted 10 minutes. For some classes, it may be appropriate to modify the assignment by specifying which problems they work on first.
Some problems do not specify a method for solving. Students solve these problems using the RDW approach used for Application Problems.

Student Debrief (10 minutes)

Lesson Objective: Share and critique peer solution strategies for *put together with result unknown* word problems.

The Student Debrief is intended to invite reflection and active processing of the total lesson experience.

Invite students to review their solutions for the Problem Set. They should check work by comparing answers with a partner before going over answers as a class. Look for misconceptions or misunderstandings that can be addressed in the Debrief. Guide students in a conversation to debrief the Problem Set and process the lesson. You may choose to use any combination of the questions below to lead the discussion.

- Compare Problem 3 to Problem 4 with your partner. How are your strategies similar and different?

- Look at Problem 1(b). How did this student solve his problem? How is it similar and different from the way we use the make ten strategy?

- Which samples use similar strategies? Explain your thinking.

- Which sample seems like it could be the most efficient strategy once you became an expert with it?

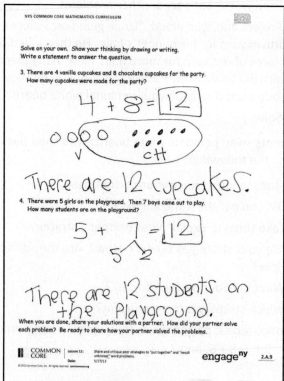

COMMON CORE | Lesson 11: | Share and critique peer solution strategies for *put together* with *result unknown* word problems. | 2.A.112
| Date: | 7/3/13 |

© 2013 Common Core, Inc. All rights reserved. **commoncore.org**

Exit Ticket (3 minutes)

After the Student Debrief, instruct students to complete the Exit Ticket. A review of their work will help you assess the students' understanding of the concepts that were presented in the lesson today and plan more effectively for future lessons. You may read the questions aloud to the students.

Lesson 11:   Share and critique peer solution strategies for *put together* with *result unknown* word problems.

Date: 7/3/13

2.A.113

Name _____   Date _____

A*Write the missing number.   Number correct: _____

1	9 + 2 = ☐		16	4 + 8 = ☐	
2	9 + 3 = ☐		17	8 + 4 = ☐	
3	9 + 5 = ☐		18	7 + 4 = ☐	
4	9 + 4 = ☐		19	7 + 5 = ☐	
5	8 + 2 = ☐		20	7 + 6 = ☐	
6	8 + 3 = ☐		21	6 + 7 = ☐	
7	8 + 5 = ☐		22	9 + 9 = ☐	
8	8 + 4 = ☐		23	9 + ☐ = 18	
9	9 + 4 = ☐		24	☐ + 4 = 13	
10	8 + 5 = ☐		25	☐ + 4 = 12	
11	9 + 5 = ☐		26	12 = 3 + ☐	
12	8 + 6 = ☐		27	16 = 8 + ☐	
13	9 + 6 = ☐		28	9 + 4 = 8 + ☐	
14	6 + 9 = ☐		29	9 + 3 = 5 + ☐	
15	9 + 6 = ☐		30	☐ + 7 = 8 + 6	

COMMON CORE | Lesson 11: | Share and critique peer solution strategies for *put together* with *result unknown* word problems.
| Date: | 7/3/13

2.A.114

Name _____   Date _____

B*Write the missing number.   Number correct: _____

1	$9 + 1 = \square$		16	$3 + 8 = \square$
2	$9 + 2 = \square$		17	$8 + 3 = \square$
3	$9 + 4 = \square$		18	$7 + 3 = \square$
4	$9 + 3 = \square$		19	$7 + 4 = \square$
5	$8 + 2 = \square$		20	$7 + 5 = \square$
6	$8 + 3 = \square$		21	$5 + 7 = \square$
7	$8 + 5 = \square$		22	$8 + 8 = \square$
8	$8 + 4 = \square$		23	$8 + \square = 16$
9	$9 + 4 = \square$		24	$\square + 3 = 12$
10	$8 + 5 = \square$		25	$\square + 4 = 12$
11	$9 + 5 = \square$		26	$12 = 3 + \square$
12	$8 + 7 = \square$		27	$14 = 7 + \square$
13	$9 + 7 = \square$		28	$9 + 3 = 8 + \square$
14	$7 + 9 = \square$		29	$9 + 3 = 5 + \square$
15	$9 + 7 = \square$		30	$\square + 7 = 8 + 5$

Lesson 11: Share and critique peer solution strategies for *put together* with *result unknown* word problems.

Date: 7/3/13

2.A.115

Name _____ Date _____

Jeremy had 7 big rocks and 8 little rocks in his pocket.

How many rocks does Jeremy have?

1. Circle all student work that correctly matches the story.

a.

7 + 8 = 15

b.

7 + 8 = 15

c.

7 + 8 = 15

d.

7 + 8 = 15

e.

7 + 8 = 15

f.

7 + 8 = 15

2. Fix the work that was incorrect by making a new drawing in the space below with the matching number sentence.

COMMON CORE | Lesson 11: Share and critique peer solution strategies for *put together* with *result unknown* word problems.
Date: 7/3/13

2.A.116

Solve on your own. Show your thinking by drawing or writing. Write a statement to answer the question.

3. There are 4 vanilla cupcakes and 8 chocolate cupcakes for the party. How many cupcakes were made for the party?

4. There were 5 girls on the playground. Then 7 boys came out to play. How many students are on the playground?

When you are done, share your solutions with a partner. How did your partner solve each problem? Be ready to share how your partner solved the problems.

 Lesson 11:   Share and critique peer solution strategies for *put together* with *result unknown* word problems.

Date: 7/3/13

2.A.117

Name _____ Date _____

John thinks the problem below should be solved using 5-group drawings and Sue thinks it should be solved using a number bond. Solve both ways and circle the strategy you think is the most efficient.

1. Kim scores 5 goals in her first soccer game and 8 runs in her softball game. How many points does she score altogether?

<u>John's work</u>   <u>Sue's work</u>

COMMON CORE™

Lesson 11: Share and critique peer solution strategies for *put together* with *result unknown* word problems.

Date: 7/3/13

2.A.118

Name _____   Date _____

Look at the student work. Correct the work. If the answer is incorrect, show a correct solution in the space below the student work.

1. Todd has 9 red cars and 7 blue cars. How many cars does he have altogether?

Mary's work	Joe's work	Len's work
9 + 7 = 16	9 + 7 = 15	9 + 7 = 16

2. Jill has 8 beta fish and 5 goldfish. How many fish does she have in total?

Frank's work	Lori's work	Mike's work
8 + 5 = 13	8 + 5 = 14	8 + 5 = 13

3. Dad baked 7 chocolate and 6 vanilla cupcakes. How many cupcakes did he bake in all?

<u>Mary's work</u>   <u>Joe's work</u>   <u>Lori's work</u>

13 = 7 + 6

10 + 3 = 13

7 + 6= 13

4. Mom caught 9 fireflies and Sue caught 8 fireflies. How many fireflies did they catch altogether?

<u>Mike's work</u>   <u>Len's work</u>   <u>Frank's work</u>

10 + 7 = 17

17 = 9 + 8

18 = 9 + 8

COMMON CORE™

Lesson 11: Share and critique peer solution strategies for *put together* with *result unknown* word problems.
Date: 7/3/13

2.A.120

COMMON CORE™

Lesson 11:   Share and critique peer solution strategies for *put together* with
Date: *result unknown* word problems.
              7/3/13

2.A.121

© 2013 Common Core, Inc. All rights reserved. commoncore.org

Topic B

Counting On or Taking from Ten to Solve *Result Unknown* Problems

1.OA.1, 1.OA.3, 1.OA.4, 1.OA.6, 1.OA.5, 1.OA.7

Focus Standard:	1.OA.1	Use addition and subtraction within 20 to solve word problems involving situations of adding to, taking from, putting together, taking apart, and comparing, with unknowns in all positions, e.g., by using objects, drawings, and equations with a symbol for the unknown number to represent the problem.
	1.OA.3	Apply properties of operations as strategies to add and subtract. (Students need not use formal terms for these properties.) *Examples: If 8 + 3 = 11 is known, then 3 + 8 = 11 is also known. (Commutative property of addition.) To add 2 + 6 + 4, the second two numbers can be added to make a ten, so 2 + 6 + 4 = 2 + 10 = 12. (Associative property of addition.)*
	1.OA.4	Understand subtraction as an unknown-addend problem. *For example, subtract 10 − 8 by finding the number that makes 10 when added to 8.*
	1.OA.6	Add and subtract within 20, demonstrating fluency for addition and subtraction within 10. Use mental strategies such as counting on; making ten (e.g., 8 + 6 = 8 + 2 + 4 = 10 + 4 = 14); decomposing a number leading to a ten (e.g., 13 − 4 = 13 − 3 − 1 = 10 − 1 = 9); using the relationship between addition and subtraction (e.g., knowing that 8 + 4 = 12, one knows 12 − 8 = 4); and creating equivalent but easier or known sums (e.g., adding 6 + 7 by creating the known equivalent 6 + 6 + 1 = 12 + 1 = 13).
Instructional Days:	10	
Coherence -Links from:	GK–M4	Number Pairs, Addition and Subtraction to 10
-Links to:	G2–M3	Place Value, Counting, and Comparison of Numbers to 1000
	G2–M5	Addition and Subtraction Within 1000 with Word Problems to 100

Topic B focuses on the take from ten Level 3 strategy (**1.OA.6**). Students begin with word problems calling on them to subtract 9 from 10 in Lessons 12 and 13, first with concrete objects, then with drawings, and then with number bonds. The problems students solve are similar to this one: "Mary has two plates of cookies, one with 10 and one with 2. At the party, 9 cookies were eaten from the plate with 10 cookies. How many cookies were left after the party?" (**1.OA.1**) 10 − 9 = 1 and 1 + 2 = 3. This allows students to use this take from ten strategy when the ten is already separated for them, and in a variety of contexts (concrete, pictorial, and abstract), which sets them up for the work of the later lessons of the topic where they must decompose teen numbers on their own to take from ten.

Lessons 14, 15, and 16 focus students on modeling subtraction of 9 from teen numbers with first manipulatives, then 5-groups drawings, and finally number bonds. Students relate counting on to subtraction in a couple of ways (pictured below) (**1.OA.4**). Students begin to realize that there is both simplicity and efficiency when they decompose the teen number into 10 and some ones, subtract the 9 from 10, and finally add the 1 left over with the some ones; this is key in Lesson 16 as students share their thinking and compare efficiency.

S: To solve 12 – 9, I count on from 9 to 12, niiiine, 10, 11, 12, three counts. → To solve 12 – 9, I make 12 into 10 and 2 and subtract 9 from ten. 1 + 2 = 3.

Level 2: Count on

Level 3: Decompose ten and compose with the ones

This same progression that occurred with subtracting 9 from teen numbers repeats itself in Lessons 17, 18, and 19, as students subtract 8 from teen numbers in concrete, pictorial, and abstract contexts. Students practice a pattern of action, take from ten and add the ones, as they face different contexts in word problems (**MP.8**), e.g., "Maria has 12 snowballs. She threw away 8 of them. How many does she have left?" (**1.OA.3**).

Lesson 20 both broadens and solidifies students' strategy use as they are faced with a combination of 7, 8, and 9 as subtrahends being taken away from teen numbers in both story problems and abstract equations. Lesson 21 closes Topic B with student-centered discussion about solution strategies as they solve both action-oriented (*take from with result unknown*) and relationship (*take apart with addend unknown*) problems. Students ask each other, "How and why did you solve it this way?" then discuss which strategies are the most efficient.

A Teaching Sequence Towards Mastery of Counting On or Taking from Ten to Solve *Result Unknown* Problems

Objective 1: Solve word problems with subtraction of 9 from 10.
(Lessons 12–13)

Objective 2: Model subtraction of 9 from teen numbers.
(Lessons 14–15)

Objective 3: Relate counting on to making ten and taking from ten.
(Lesson 16)

Objective 4: Model subtraction of 8 from teen numbers.
(Lessons 17–18)

Objective 5: Compare efficiency of counting on and taking from ten.
(Lesson 19)

Objective 6: Subtract 7, 8, and 9 from teen numbers.
(Lesson 20)

Objective 7: Share and critique peer solution strategies for *take from with result unknown* and *take apart with addend unknown* word problems from the teens.
(Lesson 21)

Lesson 12

Objective: Solve word problems with subtraction of 9 from 10.

Suggested Lesson Structure

■ Fluency Practice   (11 minutes)
■ Application Problem   (6 minutes)
■ Concept Development   (33 minutes)
■ Student Debrief   (10 minutes)
  Total Time   **(60 minutes)**

Fluency Practice (11 minutes)

■ Rewrite Expressions as 10+ Sentences **1.OA.6**   (5 minutes)
■ 5-Group Flash: Partners to Ten **1.OA.6**   (2 minutes)
■ Teen Number Bonds **1.NBT.2**   (4 minutes)

Rewrite Expressions as 10+ Sentences (5 minutes)

Materials: (S) Personal white boards

Note: This review fluency reinforces the make ten addition strategy, where students mentally decompose numbers to create equivalent but easier number sentences.

Write addition sentences with 9, 8, or 7 as an addend. Tell students to rewrite the sentence with 10 as an addend (e.g., write 9 + 2 and students write 10 + 1 = 11). Suggested sequence: 9 + 1, 9 + 2, 9 + 3, 9 + 5, 9 + 6, 8 + 2, 8 + 3, 8 + 5, 8 + 6, 7 + 3, etc.

5-Group Flash: Partners to Ten (2 minutes)

Materials: (T) 5-group row cards

Note: This activity supports Grade 1's core fluency standard of adding and subtracting within 10. Notice the shift in visual representation of ten, which will transition students into seeing ten as a single unit by the module's end.

This fluency activity focuses on the partners to ten. The following is a recommended sequence:

Flash a card for 2–3 seconds. Snap. Students say the number. Snap again.   Students say the partner to ten.

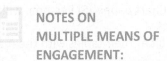

NOTES ON
MULTIPLE MEANS OF
ENGAGEMENT:

Certain fluency games that you play in class are good to play at home. Send home directions to the games, so that parents can play with their child. You can also suggest ways parents can use different numbers to challenge their child and extend their learning during the games.

Teen Number Bonds (4 minutes)

Materials: (S) Personal white boards with 5-group row template

Note: Composing teen numbers as 10 ones and some more ones prepares students for the take from ten subtraction strategy.

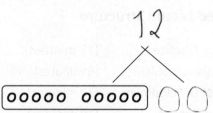

- T: Draw more circles to show a total of 12.
- S: (Draw 2 more circles.)
- T: Say 12 as a number bond, with 10 as a part.
- S: 10 and 2 make 12.
- T: Draw lines to show the total of 12 from your dots.
- S: (Draw lines to make a number bond with the numeral 12 on top.)

Continue with other numbers between 11 and 20.

Application Problem (6 minutes)

Claudia bought 8 red apples and 9 green apples. How many apples does Claudia have altogether? Make a math drawing, number sentence, and statement to show your thinking.

Extension: Claudia ate 3 red apples and her friend ate 4 green apples. How many apples does Claudia have now?

Note: This problem revisits the make ten strategy introduced in Topic A. It provides a foundation for today's work of solving word problems with subtraction of 9 from 10 using the same numbers and story problem character.

Concept Development (33 minutes)

Materials: (T) Chart paper (S) Personal white boards

Have students sit at their tables with the materials.

- T: (Project and read aloud.) When Claudia brought home her 17 apples, she put 10 in a bowl and 7 on the table. Then she decided to give 9 apples to her babysitter. How many apples did Claudia have left? (Pause.) Solve the problem on your personal board and talk with your partner about how you solved it.
- S: (Solve the problem and discuss strategies as the teacher circulates.)
- T: What strategies did you use?
- S: I drew them all and then crossed off the ones on the table and 2 more. I counted the ones that were left. 8! → I drew 10 circles for the bowl and 7 for the table. Then I took 9 from the 10 in the bowl.

Lesson 12:   Solve word problems with subtraction of 9 from 10.
Date: 7/3/13

2.B.5

7 and 1 is 8!

T: Let's all try another. (Project and read aloud, "Bailey Bunny had 10 carrots in a basket and 5 on a plate. She ate 9 carrots from the basket. How many carrots were left?")

T: On your personal white board, draw how many carrots Bailey Bunny had in the basket and label it.

S: (Draw 10 circles and write B or basket.)

T: In the next row, draw the carrots there were on the plate and label it.

S: (Draw 5 circles and write P or plate.)

T: The problem says that she ate 9 carrots from the basket. What should we do?

S: Cross off 9!

T: From where?

S: From the basket, from 10.

T: Show on your personal white board.

S: (Cross off 9 circles from 10.)

T: How many carrots are left in the basket?

S: 1 carrot!

T: How many are left on the plate?

S: 5 carrots.

T: Then how many carrots are left altogether?

S: 6 carrots.

Repeat the process using the suggested sequence: $11 - 9$, $12 - 9$, and $14 - 9$, recording the work on a chart paper for the Debrief.

T: Let's record how we solved our story problem with a number bond. (Read the story again.) Draw a number bond to show Bailey Bunny's total number of carrots, the part in the basket, and the part on the plate.

S: (Students draw.)

T: Draw circles to show the different parts.

S: (Draw.)

T: What did we do next? Show in your picture.

S: (Cross off 9 circles.) We took away 9 carrots from the basket. → We took away 9 from 10.

T: Turn and talk to your partner about how you can find how many carrots are left.

S: I counted 1, 2, 3, 4, 5, 6. → I added 1 and 5. That's 6 carrots. → I didn't use the picture. I counted on, niiine, 10, 11, 12, 13, 14, 15. That is 6 counts.

Repeat the process using the following suggested sequence: $16 - 9$, $17 - 9$, and $18 - 9$, recording the work on a chart paper for the Debrief.

NOTES ON MULTIPLE MEANS OF EXPRESSION:

At this time, students may be working at varying stages of subtracting, as depicted in the image above. As we praise students for accurate solutions, we want to encourage them to move to the next level strategy. If they are counting all, they should be encouraged to make the connection to counting on. If students are counting on, they should be encouraged towards taking from ten.

Problem Set (10 minutes)

Students should do their personal best to complete the Problem Set within the allotted 10 minutes. For some classes, it may be appropriate to modify the assignment by specifying which problems they work on first. Some problems do not specify a method for solving. Students solve these problems using the RDW approach used for Application Problems.

Student Debrief (10 minutes)

Lesson Objective: Solve word problems with subtraction of 9 from 10.

The Student Debrief is intended to invite reflection and active processing of the total lesson experience.

Invite students to review their solutions for the Problem Set. They should check work by comparing answers with a partner before going over answers as a class. Look for misconceptions or misunderstandings that can be addressed in the Debrief. Guide students in a conversation to debrief the Problem Set and process the lesson. You may choose to use any combination of the questions below to lead the discussion.

- ▪ Look at your drawings on your Problem Set. What did you notice when we took away 9 for each problem?

- ▪ Look at the chart of work from the Concept Development. What do you notice about the answers to each of these questions? (The answer is always 1 more than the second part on number bond.) Why do you think this is?

- ▪ How can solving Problem 3 help you solve Problem 4?

- ▪ After taking 9 from 10, how did you find the total amount left over? Which is the most efficient way to find out how many are left? Explain your thinking.

- ▪ Look at your Application Problem and think about what Claudia did with the apples once she got home (model this problem again). How are these problems similar? How are they different?

Exit Ticket (3 minutes)

After the Student Debrief, instruct students to complete the Exit Ticket. A review of their work will help you assess the students' understanding of the concepts that were presented in the lesson today and plan more effectively for future lessons. You may read the questions aloud to the students.

Name _____   Date _____

Make a simple math drawing. Cross out from the 10 ones or the
other part, in order to show what happens in the stories.

1. Bill has 16 grapes. 10 are on one vine and 6 are on the ground.
    Bill eats 9 grapes from the vine. How many grapes does Bill have left?

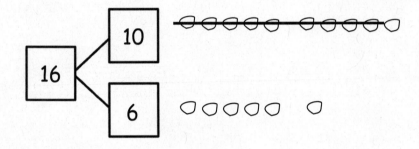

                                              Bill has _____ grapes now.

2. 12 frogs are in the pond. 10 are on a lily pad and 2 are in the water. 9 frogs hop
    away from the lily pad. How many frogs are in the pond?

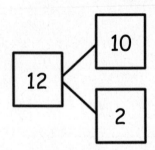

                                              There are _____ frogs still in the pond.

3. Kim has 14 stickers. 10 stickers are on the first page and 4 stickers are on the
    second page. Kim loses 9 stickers from the first page. How many stickers are still
    in her book?

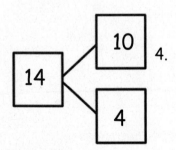   4.

                                              Kim has ____ stickers in her book.

4. 10 eggs are in a carton and 5 eggs are in a bowl. Joe's father cooks 9 eggs from the carton. How many eggs are left?

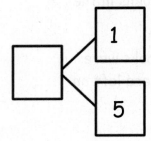

There are ____ eggs left.

5. Jana had 10 wrapped gifts on the table and 7 wrapped gifts on the floor. She unwrapped 9 gifts from the table. How many gifts are still wrapped?

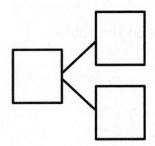

Jana has ____ gifts still wrapped.

6. There are 10 cupcakes on a tray and 8 on the table. On the tray, there are 9 vanilla cupcakes. The rest of the cupcakes are chocolate. How many cupcakes are chocolate?

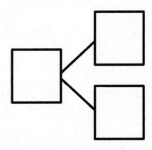

There are ____ chocolate cupcakes.

Name _____   Date _____

Make a simple math drawing. Cross out from the 10 ones to show what happens in the stories.

1. There were 16 books on the table. 10 books were about dinosaurs. 6 books were about fish. A student took 9 of the dinosaur books. How many books were left on the table?

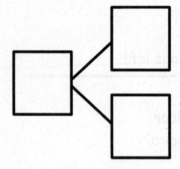

There were _____ books left on the table.

Name _____   Date _____

Make a simple math drawing. Cross out from the 10 ones to show what happens in the stories.

I had 16 grapes. I ate 9 grapes. How many grapes do I have now?

Now I have _7_ grapes.

1. There were 15 squirrels by a tree. 10 of them were eating nuts. 5 squirrels were playing. A loud noise scared away 9 of the squirrels eating nuts. How many squirrels were left by the tree?

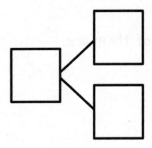

There were ____ squirrels left by the tree.

2. There are 17 ladybugs on the plant. 10 of them are on a leaf and 7 of them are on the stem. 9 of the ladybugs on the leaf crawled away. How many ladybugs are still on the plant?

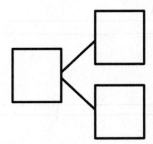

There are ____ ladybugs on the plant.

3. Use the number bond to fill in the math story. Make a simple math drawing.
    Cross out from 10 ones or some ones to show what happens in the stories.

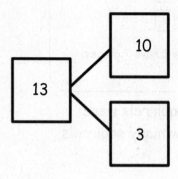

There were _____ ants in the ant hill. _____ of them are sleeping and _____ of them are
eating. 9 of the sleeping ants woke up. How many ants are <u>not</u> sleeping?

There are _____ ants <u>not</u> sleeping.

---

4. Use the number bond below to come up with your own math story. Include a simple
    math drawing. Cross out from 10 ones to show what happens.

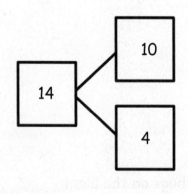

Math drawing:
Number sentences:
Statement:

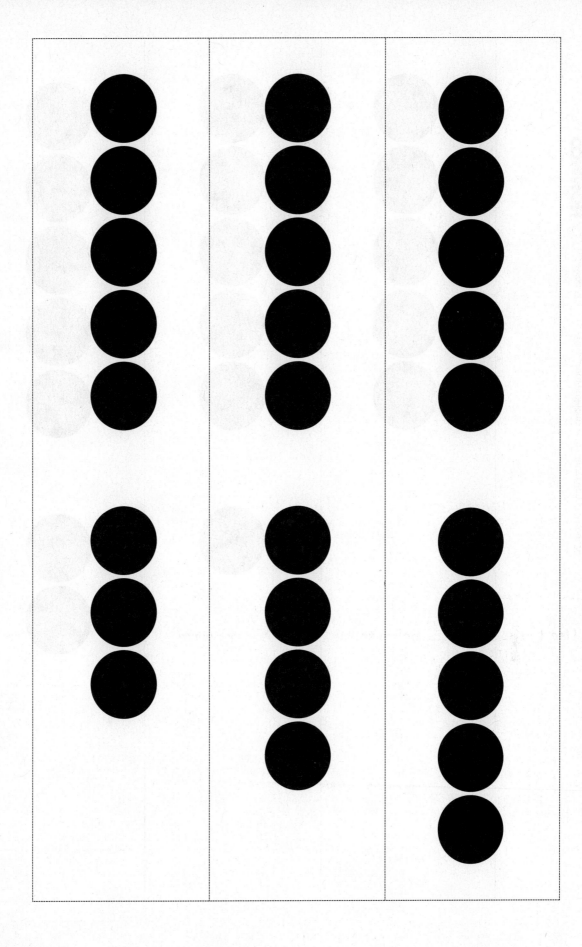

COMMON CORE™

Lesson 12:   Solve word problems with subtraction of 9 from 10.
Date: 7/3/13

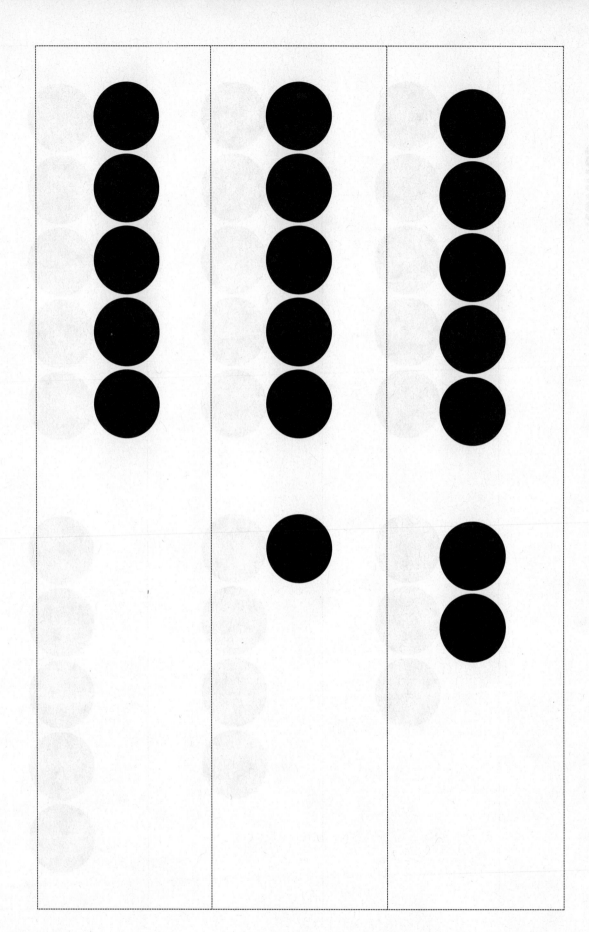

**COMMON
CORE**™

Lesson 12:
Date:

Solve word problems with subtraction of 9 from 10.

7/3/13

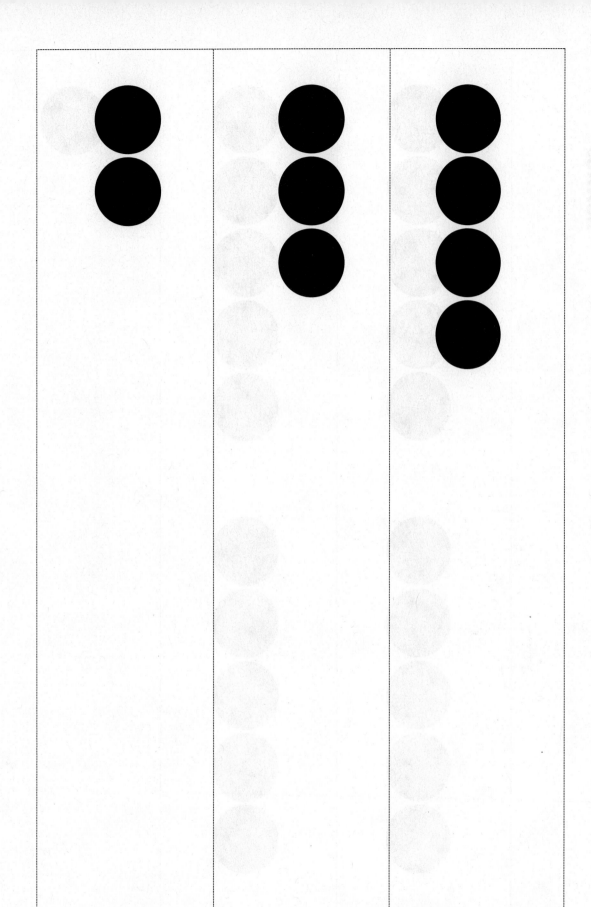

COMMON CORE™

Lesson 12:   Solve word problems with subtraction of 9 from 10.
Date: 7/3/13

COMMON CORE

Lesson 12: Solve word problems with subtraction of 9 from 10.

Date: 7/3/13

Lesson 12:
Date:

Solve word problems with subtraction of 9 from 10.

7/3/13

Lesson 13

Objective: Solve word problems with subtraction of 9 from 10.

Suggested Lesson Structure

■ Fluency Practice   (13 minutes)
■ Application Problem   (7 minutes)
  Concept Development   (30 minutes)
■ Student Debrief   (10 minutes)
  Total Time   **(60 minutes)**

Fluency Practice (13 minutes)

- 2, 3, 5 Less **1.OA.6**   (3 minutes)
- Subtraction with Cards **1.OA.6**   (5 minutes)
- 5-Group Flash: Take from Ten **1.OA.6**   (5 minutes)

2, 3, 5 Less (3 minutes)

Note: This activity supports Grade 1's core fluency standard of adding and subtracting within 10.

    T: On my signal, say the number that is 2 less.

    T: 5 (snap).

    S: 3.

Continue with numbers between 4 and 10. Then review 3 less and 5 less.

Subtraction with Cards (5 minutes)

Materials: (S) 1 deck of numeral cards with 2 extra tens for each pair of students, counters (if needed)

Note: Reviewing subtraction facts supports Grade 1's core fluency standard of adding and subtracting within 10. Provide number bond template for students who need extra support. Students can place the larger number as the whole and the smaller as a part to figure out the missing part.

Students place the deck of cards face down between them. Each partner flips over two cards and subtracts the smaller number from the larger number. The partner with the smallest difference keeps the cards played by both players that round. The player with the most cards at the end of the game wins.

5-Group Flash: Take From Ten (5 minutes)

Materials: (T) 5-group row cards (from G1–M2–Lesson 12) (S) Personal white boards with 5-group row template (from G1–M2–Lesson 12)

Note: This maintenance fluency with partners to ten facilitates the take from ten subtraction strategy that students are learning.

Flash a card (e.g., 9) for 1–3 seconds. Students cross off the number flashed from the horizontal ten-frame template and write the corresponding subtraction sentence.

Application Problem (7 minutes)

Ten snowflakes fell on Sam's mitten and 6 fell on his coat. Nine of the snowflakes on Sam's mitten melted. How many snowflakes are left? Write a subtraction sentence to show how many snowflakes are left.

Note: This problem continues the work begun in Lesson 12, asking students to subtract 9 from 10.

Concept Development (30 minutes)

Materials: (T) Image of 5-group rows (S) Personal white boards with 5-group rows

Have students come to the meeting area with their personal boards and sit in a semi-circle.

T: (Project and read aloud.) There were 10 ants on the picnic blanket and 4 ants on the grass. Nine ants from the picnic blanket went into the anthill with a breadcrumb. How many ants are not in the anthill?

T: Show me a number bond that shows how many ants were around at the beginning of the story.

S: (Write 14, 10, and 4.)

T: Using the picture from our fluency activity, I'll make a math drawing to show the parts. (Model drawing a 5-group row of 10 that is framed and labeled as 10 and 5 dark circles to the right, labeled as 4.)

T: Talk with a partner. If 9 ants left the blanket to go into the anthill, how many ants are not in the anthill?

S: (Discuss with a partner and solve.)

T: How many ants are not in the anthill?

S: 5!

NOTES ON
MULTIPLE MEANS OF
REPRESENTATION:

Reading aloud word problems facilitates problem solving for those students who have difficulty reading the text they are presented with. Hearing the word problem also helps students who are auditory learners.

T: Use my math drawing to show me how you know.

S: These 10 circles are the ants from the blanket. If I cross off 9 of them, I have 1 here (point to framed 5-group row) and 4 more here (point to 5 dark circles next to frame). → If we start from the 9 we had, we can count up. (Point to 5-group picture, starting at last circle in framed 5-group row.) 1 more to get to 10, and then 4 more to get to 14. → I knew that we had 4 black circles and I added 1 more. That's 5.

T: Which strategy is more efficient?

S: Adding 1 to the other part.

T: Turn and talk to you partner and write the number sentence that shows how we solved this problem. Explain your thinking.

S: We took away 9 ants from the 10 ants on the blanket. There was 1 ant left, plus there were 4 ants still on the grass. So, 10 – 9 = 1 and then 4 + 1 = 5. → I can write 14 – 9 = 5. In the beginning, there were 14 ants. Then 9 ants went into the anthill, so I took 9 away. There are 5 ants left.

T: Let's take a look at the math drawing. Do these 10 open circles remind you of any other drawings?

S: They look like 5-groups, except they are all in a line. We used to make them with 5 on top and 5 on the bottom.

T: You are right! Since these are all in a row, we'll call them a **5-group row**. There is a space to separate 5 circles from the other 5.

Repeat the process by having students write the number bond, draw the picture and write the number sentence using the following suggested sequence: 13 – 9, 15 – 9, 16 – 9, 17 – 9, and 18 – 9. For the first few problems, use the 5-group rows templates (with the group of 10 framed), revisiting the fluency activities from yesterday and today's lessons. Then leave the last couple of problems for students to draw their 5-group rows (with or without frames) independently.

Problem Set (10 minutes)

Students should do their personal best to complete the Problem Set within the allotted 10 minutes. For some classes, it may be appropriate to modify the assignment by specifying which problems they work on first. Some problems do not specify a method for solving. Students solve these problems using the RDW approach used for Application Problems.

NOTES ON MULTIPLE MEANS FOR ACTION AND EXPRESSION:

In this lesson, students are transitioning from drawing 5-groups to drawing 5-group rows. Some students may need some time to make the transition and complete the drawings the new way.

Student Debrief (10 minutes)

Lesson Objective: Solve word problems with subtraction of 9 from 10.

The Student Debrief is intended to invite reflection and active processing of the total lesson experience.

Invite students to review their solutions for the Problem Set. They should check work by comparing answers with a partner before going over answers as a class. Look for misconceptions or misunderstandings that can be addressed in the Debrief. Guide students in a conversation to debrief the Problem Set and process the lesson. You may choose to use any combination of the questions below to lead the discussion.

- What pattern did you notice about how we solved −9 problems? (We always took away 9 from 10. The answer is always the other part plus 1 because taking away 9 from 10 always leaves you with 1.)
- How can Problem 2 help you solve Problem 4?
- Look at Problem 6. Which part did you take the 9 from? Why? Explain your thinking.
- What new math drawing did we use today to solve subtraction problems? (5-group rows.) How is this drawing helpful?
- Look at your Application Problem. Where did you take your 9 from? Share your strategy.
- How can we use what we learned today to solve the application problem?

Exit Ticket (3 minutes)

After the Student Debrief, instruct students to complete the Exit Ticket. A review of their work will help you assess the students' understanding of the concepts that were presented in the lesson today and plan more effectively for future lessons. You may read the questions aloud to the students.

Name _____ Date _____

Solve. Use 5-group rows and cross out to show your work.

1. Mike has 10 cookies on a plate and 3 cookies in his pocket. He eats 9 cookies from the plate. How many cookies are left?

Mike has ___ cookies left.

2. Fran has 10 crayons in a box and 5 crayons on the desk. Fran lends Bob 9 crayons from the box. How many crayons does Fran have to use?

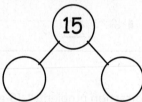

Fran has ___ crayons to use.

3. 10 ducks are in the pond and 7 ducks are on the land. 9 of the ducks in the pond are babies and all the rest of the ducks are adults. How many adult ducks are there?

There are ___ adult ducks.

With a partner, create your own stories to match and solve the number sentences. Make a number bond to show the whole as 10 and some ones. Draw with 5-group rows to match your story. Write the complete number sentence on the line.

4. 16 – 9 = ☐

_____

5. 12 – 9 = ☐

_____

6. 19 – 9 = ☐

_____

Name _____   Date _____

Solve. Fill in the number bond. Use 5-group rows and cross out to show your work.

Gabriela has 4 hair clips in her hair and 10 hair clips in her bedroom. She gives 9 of the hair clips in her room to her sister. How many hair clips does Gabriela have?

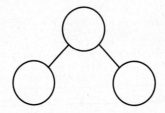

Gabriela has ____ hair clips.

Name _____   Date _____

Solve. Use 5-group rows and cross out to show your work. Write number sentences.

1. In a park, 10 dogs are running on the grass and 1 dog is sleeping under the tree. 9 of the running dogs leave the park. How many dogs are left in the park?

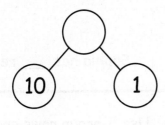

There are ____ dogs left in the park.

2. Alejandro had 9 rocks in his yard and 10 rocks in his room. 9 of the rocks in his room are gray rocks and the rest of the rocks are white. How many white rocks does Alejandro have?

Alejandro has ____ white rocks.

3. Sophia has 8 toy cars in the kitchen and 10 toy cars in her bedroom. 9 of the toy cars in the bedroom are blue. The rest of her cars are red. How many red cars does Sophia have?

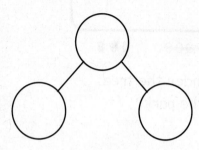

Sophia has ____ red cars.

4. Complete the number bond and fill in the math story. Use 5-group rows and cross out to show your work. Write number sentences.

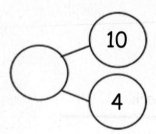

There were ____ birds splashing in a puddle and ____ birds walking on the dry grass. 9 of the splashing birds flew away. How many birds are left?

There are ____ birds left.

Lesson 14

Objective: Model subtraction of 9 from teen numbers.

Suggested Lesson Structure

■ Fluency Practice	(12 minutes)
■ Application Problem	(5 minutes)
■ Concept Development	(33 minutes)
■ Student Debrief	(10 minutes)
Total Time	**(60 minutes)**

Fluency Practice (12 minutes)

- 5-Group Flash: Partners to Ten **1.OA.6** (2 minutes)
- Sprint: Subtraction Within 10 **1.OA.6** (10 minutes)

5-Group Flash: Partners to Ten (2 minutes)

Materials: (T) 5-group row cards

Note: This activity supports Grade 1's core fluency standard of adding and subtracting within 10.

Flash a card for 2–3 seconds. Snap. Students say the number. Snap again. Students say the partner to ten.

Sprint: Subtraction Within 10 (10 minutes)

Materials: (S) Sprint: Subtraction Within 10

Note: This sprint reviews subtracting from ten, along with other subtraction facts within the Grade 1 core fluency objective of adding and subtracting within 10.

Application Problem (5 minutes)

Sarah has 6 blue beads in her bag and 4 green beads in her pocket. She gives away the 6 blue beads and 3 green beads. How many beads does she have left?

Note: This problem again asks students to subtract 9 from 10, but from two different places: some from the green bead group and some from the blue bead group. Using numbers within 10, students can explore how it is sometimes more efficient to take from a particular group(s) when subtracting. During the Student Debrief, students will have the opportunity to share their strategies.

Concept Development (33 minutes)

Materials: (T) Linking cubes (S) Personal white boards

Students sit in a semi-circle in the meeting area with their personal white boards.

NOTES ON MULITPLE MEANS OF ENGAGEMENT:

Be aware of the different learning needs in your class and adjust the lesson as necessary. Since some students may need to work at the concrete level for a longer period of time, allow access to manipulatives. Other students may grasp the take from ten strategy quickly and be able to do mental math for some number sentences.

T: (Project and read aloud.) Shayan has 12 eggs. He uses nine of them to make breakfast for his family. How many eggs are left?

T: How would you solve this problem? Use your personal white board to show your work.

S: (Solve as teacher circulates.)

T: How did you solve this problem?

S: I drew 12 eggs. I crossed off 9 and I had 3 eggs left. → I counted on from 9. (9, 10, 11, 12) I have 3 fingers up, too. → I used the strategy from yesterday. I saw that I can take apart 12 as 10 and 2. I took away 9 from 10 and did 1 + 2 = 3. Three eggs.

T: No matter which strategies these students used, did they get the same answer?

S: Yes!

T: Here is a stick of 12 linking cubes to show how many eggs Shayan had in the beginning. Just like what we practiced yesterday, let's break it off into 10 and 2. (Break off and separate into two sticks.) We need to take away…

S: 9 eggs.

NOTES ON MULTIPLE MEANS FOR ACTION AND EXPRESSION:

It is important to guide students to evaluate their thinking, as well as their partner's during the turn and talks. This provides students an opportunity to evaluate their process and analyze errors.

T: Where should I take 9 from? Turn and talk to your partner.

S: Take from 2 and then more from 10. → Take 9 from 10.

T: (Model taking away from 2.) Do I have enough? I need to take away more from 10. Help me count until we take away 9. (Count and take away 7 more.) How many do we have left?

S: 3.

T: (Model taking away from 10.) Taking away 9 from 10 will first leave us with…? (Break off 9 and shows 1.)

S: 1.

T: 1 and 2 make…?

MP.7

Lesson 14: Model subtraction of 9 from teen numbers.
Date: 7/3/13

2.B.29

MP.7

S: 3.

T: Turn and talk to your partner. Which was more efficient, simpler? Taking 9 from 10 or taking away the 2 and then some more from 10?

S: Taking 9 from 10.

T: I agree. Let's try more.

Repeat the process following the following suggested sequence: 11 – 9, 14 – 9, and 17 – 9. For each story problem, ask students which number 9 should be taken from.

T: Most of these are examples of 10 being a friendly number. When we take a number away from 10, we'll call it the take from ten strategy.

T: On your personal white board, draw a picture to show how we took 9 away from 10 to solve 17 – 9.

S: (Draw as teacher circulates and supports students.)

T: Let's do just a few more. This time, you can use drawings or the linking cubes to show how we use the take from ten strategy to solve.

Repeat with 15 – 9, 18 – 9, and 19 – 9.

Problem Set (10 minutes)

Students should do their personal best to complete the Problem Set within the allotted 10 minutes. For some classes, it may be appropriate to modify the assignment by specifying which problems they work on first. Some problems do not specify a method for solving. Students solve these problems using the RDW approach used for Application Problems.

Student Debrief (10 minutes)

Lesson Objective: Model subtraction of 9 from teen numbers.

The Student Debrief is intended to invite reflection and active processing of the total lesson experience.

Invite students to review their solutions for the Problem Set. They should check work by comparing answers with a partner before going over answers as a class. Look for misconceptions or misunderstandings that can be addressed in the Debrief. Guide students in a conversation to debrief the Problem Set and process the lesson. You may choose to use any combination of the questions below to lead the discussion.

- Look at Problems 8–10. What is happening with the difference in each of these problems? If the pattern continued, what would be the next problem? What problem would come before the first problem?

COMMON CORE   Lesson 14:   Model subtraction of 9 from teen numbers.
                         Date: 7/3/13   2.B.30

© 2013 Common Core, Inc. All rights reserved. commoncore.org

- How was setting up the problem to complete Problem 4 different from setting up the other problems? What did you need to be sure to do? Why?

- When solving 19 – 9, where can you take 9 from? Explain your answer. A student says, "Taking away 9 is like adding 1 to the part that is not 10 from the number bond. To solve 17 – 9, you can do 1 + 7." Is she correct? Explain your answer.

- What new strategy did we learn to solve our problems today? (Take from ten strategy.) Explain to your partner why it's an efficient strategy.

- Look at your application problem. How did you solve it? Do you have to add the blue beads and the green beads together to solve this problem? Why or why not? How is it like our lesson today? How is it different?

Exit Ticket (3 minutes)

After the Student Debrief, instruct students to complete the Exit Ticket. A review of their work will help you assess the students' understanding of the concepts that were presented in the lesson today and plan more effectively for future lessons. You may read the questions aloud to the students.

COMMON CORE

Lesson 14:   Model subtraction of 9 from teen numbers.
Date: 7/3/13

2.B.31

A

Number correct: ⬡

Name _____ Date _____

*Write the missing number.

1	$10 - 9 = \square$		16	$10 - \square = 5$
2	$10 - 8 = \square$		17	$9 - \square = 5$
3	$10 - 6 = \square$		18	$8 - \square = 5$
4	$10 - 7 = \square$		19	$10 - \square = 3$
5	$10 - 6 = \square$		20	$9 - \square = 3$
6	$10 - 5 = \square$		21	$8 - \square = 3$
7	$10 - 6 = \square$		22	$\square - 6 = 4$
8	$10 - 4 = \square$		23	$\square - 6 = 3$
9	$10 - 3 = \square$		24	$\square - 6 = 2$
10	$10 - 7 = \square$		25	$10 - 4 = 9 - \square$
11	$10 - 8 = \square$		26	$8 - 2 = 10 - \square$
12	$10 - 2 = \square$		27	$8 - \square = 10 - 3$
13	$10 - 1 = \square$		28	$9 - \square = 10 - 3$
14	$10 - 9 = \square$		29	$10 - 4 = 9 - \square$
15	$10 - 10 = \square$		30	$\square - 2 = 10 - 4$

B

Number correct: _____

Name _____   Date _____

*Write the missing number.

1	$10 - 8 = \square$		16	$10 - \square = 0$	
2	$10 - 9 = \square$		17	$9 - \square = 0$	
3	$10 - 8 = \square$		18	$8 - \square = 0$	
4	$10 - 9 = \square$		19	$10 - \square = 1$	
5	$10 - 7 = \square$		20	$9 - \square = 1$	
6	$10 - 9 = \square$		21	$8 - \square = 1$	
7	$10 - 8 = \square$		22	$\square - 5 = 5$	
8	$10 - 7 = \square$		23	$\square - 5 = 4$	
9	$10 - 3 = \square$		24	$\square - 5 = 3$	
10	$10 - 7 = \square$		25	$10 - 8 = 9 - \square$	
11	$10 - 6 = \square$		26	$8 - 6 = 10 - \square$	
12	$10 - 4 = \square$		27	$8 - \square = 10 - 2$	
13	$10 - 3 = \square$		28	$9 - \square = 10 - 2$	
14	$10 - 7 = \square$		29	$10 - 3 = 9 - \square$	
15	$10 - 5 = \square$		30	$\square - 1 = 10 - 3$	

COMMON CORE   Lesson 14:   Model subtraction of 9 from teen numbers.
Date: 7/3/13

2.B.33

Name _____   Date _____

1. Match the pictures with the number sentences.

a. 11 – 9 = 2

b. 14 – 9 = 5

c. 16 – 9 = 7

d. 18 – 9 = 9

e. 17 – 9 = 8

(Circle) 10 and subtract.

2.   12 - 9 = _____

3.   14 - 9 = _____

Date: 7/3/13

4. $15 - 9 = $ _____

5. $13 - 9 = $ _____

6. $16 - 9 = $ _____

7. $17 - 9 = $ _____

Draw and (circle) 10. Then subtract.

8. $12 - 9 = $ _____

9. $13 - 9 = $ _____

10. $14 - 9 = $ _____

11. $15 - 9 = $ _____

COMMON CORE

Lesson 14: Model subtraction of 9 from teen numbers.
Date: 7/3/13

2.B.35

Name _____   Date _____

Draw and (circle) 10. Solve and make a number bond.

1. 17 – 9 = _____

2. 14 – 9 = _____

3. 15 – 9 = _____

4. 18 – 9 = _____

COMMON CORE Lesson 14: Model subtraction of 9 from teen numbers.

Date: 7/3/13

2.B.36

Name _____ Date _____

(Circle) 10 and subtract. Make a number bond.

1. 15 – 9 = ___

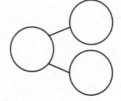

Draw and (circle) 10. Subtract and make a number bond.

2. 14 – 9 = ___

3. 12 – 9 = ___

4. 13 – 9 = ___

5. 16 – 9 = ___

COMMON CORE™   Lesson 14:   Model subtraction of 9 from teen numbers.
Date: 7/3/13

2.B.37

Complete the number bond and write the number sentence that helped you.

a.

_____

b.

_____

c.

_____

d.

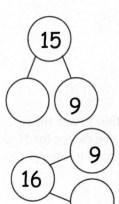

_____

Make the number bond that would come next and write a number sentence that matches.

COMMON
CORE™

Lesson 14:
Date:

Model subtraction of 9 from teen numbers.
7/3/13

2.B.38

Lesson 15

Objective: Model subtraction of 9 from teen numbers.

Suggested Lesson Structure

■ Fluency Practice   (10 minutes)
▨ Application Problem   (7 minutes)
▨ Concept Development   (33 minutes)
■ Student Debrief   (10 minutes)
   Total Time   **(60 minutes)**

Fluency Practice (10 minutes)

- 5-Group Flash: 5 Less and 4 Less **1.OA.6**   (2 minutes)
- Make It Equal: Subtraction Expressions **1.OA.6**   (5 minutes)
- Partners to Ten **1.OA.6**   (3 minutes)

5-Group Flash: 5 and 4 Less (2 minutes)

Materials: (T) 5-group row cards (from G1–M2–Lesson 12)

Note: This activity supports Grade 1's core fluency standard of adding and subtracting within 10 and helps students to see the relationship with 5 less (easy, one 5-group less) to 4 less (take out the five except for 1). For struggling students, lead them to visualize 5 less by hiding a 5-group. Make the connection to seeing the number on their fingers and hiding one hand.

Flash a card for 2–3 seconds. Students say the number that is 5 less and then 4 less.

Make It Equal: Subtraction Expressions (5 minutes)

Materials: (S) 5-group cards (from G1–M1–Lesson 5) and 1 "=" card, and 2 "–" cards per each set of partners

Note: This activity builds fluency with subtraction within 10 and promotes an understanding of equality.

Assign students partners of similar skill level. Students arrange 5-group cards from 0 to 10, including the extra 5, and place the "=" card between them. Write four numbers on the white board (e.g., 10, 9, 2, 1). Partners take the 5-group cards that match the numbers written to make two equivalent subtraction expressions (e.g., 10 – 9 = 2 – 1). Students can be encouraged to make another sentence of equivalent expressions for the same set of cards as well.

Suggested sequence: 10, 9, 2, 1   10, 3, 9, 2   10, 4, 5, 9   10, 8, 7, 9   10, 7, 9, 6   10, 8, 4, 2

| COMMON CORE | Lesson 15: | Model subtraction of 9 from teen numbers. | 2.B.39 |
| | Date: | 7/3/13 | |

Partners to Ten (3 minutes)

Materials: (S) Personal white boards with 5-group row insert

Note: This maintenance fluency with partners to ten facilitates the take from ten subtraction strategy.

Say a number between 0 and 10 (e.g., 9). Students cross off the number from the horizontal ten insert and write the corresponding subtraction sentence.

Application Problem (7 minutes)

Julian has 7 markers. His mother gives him 8 more. He loses 9 markers. How many does he have left?

Note: In the Student Debrief, students can discuss their drawings and number sentences, and share various strategies, one of which may be decomposing 15 into 10 and 5, taking 9 from 10. Though it will be covered formally in a later lesson, teachers might also choose to encourage students to see that the expressions 15 – 9 and 1 + 5 are equivalent.

Concept Development (33 minutes)

Materials: (S) Personal white boards

- T: (Project 15 – 9 = ___.) With a partner, solve this on your number board. Use words or a drawing to show how you know.
- S: (Discuss and solve with partner as teacher circulates and notices the solution strategies students are using independently.)
- T: What is the unknown number in this number sentence?
- S: Six!
- T: How do you solve that?
- S: I started at 9 and counted on until I got to 15. That took 6 fingers. → I took 9 away from 15 and had 6 left. → I know 15 is made of 10 and 5, so I took 9 from 10 and then saw that I had 6 left.
- T: I noticed that many of you used drawings on your personal white boards. How can we draw 15 so that we can tell how many we have when we look quickly?
- S: Use 5-group pictures!

NOTES ON MULTIPLE MEANS FOR ACTION AND EXPRESSION:

Some students may have trouble organizing their dots in a row with spaces in the correct places. Be sure to accommodate these students and set up a way for them to be successful with their drawings. We don't want them getting frustrated so that they are unable to focus on the math problem.

COMMON CORE

Lesson 15: Model subtraction of 9 from teen numbers.
Date: 7/3/13

2.B.40

T: Let's use 5-groups in one long row, like we did during fluency today. (Draw a 5-group row to show 15 on the board. Leave extra space between the first 10 circles and the last 5 circles.)

T: Let's frame the 10 circles we have so we can see 10 and 5 more easily. (Draw a rectangle around the first 10 circles.)

T: Now we can see 15 as 10 and 5. (Add the number 15 and the bond lines above as shown.)

T: If we want to take 9 out of 15, how can this drawing help us find a quick and easy place to take the 9 from?

S: The group of 10 inside the frame!

T: Hmm, if I take 9 out of 10, how much would that leave me in the frame?

S: Just one!

T: How much do we have when we take 9 out of 15?

S: Six! There is 1 left in the frame and 5 left on the other side, so that's 6.

T: (Project 14 − 9 = ___.) Let's all make 5-group drawings like that last one as we solve for the unknown number.

Repeat the process above with the following sequence: 16 − 9; 13 − 9; 17 − 9. Support students in drawing 5-group rows so that they can see the ten and the additional circles easily. Circulate and encourage students to share where they can find 9 quickly and easily.

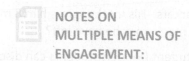

NOTES ON MULTIPLE MEANS OF ENGAGEMENT:

For those students that can fluently solve math facts within 20, cultivate excitement by connecting on-level math to higher math, presenting numbers to 100. If they can solve 15 − 9 with ease present problems such as 25 − 9 or 35 − 9.

Suggest students cover the 9 to help them move away from counting all and move towards visualizing and mental math.

After two problems, ask them to close their eyes and see if they can visualize or see in their mind's eye what is happening in the story when they subtract 9.

Have students draw the problem using 5-group drawings. Before they cross out the 9, ask them to visualize what the picture will look like once it is crossed out and determine how many will not be crossed out. Then have students cross out the 9 and see if their picture matches what they visualized.

Problem Set (10 minutes)

Students should do their personal best to complete the Problem Set within the allotted 10 minutes. For some classes, it may be appropriate to modify the assignment by specifying which problems they work on first. Some problems do not specify a method for solving. Students solve these problems using the RDW approach used for Application Problems.

Lesson 15: Model subtraction of 9 from teen numbers.
Date: 7/3/13

2.B.41

© 2013 Common Core, Inc. All rights reserved. commoncore.org

Student Debrief (10 minutes)

Lesson Objective: Model subtraction of 9 from teen numbers.

The Student Debrief is intended to invite reflection and active processing of the total lesson experience.

Invite students to review their solutions for the Problem Set. They should check work by comparing answers with a partner before going over answers as a class. Look for misconceptions or misunderstandings that can be addressed in the Debrief. Guide students in a conversation to debrief the Problem Set and process the lesson. You may choose to use any combination of the questions below to lead the discussion.

- Look at your Problem Set. How did you find an easy way to take 9 out of the teen numbers?

- Look at Problems 6–8. What do you notice is similar about the pictures in these problems? What do you notice about the numbers in these problems? If this pattern continued, what problem would come next? How can the problems help us solve 11 – 9?

- Look at Problem 10. How are the two number sentences related? What was the same or different about your drawings?

- Look at your Application Problem. How does the problem connect to today's lesson? How would you change or add to your work?

Exit Ticket (3 minutes)

After the Student Debrief, instruct students to complete the Exit Ticket. A review of their work will help you assess the students' understanding of the concepts that were presented in the lesson today and plan more effectively for future lessons. You may read the questions aloud to the students.

COMMON CORE

Lesson 15:   Model subtraction of 9 from teen numbers.
Date: 7/3/13

2.B.42

Name _____ Date _____

1. Match the pictures with the number sentences.

a. 13 – 9 = 4

b. 14 – 9 = 5

c. 17 – 9 = 8

d. 18 – 9 = 9

e. 16 – 9 = 7

Draw 5-group rows. Visualize and then cross out to solve. Complete the number sentences.

2. 11 - 9 = _____

3. 13 - 9 = _____

4. 16 - 9 = _____

5. 17 - 9 = _____

COMMON CORE | Lesson 15: | Model subtraction of 9 from teen numbers.
Date: | 7/3/13

2.B.43

6.   14 – 9 = _____

7.   13 – 9 = _____

8.   12 – 9 = _____

9.   15 – 9 = _____

10. Show making 10 and taking from 10 to complete the two number sentences.

   (a)   5 + 9 = ____

   (b)   14 – 9 = ____

11. Make a number bond for #10. Write two additional number sentences that use this number bond.

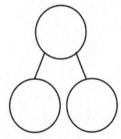   _____   _____

Name _____   Date _____

Draw 5-group rows and cross out to solve. Complete the number sentences.

1. 17 – 9 = ____

2. 19 – 9 = ____

Name _____   Date _____

Write the number sentence for each 5-group row drawing.

1.

⊖⊖⊖⊖⊖ ⊖⊖⊖⊖○   ○○○   **13 − 9 = 4**

⊖⊖⊖⊖⊖ ⊖⊖⊖⊖○   ○○○○○ ○   _____

⊖⊖⊖⊖⊖ ⊖⊖⊖⊖○   ○○○○○ ○○○○   _____

⊖⊖⊖⊖⊖ ⊖⊖⊖⊖○   ○○○○○ ○○   _____

⊖⊖⊖⊖⊖ ⊖⊖⊖⊖○   ○○○○○ ○○○   _____

⊖⊖⊖⊖⊖ ⊖⊖⊖⊖○   ○○○○   _____

Draw 5-groups to complete the number bond and write the 9– number sentence.

2.

3.

4.

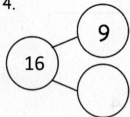

Draw 5-groups to show making ten and taking from ten to solve the two number sentences. Make a number bond and write two additional number sentences that would have this number bond.

5. 8 + 9 = ____

6. 17 – 9 = ____

_____

_____

_____

_____

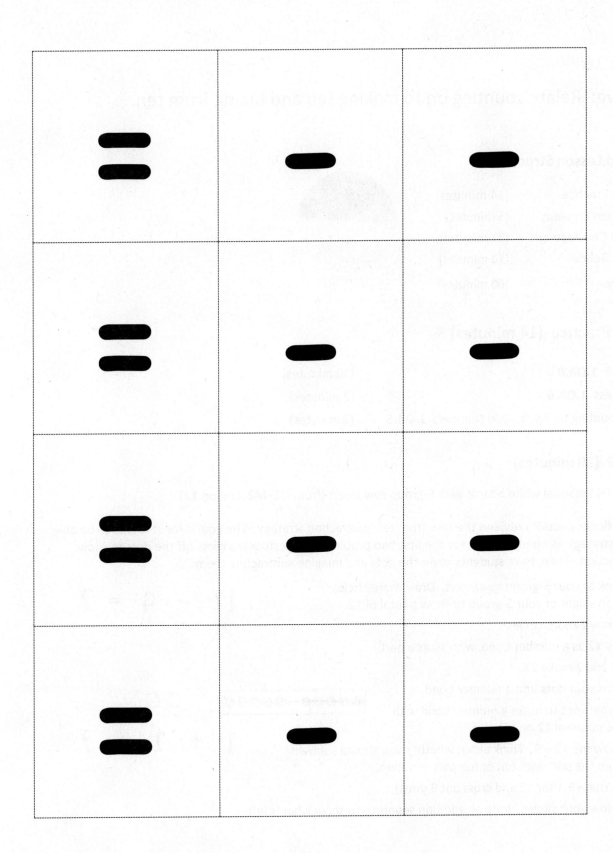

COMMON CORE™ Lesson 15: Model subtraction of 9 from teen numbers.
Date: 7/3/13

2.B.48

Lesson 16

Objective: Relate counting on to making ten and taking from ten.

Suggested Lesson Structure

■ Fluency Practice   (14 minutes)
■ Application Problem   (5 minutes)
■ Concept Development   (31 minutes)
■ Student Debrief   (10 minutes)
   Total Time   **(60 minutes)**

Fluency Practice (14 minutes)

- Subtract 9 **1.OA.6**   (10 minutes)
- 5 and 4 Less **1.OA.6**   (2 minutes)
- Happy Counting by Twos: Odd Numbers **1.OA.5**   (2 minutes)

Subtract 9 (10 minutes)

Materials: (S) Personal white boards with 5-group row insert (from G1–M2–Lesson 12)

Note: This fluency activity reviews the take from ten subtraction strategy. The goal is for students to be able to use this strategy as mental math. For the first two problems, have students cross off the dots to show their subtraction. Then, have students cover the dots and imagine subtracting them.

T: Look at your 5-group row insert. Draw more circles to the right of your 5-group to show a total of 12.

S: (Draw 2 more circles).

T: Say 12 as a number bond, with 10 as a part.

S: 10 and 2 make 12.

T: Turn your dots into a number bond.

S/T: (Draw lines to make a number bond with the numeral 12 on top.)

T: Show me 12 – 9. Think about whether you should subtract from the part with ten or the part with two.

S/T: (Write – 9 after 12 and cross out 9 dots.)

T: Below your circles, write an addition sentence to show what is left.

S: (Write 1 + 2 = 3.)

T: What is 12 – 9?

S: 3.

Continue with other numbers between 11 and 20. As soon as possible, reduce the number of steps (e.g., show me 14 – 9).

5 and 4 Less (2 minutes)

Materials: (T) 5-group row cards (from G1–M2–Lesson 12)

Note: This activity supports Grade 1's core fluency standard of adding and subtracting within 10 and helps students to see 4 less as related to 5 less (take out the five except for 1). For struggling students, lead them to visualize 5 less by hiding a 5-group. Make the connection to seeing the number on their fingers and hiding one hand.

Flash a card for two to three seconds. Students say the number that is 5 less and then 4 less.

Happy Counting by Twos: Odd Numbers (2 minutes)

Note: Reviewing counting on allows students to maintain fluency with adding and subtracting 2.

Do the Happy Counting activity from G1–M2–Lesson 4, counting by twos from 1 to 19 and back (This range may be adjusted to meet the needs of students.)

Application Problem (5 minutes)

There were 16 coats on the rack. Nine students took their coats to go outside. How many coats were still on the rack?

Extension: If 4 more students take their coat to go outside, how many coats will still be hanging?

Note: In this problem, students may use the take from ten strategy or count on strategy. While circulating, look for students who used these strategies and ask them to share during the Debrief.

Concept Development (31 minutes)

Materials: (S) Personal white boards

Students sit in a semi-circle in the meeting area with their personal white boards.

T: (Write 11 – 9 = ___.) Solve 11 – 9 on your personal white board.

S: (Solve on personal white board as the teacher circulates and selects two students, one using the count on strategy and another using the take from ten strategy.)

S: I started with 9 and counted on. Niiiine, 10, 11. Two fingers are up.

T: Let's all try counting on.

T/S: Niiiine, 10, 11. (Put up a finger for each count after 9.)

T: (Ask second student.) How did you solve 11 – 9?

S: I took 9 from 10 and did 1 + 1 and got 2.

T: Let's all use the take from ten strategy to solve on our personal white boards.

S: (Show a number bond to break apart 11 to solve.)

T: What did you do?

S: 10 – 9 is 1; 1 + 1 is 2.

T: Everyone, let's use the take from ten strategy using our fingers to check! Start by showing 11 fingers.

S: We can't! We only have 10 fingers!

T: Oh boy, we can't quite do that, can we? We'll just have to use our imagination. First, put up your 10 fingers.

S: (Show 10 fingers.)

MP.4

T: How many more fingers do we need to imagine?

S: 1.

T: Visualize, or picture, 1 more finger next to your 10. Now, take away 9, all at once.

S: (Hold 1 finger up.)

T: How many fingers do you have up?

S: 1.

T: How many imaginary fingers are still up?

S: 1.

T: So how many fingers are there altogether, real and imaginary? Let's count. Nod your head when you count your imaginary fingers so we are sure we counted them.

S/T: Ooonne, 2. (Nod head while saying 2.)

T: What is 11 – 9?

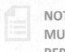

real fingers   imaginary finger

NOTES ON MULTIPLE MEANS FOR REPRESENTATION:

Sharing strategies is important for students to articulate the way they chose to solve a problem. Other students will hear how their classmates are thinking and this may guide them in understanding the strategies at a deeper level. As the teacher, you can see who is using Level 1, Level 2, or Level 3 strategies in your classroom.

Lesson 16: Relate counting on to making ten and taking from ten.
Date: 7/3/13

2.B.51

S: 2.

T: Which strategy was easier for you? Turn and talk to your partner.

S: (Discuss.)

T: I heard many students say that they were all easy. They took about the same amount of time. Let's try another problem to see if one strategy is a better shortcut than the other.

Invite all students to solve 17 – 9, using the two strategies (take from ten, modeled with a number bond and with imaginary fingers, and counting on), allowing students to experience that the take from ten strategy is more efficient. Also generate a discussion about the difficulty of trying to count 7 imaginary fingers since they are hard to keep track of. Repeat the process subtracting 9 from 12 to 18 out of sequence so that students have a chance to practice the take from ten strategy. A suggested sequence is 13 – 9, 17 – 9, 15 – 9, 12 – 9, etc. Discuss the increased efficiency of taking from ten as the minuend, or the total, gets bigger when we are subtracting 9, gradually abandoning the counting on strategy and exclusively using the take from ten strategy.

For 14 – 9 and on, use the following paradigm to demonstrate a more efficient way to count on when using imaginary fingers. Students will find that trying to keep track of more than 3 imaginary fingers through head nodding becomes difficult.

T: Let's try 14 – 9. Show 10 fingers and imagine 4 more.

S: (Show 10 fingers.)

T: Now take away 9, all at once. How many fingers do you have up?

S: 1.

T: How many imaginary fingers are still up?

S: 4.

T: Instead of nodding our heads 4 times to count on, can you see how many fingers there are altogether?

S: Yes. We can just add 1 and 4. That's 5.

As the strategy becomes more familiar, invite students to visualize the entire process instead of using their fingers.

Note: Although using take from ten strategy is more efficient than counting on one at a time, starting with 13 – 9, some students may find counting on by keeping track on their fingers easier (e.g., niiine, 10, 11, 12, 13, as they put up a finger for each number) because they have not yet mastered the take from ten strategy. It is not wrong for students to say counting on is easier, but with continued practice they may embrace the Level 3 strategy of taking from ten.

NOTES ON MULTIPLE MEANS FOR REPRESENTATION:

When using word problems in class or sending them home as homework, be sure to provide help for your non-readers. Tell parents they can read the problems to their child since you want to focus on the students' problem solving skills and not their reading ability during this part of homework.

Problem Set (10 minutes)

Students should do their personal best to complete the Problem Set within the allotted 10 minutes. For some classes, it may be appropriate to modify the assignment by specifying which problems they work on first. Some problems do not specify a method for solving. Students solve these problems using the RDW approach used for Application Problems.

Lesson 16:   Relate counting on to making ten and taking from ten.
Date: 7/3/13

2.B.52

Student Debrief (10 minutes)

Lesson Objective: Relate counting on to making ten and taking from ten.

The Student Debrief is intended to invite reflection and active processing of the total lesson experience.

Invite students to review their solutions for the Problem Set. They should check work by comparing answers with a partner before going over answers as a class. Look for misconceptions or misunderstandings that can be addressed in the Debrief. Guide students in a conversation to debrief the Problem Set and process the lesson. You may choose to use any combination of the questions below to lead the discussion.

- In Problem 3, how is the take from ten strategy similar to counting on?

- We found that counting on from 9 took different amounts of time, depending on what number we were subtracting from. Is this also true when using the take from ten strategy? Does it take longer to take from ten when the starting number is larger? Explain your reasoning.

- We used our imaginary fingers to show the take from ten strategy. (Model 12 – 9.) How is this like counting on? What did we do to make our count on strategy more efficient? Look at Problem 5. Which strategy did you choose for each problem? Explain your reasoning.

    - Guide students to see that counting on one at a time becomes less efficient as the difference becomes large.

    - As time allows, expand the discussion to point out that our modifications to counting on (mentioned in the previous bullet) do make it more efficient, and on par with the take from ten strategy.

- What new math strategy did we use today to solve subtraction problems more efficiently? (Taking from ten using fingers.)

COMMON CORE

Lesson 16:   Relate counting on to making ten and taking from ten.
Date: 7/3/13

2.B.53

- Look at your Application Problem. How did you choose to solve it? Explain your thinking. How could the strategies discussed today be used to solve this problem?

Exit Ticket (3 minutes)

After the Student Debrief, instruct students to complete the Exit Ticket. A review of their work will help you assess the students' understanding of the concepts that were presented in the lesson today and plan more effectively for future lessons. You may read the questions aloud to the students.

Name _____ Date _____

Solve the problem by counting on (a) and using a number bond to take from ten (b).

1. Lucy had 12 balloons at her birthday party. She gave balloons to 9 of her friends. How many balloons did she have left?

   (a)   12 - 9 = _____

   (b)   12 – 9 = _____
        /\

                                                Lucy had ____ balloons left.

_____

2. Justin had 15 blueberries on his plate. He ate 9 of them. How many does he have left to eat?

   (a)   15 - 9 = _____

   (b)   15 – 9 = _____
        /\

                                                Justin has ____ blueberries left to eat.

Complete the subtraction sentences by using the take from ten strategy and counting on. Tell which strategy you would prefer to use for Problems 3 and 4.

3.   (a) 11 - 9 = ____   (b) 11 - 9 = ____   ☐ take from ten
                                        ∧   ☐ count on

4.   (a) 18 - 9 = ____   (b) 18 - 9 = ____   ☐ take from ten
                                        ∧   ☐ count on

5.   Think about how to solve the following subtraction problems:

      16 – 9   12 – 9   18 – 9

      11 – 9   15 – 9   14 – 9

      13 – 9   19 – 9   17 – 9

Choose which problems you think are easier to count on from 9 and which are easier to use the take from ten strategy for.

Problems to use the *count on* strategy with:	Problems to use the *take from ten* strategy with:

Were there any problems that were just as easy using either method? Did you use a different method for any problems?

Name _____ Date _____

Complete the subtraction sentences by using the count on and take from ten strategies.

1. (a) 13 - 9 = ____   (b) 13 - 9 = ____
                                      /\

_____

2. (a) 17 - 9 = ____   (b) 17 - 9 = ____
                                      /\

Name _____   Date _____

Complete the subtraction sentences by using the count on or take from ten strategy. Tell which strategy you used.

1. 17 - 9 = _____

☐ take from ten

☐ count on

2. 12 - 9 = _____

☐ take from ten

☐ count on

3. 16 - 9 = _____

☐ take from ten

☐ count on

4. 11 - 9 = _____

☐ take from ten

☐ count on

5. Nicholas collected 14 leaves. He pasted 9 into his notebook. How many leaves did he not paste into his notebook? Choose the count on or take from ten strategy to solve.

I chose this strategy:

☐ take from ten

☐ count on

6. Sheila had 17 oranges. She gave 9 oranges to her friends. How many oranges does Sheila have left? Choose the count on or take from ten strategy to solve.

> I chose this strategy:
>
> ☐ take from ten
>
> ☐ count on

7. Paul has 12 marbles. Lisa has 18 marbles. They each rolled 9 marbles down a hill. How many marbles did each student have left? Tell which strategy you chose for each student.

Paul has _____ marbles left.   Lisa has _____ marbles left.

8. Just as you did today in class, think about how to solve the following problems and talk to your parent or caregiver about your ideas.

15 – 9	13 – 9	17 – 9
18 – 9	19 – 9	12 – 9
11 – 9	14 – 9	16 – 9

Circle the problems you think are easier to count on from 9 and put a rectangle around those that are easier to use the take from ten strategy for. Remember, some might be just as easy using either method. Underline problems you used a different strategy for.

COMMON CORE™   Lesson 16:   Relate counting on to making ten and taking from ten.
                 Date: 7/3/13

Lesson 17

Objective: Model subtraction of 8 from teen numbers.

Suggested Lesson Structure

■ Fluency Practice   (14 minutes)
■ Application Problem   (5 minutes)
■ Concept Development   (31 minutes)
■ Student Debrief   (10 minutes)
   Total Time   **(60 minutes)**

Fluency Practice (14 minutes)

- Subtract 9 **1.OA.6**   (4 minutes)
- Sprint: Subtract 9 **1.OA.6**   (10 minutes)

Subtract 9 (4 minutes)

Materials: (T) Subtract 9 Flashcards

Note: This fluency activity reviews the take from ten subtraction strategy when the subtrahend is 9.

Show a Subtract 9 Flashcard (e.g., 12 – 9).

    T: Say 12 the Say Ten way.
    S: Ten 2.
    T: 10 – 9 is ? (Snap).
    S: 1.
    T: 1 + 2 is ? (Point to the 2; snap).
    S: 3.
    T: 12 – 9 is ? (Snap).
    S: 3.

Sprint: Subtract 9 (10 minutes)

Materials: (S) Subtract 9 Sprint

Note: This Sprint reviews the take from ten subtraction strategy when the subtrahend is 9.

Lesson 17:   Model subtraction of 8 from teen numbers.
Date: 7/3/13

2.B.60

Application Problem (5 minutes)

Gisella had 13 markers in her bag. Eight markers fell out of the bag. How many markers does Gisella have now?

Note: While circulating, notice which students already recognize the application of the take from ten strategy, previously applied only to subtracting 9. Notice which students are crossing off one at a time instead of crossing off 8 quickly. Student strategy choices will be discussed in the debrief.

$13 - 8 = 5$

She has 5 markers.

Concept Development (31 minutes)

Materials: (T) Linking cubes of different colors (S) Personal white boards

Note: Using different colored linking cubes will help students realize that not all objects need to be identical in a given set.

Students sit in a semi-circle in the meeting area with their personal white boards.

T: (Project and read aloud.) Ayan had 15 building blocks. He used 8 of them to make a car. How many blocks were left?

T: How would you solve this problem? Use your personal white board to show your work.

S: (As students solve, circulate and observe student strategies.)

T: How did you solve?

S: I drew 15 squares. I crossed off 8 and I had 7 pieces left. → I counted on from 8 to 15. Eiiiight, 9, 10, 11, 12, 13, 14, 15. I have 7 fingers up, so 7 blocks. → I used the take from ten strategy. I saw that I can take apart 15 into 10 and 5. I took away 8 from 10 and did $2 + 5 = 7$. Seven blocks.

T: No matter which strategies these students used, did they get the same answer?

S: Yes!

T: (Show a stick of 15 cubes of different colors.) Here is a stick of 15 linking cubes to show how many building blocks Ayan had in the beginning. To use the take from ten strategy, let's break this apart into…

S: 10 and 5.

T: (Break off and separate into two sticks.) We need to take away…

S: 8 pieces.

T: From…

S: 10.

T: (Take away 8 from 10.) 10 minus 8 is?

NOTES ON MULTIPLE MEANS FOR ACTION AND EXPRESSION

It is important to guide students to evaluate their thinking, as well as their partner's during the turn and talk. This provides students an opportunity to evaluate their process and analyze errors.

| Lesson 17: | Model subtraction of 8 from teen numbers. |
| Date: | 7/3/13 |

2.B.61

S: 2.

T: 2 and 5 make…

S: 7.

T: Let's check by using our fingers. Show me 15 fingers. How many imaginary fingers are up?

S: (Show 10 fingers.) 5.

T: Take away 8, all at once.

S: (Show 2 fingers.)

T: How many fingers are up?

S: 2.

T: How many imaginary fingers are there?

S: 5.

T: How many fingers, real and imaginary, are there altogether?

S: 7.

T: What addition sentence helped you solve $15 - 8$?

S: $2 + 5 = 7$.

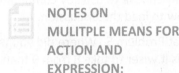

NOTES ON MULITPLE MEANS FOR ACTION AND EXPRESSION:

Adapt what you expect of certain students depending on their level of understanding. Some students may be ready to move away from draw and circle 10 to just break apart the teen number with a number bond in their work.

Repeat the process following the suggested sequence: $11 - 8$, $12 - 8$, $14 - 8$, $15 - 8$, $17 - 8$, $18 - 8$ (take 8 from 8 rather than 10), and $19 - 8$ (take 8 from 9). You may want to use linking cubes to aid student understanding for the first few problems but move towards using fingers. At $18 - 8$ and $19 - 8$, reintroduce the linking cubes, as they will provide a more clear visual representation for determining from where to quickly subtract 8. If time allows, have students work with a partner and practice subtracting 8 using the take from ten strategy with fingers and writing the addition sentence to help solve.

Problem Set (10 minutes)

Students should do their personal best to complete the Problem Set within the allotted 10 minutes. For some classes, it may be appropriate to modify the assignment by specifying which problems they work on first. Some problems do not specify a method for solving.   Students solve these problems using the RDW approach used for Application Problems.

Student Debrief (10 minutes)

Lesson Objective: Model subtraction of 8 from teen numbers.

The Student Debrief is intended to invite reflection and active processing of the total lesson experience.

COMMON CORE

Lesson 17: Model subtraction of 8 from teen numbers.
Date: 7/3/13

2.B.62

Invite students to review their solutions for the Problem Set. They should check work by comparing answers with a partner before going over answers as a class. Look for misconceptions or misunderstandings that can be addressed in the Debrief. Guide students in a conversation to debrief the Problem Set and process the lesson. You may choose to use any combination of the questions below to lead the discussion.

- Look at Problem 5. Where did you take 8 from? Why is it wiser to take 8 from 9 than 10?

- Look at the way a student solved Problem 6. How is her solution similar to and different from yours?

- How can knowing $15 - 9 = 6$ help you solve $15 - 8$? Explain your thinking.
  - When we take from ten to solve these two problems, what is different about how we get our solution? (In $15 - 9$, we add 1 to 5. In $15 - 8$, we add 2 to 5.)
  - How is $15 - 9$ different from $15 - 8$? How much less are we taking away? How would that change the answer? (We took away 1 less, so the answer will have 1 more.) Extension: Following this pattern, how would you solve $15 - 7$?
- Look at the Application Problem. How did you choose to solve it? Explain your thinking. How could the strategy discussed today be used to solve this problem?

Exit Ticket (3 minutes)

After the Student Debrief, instruct students to complete the Exit Ticket. A review of their work will help you assess the students' understanding of the concepts that were presented in the lesson today and plan more effectively for future lessons. You may read the questions aloud to the students.

A

Name _____   Date _____

*Write the missing number. Pay attention to the addition or subtraction sign.

1	$10 - 9 = \square$		16	$10 - 9 = \square$	
2	$1 + 2 = \square$		17	$11 - 9 = \square$	
3	$10 - 9 = \square$		18	$12 - 9 = \square$	
4	$1 + 3 = \square$		19	$15 - 9 = \square$	
5	$10 - 9 = \square$		20	$14 - 9 = \square$	
6	$1 + 1 = \square$		21	$13 - 9 = \square$	
7	$10 - 9 = \square$		22	$17 - 9 = \square$	
8	$1 + 2 = \square$		23	$18 - 9 = \square$	
9	$12 - 9 = \square$		24	$9 + \square = 13$	
10	$10 - 9 = \square$		25	$9 + \square = 14$	
11	$1 + 3 = \square$		26	$9 + \square = 16$	
12	$13 - 9 = \square$		27	$9 + \square = 15$	
13	$10 - 9 = \square$		28	$9 + \square = 17$	
14	$1 + 5 = \square$		29	$9 + \square = 18$	
15	$15 - 9 = \square$		30	$9 + \square = 19$	

COMMON CORE™   Lesson 17:   Model subtraction of 8 from teen numbers.

Date: 7/3/13

2.B.64

B

Number correct:

Name _____   Date _____

*Write the missing number. Pay attention to the addition or subtraction sign.

1	10 - 9 = ☐		16	10 - 9 = ☐	
2	1 + 1 = ☐		17	11 - 9 = ☐	
3	10 - 9 = ☐		18	13 – 9 = ☐	
4	1 + 2 = ☐		19	14 - 9 = ☐	
5	10 - 9 = ☐		20	13 - 9 = ☐	
6	1 + 3 = ☐		21	12 - 9 = ☐	
7	10 - 9 = ☐		22	15 - 9 = ☐	
8	1 + 4 = ☐		23	16 - 9 = ☐	
9	14 - 9 = ☐		24	9 + ☐ = 12	
10	10 - 9 = ☐		25	9 + ☐ = 13	
11	1 + 3 = ☐		26	9 + ☐ = 15	
12	13 - 9 = ☐		27	9 + ☐ = 14	
13	10 - 9 = ☐		28	9 + ☐ = 15	
14	1 + 2 = ☐		29	9 + ☐ = 17	
15	12 - 9 = ☐		30	9 + ☐ = 16	

Name _____   Date _____

1. Match the pictures with the number sentences.

a.   12 – 8 = 4

b.   17 – 8 = 9

c.   16 – 8 = 8

d.   18 – 8 = 10

e.   14 – 8 = 6

Circle 10 and subtract.

2.   13 – 8 = _____

3.   11 – 8 = _____

4.   15 – 8 = _____

5.   19 – 8 = _____

6.   16 – 8 = _____

7.   17 – 8 = _____

Draw and circle 10, **or** break apart the teen number with a number bond. Then subtract.

8.   12 – 8 = _____

9.   13 – 8 = _____

10.   14 – 8 = _____

11.   15 – 8 = _____

COMMON CORE | Lesson 17:   Model subtraction of 8 from teen numbers.
Date: 7/3/13

2.B.67

Name _____   Date _____

1. Draw and (circle) 10. Then subtract.

a) 12 – 8 = _____	b) 14 – 8 = _____

2. Use a number bond to break apart the teen number. Then subtract.

   15 – 8 = _____

COMMON CORE   Lesson 17:   Model subtraction of 8 from teen numbers.
Date: 7/3/13

2.B.68

Name _____ Date _____

1. Match the number sentence to the picture or to the number bond.

a. 13 – 7 = _____

13	10 – 7 = 3
/\	
10 3	3 + 3 = 6

b. 16 – 8 = _____

c. 11 – 8 = _____

13	10 – 8 = 2
/\	
10 3	2 + 3 = 5

d. 13 – 8 = _____

2. Show how you would solve 14 – 8, either with a number bond or a drawing.

Circle 10. Then subtract.

3. Milo has 17 rocks. He throws 8 of them into a pond. How many does he have left?

Milo has _____ rocks left.

Lesson 17: Model subtraction of 8 from teen numbers.
Date: 7/3/13

2.B.69

Draw and circle 10. Then subtract.

Lucy has $12. She spends $8. How much money does she have now?

Lucy has $_____ now.

Draw and circle 10, or use a number bond to break apart the teen number and subtract.

4. Sean has 15 dinosaurs. He gives 8 to his sister. How many dinosaurs does he keep?

Sean keeps _____ dinosaurs.

---

5. Use the picture to fill in the math story. Show a number sentence.

| Olivia saw _____ clouds in the sky. _____ clouds went away. How many clouds are left? | Try it! Can you show how to solve this problem with a number bond? |

COMMON CORE

Lesson 17: Model subtraction of 8 from teen numbers.
Date: 7/3/13

2.B.70

10 - 9	11 - 9
12 - 9	13 - 9
14 - 9	15 - 9
16 - 9	17 - 9
18 - 9	19 - 9

Lesson 18

Objective: Model subtraction of 8 from teen numbers.

Suggested Lesson Structure

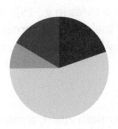

■ Fluency Practice	(12 minutes)
■ Application Problem	(5 minutes)
■ Concept Development	(33 minutes)
■ Student Debrief	(10 minutes)
Total Time	**(60 minutes)**

Fluency Practice (12 minutes)

- Cold Call: Subtract 9 **1.OA.6**   (4 minutes)
- Hide Zero Number Sentences **1.NBT.2**   (2 minutes)
- Number Path **1.OA.6**   (6 minutes)

Cold Call: Subtract 9 (4 minutes)

Materials: (T) Subtract 9 Flashcards (from G1–M2–Lesson 17)

Note: This fluency activity reviews the take from ten subtraction strategy when the subtrahend is 9.

Show a Subtract 9 Flashcard (e.g., 12 – 9). Play Cold Call, where you flash a card and cold call a student or group of students to answer. If students continue to need help subtracting 9, use the following paradigm.

    T: Say 12 the Say Ten way.
    S: Ten 2.
    T: 10 – 9 is? (Snap.)
    S: 1.
    T: 1 + 2 is? (Point to the 2, snap.)
    S: 3.
    T: So 12 – 9 is? (Snap.)
    S: 3.

Lesson 18:   Model subtraction of 8 from teen numbers.
Date: 7/3/13

2.B.72

Hide Zero Number Sentences (2 minutes)

Materials: (S) Hide Zero cards (from G1–M1–Lesson 38)

Note: This fluency activity strengthens the understanding of place value and prepares students to understand ten as a unit by the module's end.

Show students numbers from 10 to 19 with Hide Zero cards (e.g., 15). Students say an addition sentence with 10 as an addend (e.g., 10 + 5 = 15). As students say the sentence, break apart the Hide Zero cards to model the equation. They can also say the numbers the Say Ten way and the regular way.

Number Path (6 minutes)

Materials: (T/S) Personal white boards with number path insert, a counter

Note: Using a number path to get to and from 10 will prepare students to relate counting on and taking from ten in G1–M2–Lesson 19.

    T: Put your counter on 8.
    S: (Place counters on 8.)
    T: How many spaces will you need to move to land on 10? (Pause to provide thinking time.)
    S: 2.
    T: Let's check. Move your counter to 10.
    S   (Move counters to 10)
    T: Were you right?
    S: Yes!
    T: Write an equation to show what you did.
    S: (Write 8 + 2 = 10.)

Continue moving to and from 10, within 10. Then, try starting at 10 and moving counters to and from teen numbers. Ask questions about how students determined the number of spaces they moved. Did they count each space, or did they "just know"?

Application Problem (5 minutes)

Juliana rolls 8 cars down a ramp. If she started with 15 cars at the top of the ramp, how many cars does Juliana still have at the top of the ramp?

Note: This Application Problem provides another context for students to subtract 8 from a teen number. While it is still a *take from with result unknown* problem type, the problem is somewhat more complex based on the order of the sentences within the story. In this story, the quantity being subtracted is given first.

Lesson 18:   Model subtraction of 8 from teen numbers.
Date: 7/3/13

2.B.73

Concept Development (33 minutes)

Materials: (S) Personal white boards

Students gather in the meeting area with their personal white boards.

T: (Project 15 − 8 = ___.) Show me 15 fingers. How many imaginary fingers are up?

S: (Show 10 fingers.) 5.

T: Take away 8 all at once. How many fingers, real and imaginary, are there now?

S: 7.

T: What addition sentence helped you solve 15 − 8?

S: 2 + 5 = 7.

T: Let's use 5-group drawings to show how we used our fingers. How did we show 15 with our fingers?

S: We used 10 real fingers and 5 imaginary fingers.

T: (Decompose 15 by drawing a 5-group row on the board. Leave extra space between the first 10 circles and the last 5 circles.)

T: (Draw a frame around 10 circles.) This is so everyone can see 10 and 5 more easily, just like how we've framed 10 objects together in the past.

T: How did you take away 8 all at once using your fingers? How can we show that in our drawing?

S: We took down 8 real fingers. So cross off 8 from the ten. → We can just hide 8 circles from the ten.

T: If we cross off or hide 8 circles from 10, how many circles would that leave us in the frame?

S: 2.

T: Great. (Hide 8 circles.) How many circles do you see now?

S: 7.

T: What addition sentence do you see in your picture?

S: 2 + 5 = 7.

Repeat the process above with the following sequence: 11 − 8, 16 − 8, 13 − 8, 17 − 8, 12 − 8, 14 − 8, 18 − 8, and 19 − 8. Invite students to draw 5-group rows on their personal white boards. After solving a few problems using both strategies as a whole class, have students work with their partners. Alternate having Student A solve the problem using real and imaginary fingers while Student B shows her work with 5-group row drawings.

When it seems appropriate, ask students to close their eyes and see if they can visualize what is happening when they subtract 8, encouraging them to move away from using their fingers or drawings and work towards using mental math. Have students share what they are picturing in their minds when they are solving.

NOTES ON
MULTIPLE MEANS FOR
ENGAGEMENT:

Having students work in partners frequently develops their cooperative learning skills. Some students will have trouble working together with a partner while others will shine through as leaders. Be sure to talk about how to work well in a team if you see any problems develop.

MP.4

COMMON CORE | Lesson 18: | Model subtraction of 8 from teen numbers.

Date: | 7/3/13

2.B.74

© 2013 Common Core, Inc. All rights reserved. commoncore.org

Problem Set (10 minutes)

Students should do their personal best to complete the Problem Set within the allotted 10 minutes. For some classes, it may be appropriate to modify the assignment by specifying which problems they work on first. Some problems do not specify a method for solving. Students solve these problems using the RDW approach used for Application Problems.

Student Debrief (10 minutes)

Lesson Objective: Model subtraction of 8 from teen numbers.

The Student Debrief is intended to invite reflection and active processing of the total lesson experience.

Invite students to review their solutions for the Problem Set. They should check work by comparing answers with a partner before going over answers as a class. Look for misconceptions or misunderstandings that can be addressed in the Debrief. Guide students in a conversation to debrief the Problem Set and process the lesson. You may choose to use any combination of the questions below to lead the discussion.

- What pattern did you notice every time we took away 8 from a teen number?
- How did you solve 18 – 8 and 19 – 8? How is solving these problems different from solving the other – 8 problems?
- How did solving Problem 7 help you solve Problem 8?
- Look at Problem 9. How are they related? Using this problem, explain how the make ten strategy is related to take from ten strategy.
- How can we use what we learned about taking away 8 from a teen number to solving a –7 problem?
- What tools did we use today to help us subtract 8 from a teen number? (Our fingers and 5-group drawings.) How did it help us?
- How is the way you subtract 8 from a teen number different from the way you subtract 9?

COMMON CORE   Lesson 18:   Model subtraction of 8 from teen numbers.
Date: 7/3/13

2.B.75

© 2013 Common Core, Inc. All rights reserved. **commoncore.org**

- Look at the Application Problem. How did you choose to solve it? Explain your thinking. How could the strategies discussed today be used to solve this problem?

Exit Ticket (3 minutes)

After the Student Debrief, instruct students to complete the Exit Ticket. A review of their work will help you assess the students' understanding of the concepts that were presented in the lesson today and plan more effectively for future lessons. You may read the questions aloud to the students.

Lesson 18:   Model subtraction of 8 from teen numbers.
Date: 7/3/13

2.B.76

Name _____ Date _____

1. Match the pictures with the number sentences.

   a. 13 – 8 = 5

   b. 14 – 8 = 6

   c. 17 – 8 = 9

   d. 18 – 8 = 10

   e. 16 – 8 = 8

Make a math drawing of a 5-group row and some ones to solve the following problems. Write the addition sentence that shows how you add the parts after subtracting 8 or 9.

2. 11 - 8 = ____

   _____

3. 12 - 8 = ____

   _____

4. 15 - 8 = ____

   _____

5. 19 - 8 = ____

   _____

6. 16 – 8 = _____   _____

7. 16 – 9 = _____   _____

8.   14 – 9 = _____   _____

9. Show how to make ten and take from ten to solve the two number sentences.

   (a)   6 + 8 = _____ | (b) 14 – 8 = _____

Name _____ Date _____

Draw 5-group rows and cross out to solve. Complete the number sentences. Write the 2+ addition sentence that helped you add the two parts.

1. 14 – 8 = _____

2 + _____ = _____

_____

2. 17 – 8 = _____

2 + _____ = _____

COMMON CORE™ | Lesson 18: | Model subtraction of 8 from teen numbers.
Date: | 7/3/13

2.B.79

Name _____   Date _____

Draw 5-group rows and cross out to solve. Write the 2+ addition sentence that helped you add the two parts.

1. Annabelle had 13 goldfish. 8 goldfish ate fish food. How many goldfish did not eat fish food?

_____ goldfish did not eat fish food.

2. Sam collected 15 buckets of rain water. He used 8 buckets to water his plants. How many buckets of rain water does Sam have left?

Sam has _____ buckets of rain water left.

3. There were 19 turtles swimming in the pond. Some turtles climbed up onto the dry rocks and now there are only 8 turtles swimming. How many turtles are on the dry rocks?

There are _____ turtles on the dry rocks.

Show making ten or taking from ten to solve the number sentences.

4. 7 + 8 = _____	5. 15 – 8 = _____

Find the missing number by drawing 5-group rows.

6. 11 – 9 = _____	7. 14 – 9 = _____

8. Draw 5-group rows to show the story. Cross out or use number bonds to solve.
   Write a number sentence to show how you solved the problem.

There were 14 people at home. 10 people are watching a football game. 4 people are playing a board game. 8 people left. How many people stayed?

_____ people stayed at home.

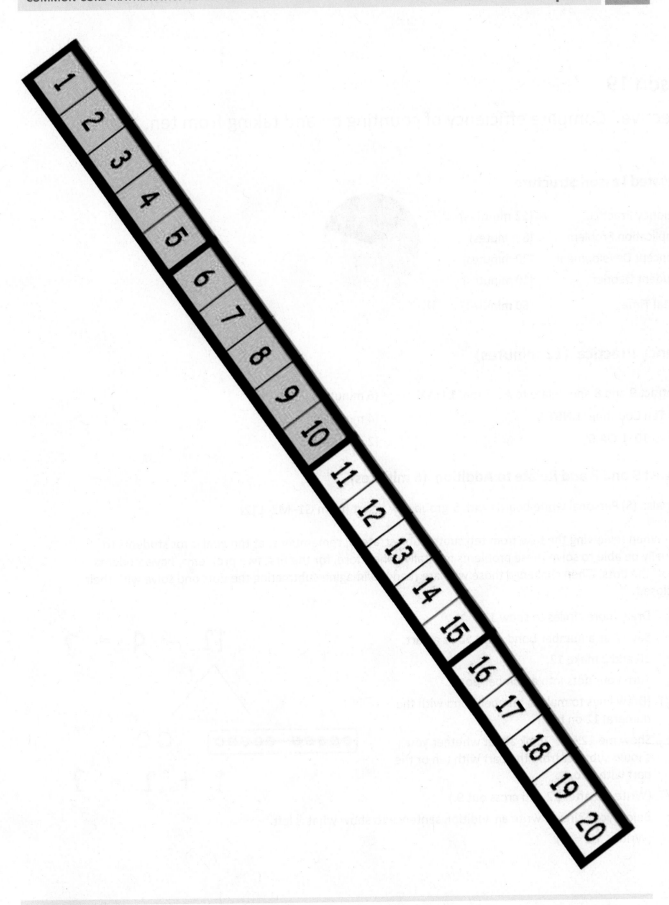

COMMON CORE™

Lesson 18:
Date:

Model subtraction of 8 from teen numbers.
7/3/13

2.B.82

© 2013 Common Core, Inc. All rights reserved. **commoncore.org**

Lesson 19

Objective: Compare efficiency of counting on and taking from ten.

Suggested Lesson Structure

■ Fluency Practice   (12 minutes)
■ Application Problem   (8 minutes)
□ Concept Development   (30 minutes)
■ Student Debrief   (10 minutes)
  Total Time   **(60 minutes)**

Fluency Practice (12 minutes)

- Subtract 9 and 8 and Relate to Addition **1.OA.6**   (6 minutes)
- Say Ten Counting **1.NBT.5**   (4 minutes)
- Get to 10 **1.OA.6**   (2 minutes)

Subtract 9 and 8 and Relate to Addition (6 minutes)

Materials: (S) Personal white boards with 5-group row insert (from G1–M2–L12)

Note: When reviewing the take from ten subtraction strategy, remember that the goal is for students to eventually be able to solve these problems mentally. Therefore, for the first two problems, have students cross off the dots. Then challenge those who are ready to imagine subtracting the dots and solve with their eyes closed.

T: Draw more circles to show 12.
T: Say 12 as a number bond, with 10 as a part.
S: 10 and 2 make 12.
T: Turn your dots into a number bond.
S/T: (Draw lines to make a number bond with the numeral 12 on top.)
T: Show me 12 – 9. Think about whether you should subtract from the part with ten or the part with two.
S/T: (Write – 9 after 12 and cross out 9.)
T: Below your circles, write an addition sentence to show what is left.
S: (Write 1 + 2 = 3.)

T: What is 12 – 9?

S   3.

T: Can anybody say 12 – 9 = 3 as an addition sentence? (Call on a student.)

S: 9 + 3 = 12.

Continue with other numbers between 11 and 20, alternating between subtracting 9 and subtracting 8. As soon as possible, reduce steps (e.g., show me 11 – 8).

Say Ten Counting (4 minutes)

Materials: (S) Personal white boards

Note: Say Ten counting strengthens understanding of place value. It is used throughout Grade 1 fluency, beginning in G1–M1–Lesson 4. A description of Say Ten counting, as shared with children in kindergarten, can be found in GK–M5–Lesson 4.

Do Say Ten counting from 0 to 40 and back. Count for two minutes. Then, have students see how many numbers they can write from 10 to 40 in two minutes.

Get to 10 (2 minutes)

Materials: (T) 20-bead Rekenrek

Note: Practicing getting to 10 from single-digit and teen numbers prepares students for today's lesson, as they will be encouraged to count on or back strategically, stopping at 10 and continuing to the desired number.

T: (Show 8 on the Rekenrek.) What number do you see?

S: 8.

T: How can I get to 10?

S: Add 2.

T: (Move 2 beads to make ten.) Good.

T: (Show 12.) What number do you see?

S: 12.

Continue with other numbers within 20.

Application Problem (8 minutes)

Carla, Jose, and Yannis each have 8 cherries. They all get more cherries to put in their bowls. Now Carla has 12 cherries, Jose has 14 cherries, and Yannis has 16 cherries. How many more cherries did each child put in his or her bowl? Write a number sentence for each answer.

C
$8+\boxed{4}=12$
Carla took
4 cherries.

J
$8+\boxed{6}=14$
Jose took
6 cherries.

Y
$8+\boxed{8}=16$
Yannis took
8 cherries.

Note: This Application Problem enables students to consider three different missing addends all starting from 8. Consider adjusting the story to include only Carla or only Carla and Jose, depending on student need. During the Debrief, students will connect their solution to one child's quantity of cherries as a possible stepping stone for solving the other children's quantity of cherries.

Concept Development (30 minutes)

Materials: (T) Number path (S) Personal white boards with number path insert (from G1–M2–Lesson 18)

Have students come to the meeting area and sit in a semi-circle with their materials.

T: (Write 13 – 8 = ___.) Let's count on by tracking on our fingers to solve 13 – 8.

S: Eiiight, 9, 10, 11, 12, 13. (Put up a finger for each number starting with 9.)

T: What is 13 – 8?

S: 5.

T: Let's count on using a more effient strategy. You are an expert at making ten, so let's count on from 8 to 13, but this time, by making ten.   Show me 8 fingers.

S: (Extend 8 fingers.)

T: How many fingers do we need to pop up to make ten? Show me.

S: 2. (Extend the rest of the fingers.)

T: We need to now imagine more fingers popping up. How many more imaginary fingers do we need to get to 13?

S: 3.

T: How many more fingers, real and imaginary, did we need to get from 8 to 13?

S: 5.

T: Let's use the number path to show what we did with our fingers.

COMMON CORE   Lesson 19:   Compare efficiency of counting on and taking from ten.
Date: 7/3/13

2.B.85

T: (Project number path.) Let's see what counting up by making ten looks like on the number path. How many do we need to get from 8 to 10?

S: 2.

T: I can just jump 2 squares to get to 10 from 8. (Draw a curved arrow from 8 to 10, write +2.)

T: I need to get to 13. What is 13 in Say Ten way?

S: Ten 3.

T: How many do we need to get from 10 to 13?

S: 3.

T: I don't need to count on tennnn, 11, 12, 13. I can just jump 3 squares to get to 13 from 10. (Draw a curved arrow from 10 to 13, write +3.)

T: How many squares did we jump in all from 8 to 13?
     How many do we need to get from 8 to 13?

S: 5.

T: How did you know so quickly?

S: 2 and 3 is 5. → 2 + 3 = 5.

T: Great job counting on to make ten first.

T: Let's check this work using the take from ten strategy using our fingers and a number bond. Put up 13 fingers. How many real and imaginary fingers are up?

S: 10 fingers and 3 imaginary ones.

T: (Write the number bond for 13.) Subtract 8 fingers all at once.

S: (Show 2 fingers.)

T: Where did you take away the 8 from?

S: From the 10 fingers.

T: What is 10 − 8? (Point to 10 in the number bond and 8 in the expression.)

S: 2.

T: How many more imaginary fingers do you have?

S: 3.

T: (Point to 3 in the number bond.) What is 2 and 3?

S: 5.

T: So what is 13 − 8? Say the number sentence.

S: 13 − 8 = 5.

NOTES ON
MULITPLE MEANS OF
REPRESENTATION:

As the teacher, you should feel a sense of pride as your students use strategies to make math easy. It is also exciting when students are able to explain how they are thinking and relate counting on to make ten and taking from ten. Use these students to show others who may want or need some extra help.

Repeat the process using the number path and the take from ten strategy following the suggested sequence: 11 − 8, 14 − 8, 15 − 8, 12 − 8, 17 − 8, and 16 − 8. When it seems appropriate, encourage students to imagine using their fingers and move towards using only the number bond to solve. This is an opportunity for partner work. After a few modeled problems, allow students to work in partnerships with Partner A solving and Partner B checking, then changing roles.

MP.4

Problem Set (10 minutes)

Note: If needed, allow students to use their personal white boards with the number path insert to help them complete the Problem Set.

Students should do their personal best to complete the Problem Set within the allotted 10 minutes. For some classes, it may be appropriate to modify the assignment by specifying which problems they work on first. Some problems do not specify a method for solving. Students solve these problems using the RDW approach used for Application Problems.

Student Debrief (10 minutes)

Lesson Objective: Compare efficiency of counting on and taking from ten.

The Student Debrief is intended to invite reflection and active processing of the total lesson experience.

Invite students to review their solutions for the Problem Set. They should check work by comparing answers with a partner before going over answers as a class. Look for misconceptions or misunderstandings that can be addressed in the Debrief. Guide students in a conversation to debrief the Problem Set and process the lesson. You may choose to use any combination of the questions below to lead the discussion.

- Look at Problems 6 through 9. Which strategy do you prefer, counting on or the take from ten strategy? (It is important to emphasize that they are both good shortcuts rather than discussing which strategy is more efficient.) Why?

- How are these two strategies, counting on to make ten and take from ten, similar to each other? Use 15 – 8 and turn and talk to your partner. (For both of them, we do 2 + 5. For counting on, we are adding 2 to 8 to get to 10 and then adding 5 to get to 15. In the take from ten strategy, you take 8 from 10 and get 2. You add 2 to 5 that's still left and get 7.)

- Explain to your partner how counting on to make ten is related to taking from ten.

Lesson 19:   Compare efficiency of counting on and taking from ten.
Date: 7/3/13

2.B.87

- What new math tool did we use today to show counting on to make ten? (Using the number path to count on by using 2 hops to get to 10 and then adding the hops used to get to the teen number.)
- Look at the Application Problem. How did you solve it? How could we use today's strategies to solve the problem? How could knowing how many cherries Carla took help you solve how many cherries the other children took?

Exit Ticket (3 minutes)

After the Student Debrief, instruct students to complete the Exit Ticket. A review of their work will help you assess the students' understanding of the concepts that were presented in the lesson today and plan more effectively for future lessons. You may read the questions aloud to the students.

Lesson 19:   Compare efficiency of counting on and taking from ten.
Date: 7/3/13

2.B.88

Name _____ Date _____

Use a number bond to show how you used the take from ten strategy to solve the problem.

1. Kevin had 14 crayons. 8 of the crayons were broken. How many of his crayons were not broken?

14 - 8 = _____

Kevin had ____ crayons that were not broken.

Use number bonds to show your thinking.

2. 17 - 8 = _____

3. 18 - 8 = _____

Count on to solve.

4. 13 - 8 = _____

| 1 | 2 | 3 | 4 | 5 | 6 | 7 | 8 | 9 | 10 | 11 | 12 | 13 | 14 | 15 | 16 | 17 | 18 | 19 | 20 |

5. 15 - 8 = _____

Complete the subtraction sentences by using the take from ten and count on strategies. Check the strategy that seemed easiest to you.

6. (a) 12 - 8 = ___   (b) 8 + ___ = 12   ☐ take from ten

    ∧   ☐ count on

_____

7. (a) 11 - 8 = ___   (b) 8 + ___ = 11   ☐ take from ten

    ∧   ☐ count on

_____

8. (a) 16 - 8 = ___   (b) 8 + ___ = 16   ☐ take from ten

    ∧   ☐ count on

| Did you use a different strategy? |

_____

9. (a) 19 - 8 = ___   (b) 8 + ___ = 19   ☐ take from ten

    ∧   ☐ count on

| Did you use a different strategy? |

Lesson 19:   Compare efficiency of counting on and taking from ten.
Date: 7/3/13

2.B.90

Name _____   Date _____

Complete the subtraction sentences by using the take from ten strategy and count on.

| 1 | 2 | 3 | 4 | 5 | 6 | 7 | 8 | 9 | 10 | 11 | 12 | 13 | 14 | 15 | 16 | 17 | 18 | 19 | 20 |

1. (a) 11 - 8 = ____   (b) 8 + ____ = 11

    $\wedge$

_____

2. (a) 15 - 8 = ____   (b) 8 + ____ = 15

    $\wedge$

Name _____ Date _____

Complete the subtraction sentences by using the take from ten strategy and count on.

1. (a) 12 - 8 = ____   (b) 8 + ____ = 12
   $\wedge$

_____

2. (a) 15 - 8 = ____   (b) 8 + ____ = 18
   $\wedge$

_____

Choose the count on strategy or the take from ten strategy to solve.

3. 11 - 8 = ____

4. 17 - 8 = ____

COMMON CORE™   Lesson 19:   Compare efficiency of counting on and taking from ten.
Date: 7/3/13

2.B.92

Use a number bond to show how you solved using the take from ten strategy.

5. Elise counted 16 worms on the pavement. 8 worms crawled into the dirt. How many worms did Elise still see on the pavement?

$$16 - 8 = \underline{\hspace{1.5cm}}$$

| Elise saw _____ worms on the pavement. |

6. John ate 8 orange slices. If he started with 13, how many orange slices does he have left?

| John has _____ orange slices left. |

7. Match the addition number sentence to the subtraction number sentence. Fill in the missing numbers.

a. 12 – 8 = _____

| $8 +$ _____ $= 11$ |

b. 15 – 8 = _____

| $8 +$ _____ $= 18$ |

c. 18- 8 = _____

| $8 +$ _____ $= 12$ |

d. 11 – 8 =_____

| $8 +$ _____ $= 15$ |

Lesson 20

Objective: Subtract 7, 8, and 9 from teen numbers.

Suggested Lesson Structure

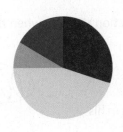

- ■ Fluency Practice   (18 minutes)
- ■ Application Problems   (5 minutes)
- ■ Concept Development   (27 minutes)
- ■ Student Debrief   (10 minutes)

  Total Time   **(60 minutes)**

Fluency Practice (18 minutes)

- Number Path: Get to 10 **1.OA.6**   (8 minutes)
- Sprint: Subtract 8 **1.OA.6**   (10 minutes)

Number Path: Get to 10 (8 minutes)

Materials: (T) Subtract 9 flashcards (from G1–M2–Lesson 17) and Subtract 8 Flashcards (S) Personal white boards with number path insert (from G1–M2–Lesson 18)

Note: Using a number path to get to and from 10 reviews yesterday's lesson, where students were encouraged to relate taking from ten to counting on.

T: (Show the flashcard 15 – 8.)

T: Write 15 – 8 as an addition sentence. Use a box for the number we don't know.

S: (Write 8 + □ = 15.)

T: How many spaces will you need to move to land on 10?

S: 2.

T: Hop from 8 to 10. Use your finger if you need help. Were you right?

S: Yes!

T: Now, hop to 15. How many spaces will you move?

$$8 + \boxed{} = 15$$

S: 5.

T: 2 + 5 = ?

| 1 | 2 | 3 | 4 | 5 | 6 | 7 | 8 | 9 | 10 | 11 | 12 | 13 | 14 | 15 | 16 | 17 | 18 | 19 | 20 |

S: 7.

T: So what is the missing number in your addition sentence?

S: 7.

T: Say the subtraction sentence.

S: 15 – 8 = 7.
Repeat sequence with other flash cards.

Sprint: Subtract 8 (10 minutes)

Materials: (S) Subtract 8 Sprint

Note: This Sprint reviews the take from ten subtraction strategy when the subtrahend is 8.

Application Problem (5 minutes)

Imran has 8 crayons in his pencil box and 7 crayons in his desk. How many crayons does Imran have in total?

Note: Because students have been focusing on subtraction, some students may try to subtract 7 from 8 to solve. Look for such misunderstandings that can be addressed through discussion during the Student Debrief or individual support.

Concept Development (27 minutes)

Materials: (S) Personal white boards with the number path insert, numeral cards 7–9, subtraction sign card

Have students come to the meeting area and sit in a semi-circle with their personal white boards.

T: (Write 13 – 9 = ____.) Solve and share with your partner what you did to get your answer.

S: (Discuss solution and strategies.)

T: Explain what you did to get your answer.

S: We made a 5-group drawing. → We used the take from ten strategy using fingers. → We made a picture in our minds. We just took away 9 from 10 and did 1 + 3. That's 4.

T: Everyone, use the number path to show how you can count on to make ten first. Don't forget to use two arrows to show your thinking.

S: (Solve by starting from 9. Arrows land on 10 and 13.)

T: What addition number sentence helped you to solve 13 – 9?

S: 1 + 3 = 4.

T: How is counting on the number path similar to using our real and imaginary fingers?

NOTES ON
MULTIPLE MEANS FOR
ACTION AND
EXPRESSION:

To support students who need extra pictorial support, draw a picture number bond (e.g., 12 decomposed to 10 and 2 circles in 5-group rows) along with the number bond.

Lesson 20:   Subtract 7, 8, and 9 from teen numbers.
Date: 7/3/13

2.B.95

S: After we drop 9 fingers, we have 1 more finger left from 10 fingers. We then add 1 to 3 imaginary fingers. This is just like hopping 1 square to get to 10 and 3 more to get to 13. We had to add 1 and 3 both times.

Continue by following the suggested sequence: 13 – 7, 13 – 8, 15 – 9, and 15 – 7. Have Partner A and Partner B alternate between using the number path and their fingers to show their work.

T: (Write 12 – 7 = ___.) Let's use a number bond to solve 12 – 7. Visualize 5-group rows showing 12. What two parts do you see? (Encourage partners to show their work to each other and check it.)

S: 10 and 2.

T: (Make a number bond for 12. Point to – 7.) Where would you take 7 away from?

S: Take 7 away from 10.

T: (Point to 10, then 7 on the board.) Take 7 away in your mind. What is 10 – 7?

S: 3.

T: How many circles are there altogether? What two parts can you picture?

S: There are 5 circles. Two and 3 make 5.

Continue the process and invite students to solve using a number bond by following the suggested sequence: 11 – 7, 11 – 8, 13 – 9, 12 – 8, 17 – 8, 16 – 7, 19 – 7, and 19 – 8.

T: Now we are going to play Simple Strategies! (Assign partners based on readiness levels. Instruct each pair to combine their numeral cards and make two piles: digits 11–19 and digits 7–9.) Here's how you play:

1. Partner A picks a card from the teen numbers pile.
2. Partners use the 9 card and the subtraction sign to make a subtraction fact. (Put 8 and 7 cards aside for later use.)
3. Partner A solves by using any of the strategies from today's lesson.
4. Partner B writes down the addition fact that helped to solve the problem (e.g., for 13 – 9, write 1 + 3).
5. Switch roles. Keep the 9 card up each time the partners begin a new expression using a new teen number card.

As students play, the teacher circulates and moves students to working with – 8, then – 7, as appropriate.

Problem Set (10 minutes)

Students should do their personal best to complete the Problem Set within the allotted 10 minutes. For some classes, it may be appropriate to modify the assignment by specifying which problems they work on first. Some problems do not specify a method for solving. Students solve these problems using the RDW approach used for Application Problems.

Note: Students may use drawings that reflect the strategies they learned from the past few days. For example, they may use 5-group drawings, arrows on a number path, or drawings of fingers.

Student Debrief (10 minutes)

Lesson Objective: Subtract 7, 8, and 9 from teen numbers.

The Student Debrief is intended to invite reflection and active processing of the total lesson experience.

Invite students to review their solutions for the Problem Set. They should check work by comparing answers with a partner before going over answers as a class. Look for misconceptions or misunderstandings that can be addressed in the Debrief. Guide students in a conversation to debrief the Problem Set and process the lesson. You may choose to use any combination of the questions below to lead the discussion.

- Look at your work from Simple Strategies! What did you notice about the addition facts for – 9 problems? – 8 problems? – 7 problems?

- Look at Problem 5 on your Problem Set. What is happening to the solution as you move from Part (a) to Part (c)? Explain why this is happening.

- Look at Problem 5 and 6. What do you notice? Explain how Problem 6 (a) and (b) relate to Problem 5 (a) and (b).

- Look at Problem 6 and 7. What do you notice? Explain how the rows are related. If there was a Column (d) here, what might the number sentences be?

- Look at Problem 8(a) and Problem 9(a). How are these related?

- Look at Problem 9. What did you do to solve these? Explain your thinking.

- How could knowing Problem 9(b) help you solve Problem 9(c)?

- Share your Application Problem with a partner. How did you solve it?

COMMON CORE

Lesson 20:   Subtract 7, 8, and 9 from teen numbers.
Date: 7/3/13

2.B.97

Exit Ticket (3 minutes)

After the Student Debrief, instruct students to complete the Exit Ticket. A review of their work will help you assess the students' understanding of the concepts that were presented in the lesson today and plan more effectively for future lessons. You may read the questions aloud to the students.

Lesson 20:   Subtract 7, 8, and 9 from teen numbers.
Date: 7/3/13

2.B.98

A

Name _____   Date _____

*Write the missing number. Pay attention to the addition or subtraction sign.

1	10 - 8 = ☐		16	10 - 8 = ☐	
2	2 + 2 = ☐		17	11 - 8 = ☐	
3	10 - 8 = ☐		18	12 - 8 = ☐	
4	2 + 3 = ☐		19	15 - 8 = ☐	
5	10 - 8 = ☐		20	14 - 8 = ☐	
6	2 + 4 = ☐		21	13 - 8 = ☐	
7	10 - 8 = ☐		22	17 - 8 = ☐	
8	2 + 1 = ☐		23	18 - 8 = ☐	
9	11 - 8 = ☐		24	8 + ☐ = 11	
10	10 - 8 = ☐		25	8 + ☐ = 12	
11	2 + 2 = ☐		26	8 + ☐ = 15	
12	12 - 8 = ☐		27	8 + ☐ = 14	
13	10 - 8 = ☐		28	8 + ☐ = 16	
14	2 + 5 = ☐		29	8 + ☐ = 17	
15	15 - 8 = ☐		30	8 + ☐ = 18	

COMMON CORE   Lesson 20:   Subtract 7, 8, and 9 from teen numbers.
Date: 7/3/13

2.B.99

B

Name _____   Date _____

*Write the missing number. Pay attention to the addition or subtraction sign.

1	10 - 8 = ☐		16	10 - 8 = ☐	
2	2 + 1 = ☐		17	11 - 8 = ☐	
3	10 - 8 = ☐		18	13 – 8 = ☐	
4	2 + 2 = ☐		19	14 - 8 = ☐	
5	10 - 8 = ☐		20	13 - 8 = ☐	
6	2 + 3 = ☐		21	12 - 8 = ☐	
7	10 - 8 = ☐		22	15 - 8 = ☐	
8	2 + 2 = ☐		23	16 - 8 = ☐	
9	12 - 8 = ☐		24	8 + ☐ = 10	
10	10 - 8 = ☐		25	8 + ☐ = 11	
11	2 + 3 = ☐		26	8 + ☐ = 13	
12	13 - 8 = ☐		27	8 + ☐ = 12	
13	10 - 8 = ☐		28	8 + ☐ = 13	
14	2 + 2 = ☐		29	8 + ☐ = 15	
15	12 - 8 = ☐		30	8 + ☐ = 16	

Name _____   Date _____

Solve the problems below. Use drawings or number bonds.

1. $11 - 9 = $ _____

2. $11 - 8 = $ _____

3. $13 - 9 = $ _____

4. $13 - 8 = $ _____

5. $13 - 7 = $ _____

6. $12 - 7 = $ _____

7. Match the equal expressions.

a. $16 - 7$ $13 - 9$

b. $17 - 7$ $18 - 9$

c. $12 - 8$ $15 - 9$

d. $14 - 8$ $18 - 8$

COMMON CORE™

Lesson 20:   Subtract 7, 8, and 9 from teen numbers.
Date: 7/3/13

2.B.101

Complete the subtraction sentences to make them true.

	(a)	(b)	(c)
1.	12 - 9 = ___	13 - 9 = ___	14 - 9 = ___
2.	12 - 8 = ___	13 - 8 = ___	14 – 8 = ___
3.	11 - 7 = ___	12 – 7 = ___	13 – 7 = ___
4.	16 – 9 = ___	18 – 9 = ___	17 – 9 = ___
5.	16 - ___ = 9	15 - ___ = 9	15 - ___ = 7
6.	15 - ___ = 6	11 - ___ = 3	16 - ___ = 7

COMMON CORE

Lesson 20:   Subtract 7, 8, and 9 from teen numbers.
Date: 7/3/13

2.B.102

Name _____ Date _____

Solve the problems below. Use drawings or number bonds.

a. $14 - 9 =$ _____   b. $14 - 7 =$ _____   c. $14 - 8 =$ _____

_____

d. $16 - 7 =$ _____   e. $16 - 9 =$ _____   f. $16 - 8 =$ _____

Name _____   Date _____

Complete the number sentences to make them true.

1. 15 – 9 = _____   2. 15 – 8 = _____   3. 15 – 7 = _____

_____

4. 17 – 9 = _____   5. 17 – 8 = _____   6. 17 – 7 = _____

_____

7. 16 – 9 = _____   8. 16 – 8 = _____   9. 16 – 7 = _____

_____

10. 19 – 9 = _____   11. 19 – 8 = _____   12. 19 – 7 = _____

_____

13. Match equal expressions.

    a.   19 – 9   12 - 7

    b.   13 – 8   18 - 8

COMMON CORE | Lesson 20: Subtract 7, 8, and 9 from teen numbers.
Date: 7/3/13

2.B.104

14. Read the math story. Use a drawing or a number bond to show how you know who is right.

a. Elsie says that the expressions 17 – 8 and 18 – 9 are equal. John says they are not equal. Who is right?

b. John says that the expressions 11 – 8 and 12 – 8 are not equal. Elsie says they are. Who is right?

c. Elsie says to solve 17 – 9, I can take one from 17 and give it to 9 to make 10. So 17 – 9 is equal to 16 – 10. John thinks Elsie made a mistake. Who is correct?

d. John and Elsie are trying to find several subtraction number sentences that start with numbers larger than 10 and always have an answer of 7. Help them figure out number sentences. They started the first one.

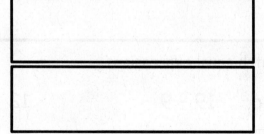

16 – 9 = ____

COMMON CORE™

Lesson 20:   Subtract 7, 8, and 9 from teen numbers.
Date: 7/3/13

2.B.105

$$10 - 8 =$$

$$11 - 8 =$$

$$12 - 8 =$$

$$13 - 8 =$$

$$14 - 8 =$$

$$15 - 8 =$$

$$16 - 8 =$$

$$17 - 8 =$$

$$18 - 8 =$$

COMMON CORE™

Lesson 20:
Date:

Subtract 7, 8, and 9 from teen numbers.
7/3/13

2.B.106

Numeral Cards

7	8	9	10
11	12	13	14
15	16	17	18
19	–		

Lesson 21

Objective: Share and critique peer solution strategies for *take from with result unknown* and *take apart with addend unknown* word problems from the teens.

Suggested Lesson Structure

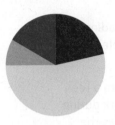

■ Fluency Practice	(13 minutes)
■ Application Problems	(5 minutes)
■ Concept Development	(32 minutes)
■ Student Debrief	(10 minutes)
Total Time	**(60 minutes)**

Fluency Practice (13 minutes)

- Subtraction with Hide Zero Cards **1.OA.6**   (3 minutes)
- Sprint: Subtract 7, 8, 9 **1.OA.6**   (10 minutes)

Subtraction with Hide Zero Cards (3 minutes)

Materials: (T) Hide Zero cards (from G1–M1–Lesson 38)

Note: This fluency reviews subtracting 7, 8, and 9 using the Hide Zero cards, which will help prepare students to understand ten as a unit by the module's end.

     T: (Show 15.) Say 15 the Say Ten way.

     S: Ten 5.

     T: (Break apart the cards to show 10 and 5. Hold up 10.) 10 – 9 = ?

     S: 1.

     T: (Hold up 5.) 1 + 5 = ?

     S: 6.

     T: (Put the cards back together to show 15.) So 15 – 9 = ?

     S: 6.

Continue subtracting 9, 8, and then 7 from teen numbers.

Sprint: Subtract 7, 8, 9 (10 minutes)

Materials: (S) Subtract 7, 8, 9 Sprint

Note: Subtracting 7, 8, and 9 from a teen numbers allows students to practice the take from ten subtraction strategy.

Application Problem (5 minutes)

There are 16 reading mats in the classroom. If 9 reading mats are being used, how many reading mats are available?

Note: While the Application Problem provides the opportunity to continue exploring subtracting 9 from a teen number, it also directly connects with students' work during today's Problem Set. By using the same quantities as the upcoming problem set, students will have a context for comparing and analyzing other student samples.

Concept Development (32 minutes)

Materials: (T) Student work sample (S) Personal white boards

Have students come to the meeting area and sit in a semi-circle.

T: (Project and read.) Colby is reading a book that is 14 pages long. She already read 8 pages. How many more pages does Colby need to read to finish the book? Turn and talk to your partner about how you would solve this problem.

T: (Project Student A's sample.) How did Student A solve this problem? Explain to your partner what this student was thinking. What strategy did Student A use?

S: She drew 14 fingers as 10 and 4. She took away 8 fingers from 10 and got 2. She then added 2 and 4 to get 6. She used the take from ten strategy! That's the right answer!

COMMON
CORE

Lesson 21:

Date:

Share and critique peer solution strategies for *take from with result unknown* and *take apart with addend unknown* word problems from the teens.

7/3/13

2.B.109

T: (Label Student A's work sample *Take from Ten Strategy.*)

T: Can you think of another good way to make a math drawing?

S: Use a 5-group row drawing. That's another easy way to see the take from ten strategy.

T: (Project Student B's sample.) How did Student B solve the problem?

S: He drew a picture but it's a little hard to see because the shapes are not organized. He drew 14 circles and took away 8 and circled the left overs. He counted the left overs, 1, 2, 3, 4, 5, 6.

T: (Label Student B's sample *Draw a Picture.*)

T: (Project Student C's sample.) Take a look at Student C's work. Her answer is 14. Is that correct? Did she do her work correctly? Turn and talk to your partner.

S: No!

T: What do you mean? What did she do wrong here? Well, did she do anything right?

S: She broke apart 14 into 10 and 4. That's correct. But look at her number sentence. She says $4 - 8 = 4$. This is not correct.

T: (Use fingers or the number path to show students her mistake , if she were to take 8 from 4 the answer is less than 0).

S: Her answer is 14, that doesn't make sense. We started with 14 and took away 8. Her answer has to be 8 less than 14.

T: I love the way you looked at her work so carefully. How can you help her get the correct answer? How would you teach her? What strategy did she try to use? Turn and talk to your partner.

S: I would tell her that you should always check what number you are taking away. In this problem, you have to take away 8. You need to subtract 8 from 10.

T: (Label Student C's sample work *Take from 10.*)

Repeat the process and analyze Students D's and E's work samples. Ask students to compare the strategies in these last two samples. Be sure to label the strategy used for each students' sample work.

NOTES ON MULTIPLE MEANS OF ACTION AND EXPRESSION:

Direct students to analyze errors so they understand why they made a mistake. Being able to articulate the mistake will help develop their math comprehension at a deeper level.

NOTES ON MULTIPLE MEANS OF ENGAGEMENT:

Make sure to validate different accurate and efficient strategies students are using or attempting to use. Be aware that students think in different ways. Encourage and cultivate strategic competence in your classroom by allowing students to explain their thinking and help them understand their missteps.

COMMON CORE™   Lesson 21:   Share and critique peer solution strategies for *take from with result unknown* and *take apart with addend unknown* word problems from the teens.   **2.B.110**

Date: 7/3/13

© 2013 Common Core, Inc. All rights reserved. commoncore.org

T: Except for Student C's work, do these all show ways to solve the problem correctly? Which way seems like it's a better shortcut? Turn and talk to your partner.

S: (Discuss while teacher circulates.)

T: (Project and read aloud.) Antalya collected 15 leaves. Nine are yellow. The rest are red. How many leaves are red? Solve this problem by showing your work clearly on your personal board.

Have students swap boards with their partner and discuss the following:

MP.2

- Study what strategy your partner used.
- Did you get the same answer?
- Take turns to explain your partner's strategy.
- Are your strategies similar? How? Are they different? How?
- What did your partner do well?
- Was one strategy a better shortcut than the other? Explain.

If time allows, repeat partner work following the suggested sequence: 12 – 7, 18 – 7 (What did you take 7 away from?), and 15 – 9.

Problem Set (10 minutes)

Students should do their personal best to complete the Problem Set within the allotted 10 minutes. For some classes, it may be appropriate to modify the assignment by specifying which problems they work on first. Some problems do not specify a method for solving. Students solve these problems using the RDW approach used for Application Problems.

Student Debrief (10 minutes)

Lesson Objective: Share and critique peer solution strategies for *take from with result unknown* and *take apart with addend unknown* word problems from the teens.

The Student Debrief is intended to invite reflection and active processing of the total lesson experience.

Invite students to review their solutions for the Problem Set. They should check work by comparing answers with a partner before going over answers as a class. Look for misconceptions or misunderstandings that can be addressed in the Debrief. Guide students in a conversation to debrief the Problem Set and process the lesson.

COMMON CORE

Lesson 21: Share and critique peer solution strategies for *take from with result unknown* and *take apart with addend unknown* word problems from the teens.

Date: 7/3/13

engage^ny 2.B.111

You may choose to use any combination of the questions below to lead the discussion.

- Compare your solution to Problems 2 and 3 with your partner. How is your work similar or different from your partner's?

- Explain how your partner solved Problem 3.

- Study the ways 16 – 7 was solved. Which solutions seem to be the longest way to solve the problem? Which seem to be the best shortcut?

- (Project Sample C and Problem 1(d).) What have you learned from studying the mistakes from these students' work?

- Look at your Application Problem with a partner. Did you solve it the same way or a different way? Is your strategy or your partner's strategy similar to one of the samples in our Problem Set? If so, explain how it is similar. Is your strategy or your partner's strategy different from all of the samples in the Problem Set? If so, explain your strategy.

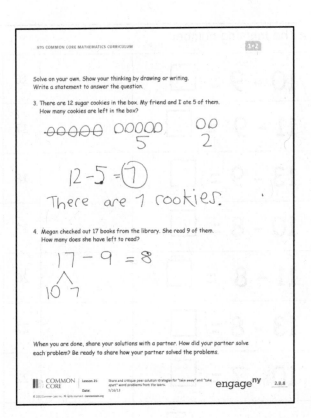

Exit Ticket (3 minutes)

After the Student Debrief, instruct students to complete the Exit Ticket. A review of their work will help you assess the students' understanding of the concepts that were presented in the lesson today and plan more effectively for future lessons. You may read the questions aloud to the students.

COMMON CORE

Lesson 21: Share and critique peer solution strategies for *take from with result unknown* and *take apart with addend unknown* word problems from the teens.

Date: 7/3/13

2.B.112

© 2013 Common Core, Inc. All rights reserved. commoncore.org

A

Number correct: ___

Name _____ Date _____

*Write the missing number.

1	10 - 9 = ☐		16	12 - 7 = ☐
2	11 - 9 = ☐		17	13 - 7 = ☐
3	13 - 9 = ☐		18	14 - 7 = ☐
4	10 - 8 = ☐		19	15 - 9 = ☐
5	11 - 8 = ☐		20	15 - 8 = ☐
6	13 - 8 = ☐		21	15 - 7 = ☐
7	10 - 7 = ☐		22	17 - 7 = ☐
8	11 - 7 = ☐		23	16 - 7 = ☐
9	13 - 7 = ☐		24	17 - 7 = ☐
10	12 - 9 = ☐		25	16 - ☐ = 9
11	13 - 9 = ☐		26	16 - ☐ = 8
12	14 - 9 = ☐		27	17 - ☐ = 8
13	12 - 8 = ☐		28	17 - ☐ = 9
14	13 - 8 = ☐		29	17 - ☐ = 16 - 8
15	14 - 8 = ☐		30	☐ - 7 = 17 - 8

Lesson 21: Share and critique peer solution strategies for *take from with result unknown* and *take apart with addend unknown* word problems from the teens.

Date: 7/3/13

2.B.113

© 2013 Common Core, Inc. All rights reserved. commoncore.org

B

Name _____   Date _____

Number correct:

*Write the missing number.

1	$10 - 9 = \square$		16	$11 - 7 = \square$
2	$11 - 9 = \square$		17	$12 - 7 = \square$
3	$12 - 9 = \square$		18	$15 - 7 = \square$
4	$10 - 8 = \square$		19	$15 - 9 = \square$
5	$11 - 8 = \square$		20	$15 - 8 = \square$
6	$12 - 8 = \square$		21	$15 - 7 = \square$
7	$10 - 7 = \square$		22	$15 - 8 = \square$
8	$11 - 7 = \square$		23	$16 - 8 = \square$
9	$12 - 7 = \square$		24	$16 - 7 = \square$
10	$11 - 9 = \square$		25	$16 - \square = 9$
11	$12 - 9 = \square$		26	$16 - \square = 8$
12	$15 - 9 = \square$		27	$16 - \square = 7$
13	$11 - 8 = \square$		28	$16 - \square = 9$
14	$12 - 8 = \square$		29	$16 - \square = 15 - 8$
15	$15 - 8 = \square$		30	$\square - 8 = 15 - 7$

COMMON CORE™

Lesson 21:   Share and critique peer solution strategies for *take from with result unknown* and *take apart with addend unknown* word problems from the teens.

Date: 7/3/13

2.B.114

Name _____   Date _____

There are 16 dogs playing at the park. 7 of the dogs went home.

How many of the dogs are still at the park?

1. Circle all student work that correctly matches the story.

(a)

$$16 - 7 = 9$$
$$\overset{\wedge}{10\quad 6}$$

(b)

3 + 6

(c)

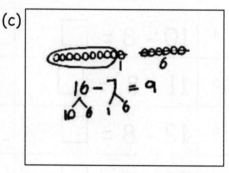

$$16 - 7 = 9$$
10 6 1 6

(d)

⑦ 8 9 10 11 12 13 14 15 16
   ⑧ 16 - 7 = 8

(e)

$$7 + \boxed{9} = 16$$
6 1   10 6

(f)

$$16 - 7$$
7 OOOOOOOOOO
    ⑨

2. Fix the work that was incorrect by making a new drawing in the space below with the matching number sentence.

COMMON CORE™

Lesson 21:   Share and critique peer solution strategies for *take from with result unknown* and *take apart with addend unknown* word problems from the teens.

Date: 7/3/13

2.B.115

Solve on your own. Show your thinking by drawing or writing.
Write a statement to answer the question.

3. There are 12 sugar cookies in the box. My friend and I ate 5 of them. How many cookies are left in the box?

4. Megan checked out 17 books from the library. She read 9 of them. How many does she have left to read?

When you are done, share your solutions with a partner. How did your partner solve each problem? Be ready to share how your partner solved the problem.

COMMON CORE™

Lesson 21: Share and critique peer solution strategies for *take from with result unknown* and *take apart with addend unknown* word problems from the teens.

Date: 7/3/13

2.B.116

Name _____ Date _____

Meg thinks solving the following word problem using the take from ten strategy is the best way to solve. Bill thinks that solving the problem using the count on strategy is a better way. Solve both ways and explain which strategy you think is best.

Mike and Sally have 6 cats. They have 14 pets in all. How many pets do they have that are _not_ cats?

| Meg's strategy | Bill's strategy |

I think _____ strategy is best because _____

_____

_____

COMMON CORE™

Lesson 21:   Share and critique peer solution strategies for _take from with result unknown_ and _take apart with addend unknown_ word problems from the teens.

Date: 7/3/13

2.B.117

Name _____   Date _____

Olivia and Jake both solved the word problems.
Write the strategy used under their work.
Check their work. If incorrect, solve correctly.
If solved correctly, solve using a different strategy.

Strategies:
• Take from 10
• Make 10
• Count on
• I just knew

Mike ate 6 apples from the fruit bowl. If the fruit bowl had 13 apples, how many apples are left?

Olivia's work

Strategy: _____

a.

Jake's work

Strategy: _____

b.

Explain why you chose to use these strategies.

a.   b.

Drew has 17 baseball cards in a box. He has 8 cards with Red Sox players and the rest are Yankee players. How many Yankee player cards does Drew have in his box?

Olivia's work

$17 - 8 = 9$

Jake's work

$17 + 8 = 25$

Strategy: _____

a.

Strategy: _____

b.

Explain why you chose to use these strategies.

a.

b.

COMMON CORE™

Lesson 21: Share and critique peer solution strategies for *take from with result unknown* and *take apart with addend unknown* word problems from the teens.

Date: 7/3/13

2.B.119

COMMON CORE | **Lesson 21:**   Share and critique peer solution strategies for *take from with result unknown* and *take apart with addend unknown* word problems from the teens.

Date: 7/3/13

2.B.120

Topic C

Strategies for Solving *Change* or *Addend Unknown* Problems

1.OA.1, 1.OA.3, 1.OA.4, 1.OA.6, 1.OA.5, 1.OA.7, 1.OA.8

Focus Standard:	1.OA.1	Use addition and subtraction within 20 to solve word problems involving situations of adding to, taking from, putting together, taking apart, and comparing, with unknowns in all positions, e.g., by using objects, drawings, and equations with a symbol for the unknown number to represent the problem.
	1.OA.3	Apply properties of operations as strategies to add and subtract. (Students need not use formal terms for these properties.) *Examples: If 8 + 3 = 11 is known, then 3 + 8 = 11 is also known. (Commutative property of addition.) To add 2 + 6 + 4, the second two numbers can be added to make a ten, so 2 + 6 + 4 = 2 + 10 = 12. (Associative property of addition.)*
	1.OA.4	Understand subtraction as an unknown-addend problem. *For example, subtract 10 – 8 by finding the number that makes 10 when added to 8.*
	1.OA.6	Add and subtract within 20, demonstrating fluency for addition and subtraction within 10. Use mental strategies such as counting on; making ten (e.g., 8 + 6 = 8 + 2 + 4 = 10 + 4 = 14); decomposing a number leading to a ten (e.g., 13 – 4 = 13 – 3 – 1 = 10 – 1 = 9); using the relationship between addition and subtraction (e.g., knowing that 8 + 4 = 12, one knows 12 – 8 = 4); and creating equivalent but easier or known sums (e.g., adding 6 + 7 by creating the known equivalent 6 + 6 + 1 = 12 + 1 = 13).
Instructional Days:	4	
Coherence -Links from:	GK–M4	Number Pairs, Addition and Subtraction to 10
-Links to:	G2–M3	Place Value, Counting, and Comparison of Numbers to 1000
	G2–M5	Addition and Subtraction Within 1000 with Word Problems to 100

Topic C provides students with practice solving *add to with change unknown, take from with change unknown, put together with addend unknown,* and *take apart with addend unknown* word problems (**1.OA.1**). Drawing on the momentum gained from Topic B, Lesson 22 allows students to attack *put together/take apart with addend unknown* word problems such as, "Maria has 15 baseballs, 8 of them are old, and some of them are brand new birthday presents. How many brand new baseballs does Maria have?" Students solve these problems using both the Level 2 counting on strategy and Level 3 subtraction strategies (**1.OA.4**).

Lesson 23 allows students to use counting on as it relates to subtraction, take from ten strategies, or the get to ten Level 3 strategy, as they solve *add to with change unknown* problems (**1.OA.6**). The get to ten strategy has students solving $12 - 3$ as $12 - 2 - 1$, understanding that decomposing the subtrahend to easily get to the ten yields a simpler, more manageable subtraction problem. It is the way a student can make ten when there is an unknown addend. It is a step away from counting on, where, rather than counting on by ones, students consider how much it takes to get to ten and then add on the rest to the teen number. For many students, the language of get to ten helps them bridge from counting on to a more efficient strategy. Up to this point, make ten for the students has shown both addends, and they are strategic about which number to break apart so that they can bond two numbers to make ten. This is a different, though related, process.

Lesson 24 presents students with *take from with change unknown* problems where they continue to select various strategies for solving. Students again relate various addition strategies to their recently acquired subtraction strategies, but in this new word problem type, the strategies they select and discuss help them better make sense of these problems. Students begin to recognize that although stories may be *take from with change unknown* problems, they can apply many strategies such as counting on, counting back, taking from ten, or getting to ten to accurately solve this challenging problem type.

Topic C closes with Lesson 25, where students move away from the context of story problems, to find matching expressions to create true number sentences. They work solely with equations to show and talk about how they would re-represent a given addition or subtraction problem using a Level 2 or Level 3 strategy. For example, when given $9 + 6$, students decompose the 6 into 1 and 5, and then can add using their new number sentence $10 + 5$, (i.e., $9 + 6 = 10 + 5$) (**1.OA.7**), using pictures and words.

A Teaching Sequence Towards Mastery of Strategies for Solving *Change* or *Addend Unknown* Problems

Objective 1: Solve *put together/take apart with addend unknown* word problems and relate counting on to the take from ten strategy.
(Lesson 22)

Objective 2: Solve *add to with change unknown* problems, relating varied addition and subtraction strategies.
(Lesson 23)

Objective 3: Strategize to solve *take from with change unknown* problems.
(Lesson 24)

Objective 4 Strategize and apply understanding of the equal sign to solve equivalent expressions.
(Lesson 25)

Lesson 22

Objective: Solve *put together/take apart with addend unknown* word problems and relate counting on to the take from ten strategy.

Suggested Lesson Structure

■ Fluency Practice   (15 minutes)
▧ Concept Development   (35 minutes)
■ Student Debrief   (10 minutes)
   Total Time   **(60 minutes)**

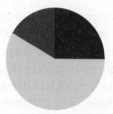

Fluency Practice (15 minutes)

- Subtract with Hide Zero Cards **1.OA.6**   (3 minutes)
- Count by Fives **1.OA.5**   (2 minutes)
- Sprint: Missing Addend Within 10 **1.OA.6**   (10 minutes)

Subtraction with Hide Zero Cards (3 minutes)

Materials: (T) Hide Zero cards (from G1–M1–Lesson 38)

Note: This fluency reviews subtracting 7, 8, and 9 using the Hide Zero cards, which will help prepare students to understand ten as a unit by the module's end. Since this is the second time students are doing this activity, get volunteers to describe the steps necessary to apply the take from ten strategy.

T: (Show 15.) What do I need to do if I want to subtract 9?
S: Take apart 15.
T: (Break apart the cards to show 10 and 5.) Now what?
S: Take 9 from 10.
T: $10 - 9 = ?$
S: 1.
T: What should I do next?
S   Add 1 to the 5.
T: $1 + 5 = ?$
S: 6.
T: (Put the cards back together to show 15.) So, $15 - 9 = ?$
S: 6.

Continue subtracting 9, 8, and then 7 from teen numbers.

Count by Fives (2 minutes)

Materials: (T) 100-bead Rekenrek

Note: Counting by fives promotes fluency with adding and subtracting 5.

Use the Rekenrek to count up and down by fives within 40. Students say the numbers as you move the beads. This time, count both forward and backward on your way up to 40 (e.g., 5, 10, 5, 10, 15, 20, 15, 20, etc.). Alternate between counting the Say Ten and regular way.

Sprint: Missing Addend Within 10 (10 minutes)

Materials: (S) Missing Addend Within 10 Sprint

Note: This review fluency is intended to strengthen students' ability to fluently add and subtract within 10, while preparing students for the problem types that will be presented in today's lesson.

Concept Development (35 minutes)

Materials: (S) Personal white boards

Note: The Application Problem is embedded within the Concept Development since it directly pertains to the objective of today's lesson.

Students may sit with a partner in the meeting area (or at their seats) with their materials.

T: (Project the following problem: Mark has 14 crayons. Eight of the crayons are on the table and some more crayons are in the box. How many crayons are in the box?)

S: (Students solve, and then share work. Circulate, noticing students' accuracy with creating a drawing that matches the story, and taking note of the varying ways students solved the problem.)

T: With a partner, explain your Application Problem drawing to your partner, and discuss how you solved the problem.

S: (Share work.)

T: (Circulate, noticing students' accuracy with creating a drawing that matches the story, and taking note of the varying ways students solved the problem.)

T: (Project today's Application Problem.) Step 1: When we want to solve a problem, we read or listen to the problem. Let's read it together again. (Write *1. Read* on the board.)

S/T: Mark has 14 crayons. Eight of the crayons are on the table and some more crayons are in the box. How many crayons are in the box?

T: Step 2: Draw as much of the math story as you can. You made some great drawings to match this story. What did you draw? (Write *2. Draw* on the board.)

Lesson 22: Solve *put together/take apart with addend unknown* word problems and relate counting on to the take from ten strategy.

Date: 7/3/13

2.C.4

S: (As students share, project work with a document camera or redraw on the board as they explain their drawing.) I drew 14 lines in a row, like the 14 crayons in the problem. I circled 8 of them and labeled those with a *T* to show they were the ones on the table. → I started by drawing 8 circles for the 8 crayons on the table. Then I started drawing dark circles until I got to 14.

T: Everyone look at your work. As I read the story, find the part of your math drawing that matches the sentence.

T: (Read from projection.) *Mark has 14 crayons.* Does your drawing show Mark has 14 crayons? Point to where your drawing shows the 14 crayons. Circle it with your finger.

T: *Eight of the crayons are on the table.* Where does your picture show the 8 crayons that are on the table?

T: Are these 8 **more** crayons, or are they a **part** of Mark's 14 crayons?

S: They are a part of Mark's crayons!

T: How can we tell these crayons from the other crayons in the story?

S: We can make those crayons circles and the other ones dots. → We can label these crayons with a *T* since they are on the table. → We can circle them.

T: If you didn't already label them with a *T* or with the word *table*, add a label. Let's put a box around them too, so we can see them together clearly. (Write *and label* after *2. Draw.*)

T: "...*and some more crayons are in the box.* Can you find these crayons in your drawing? Point to them and circle them with your finger.

T: What could we label this set of crayons?

S: *B* for box.

T: If you didn't label these crayons, add *B* or the word *Box,* to show these are the crayons in the box.

T: Now, we come to the question part of the word problem. *How many crayons are in the box?* Can we find the answer to this question in our drawing?

S: Yes, 6 crayons!

T: What number sentence would match this story? (Write *3. Write a number sentence.*)

S: 8 + 6 = 14.

T: Which number in the number sentence is the answer, or solution, to the question?

S: 6.

T: We have to make sure we put a rectangle around this number so we know it is the solution. If you didn't add a box, do that now.

T: What is the answer to our question? (Write *Write or tell a statement of the solution.*)

S: There are 6 crayons in the box.

MP.2

NOTES ON MULTIPLE MEANS FOR ACTION AND EXPRESSION:

When students are required to draw, remind them to complete math drawings so they do not spend time making beautiful pictures. The use of lines or dots with labels is very efficient.

Lesson 22: Solve *put together/take apart with addend unknown* word problems and relate counting on to the take from ten strategy.

Date: 7/3/13

2.C.5

T: When we read the problem and draw the parts of the story, it can help us understand the problem and help us write the number sentence and the answer, or solution, sentence. Let's try to **read, draw, and write (RDW)** (point to list of steps now listed on board) to solve more problems.

Use the steps listed on the board as you repeat the process above with three more *put together/take apart with addend unknown* problems using the suggested sequence of story problems:

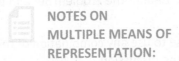

NOTES ON
MULTIPLE MEANS OF
REPRESENTATION:

- There are 12 milk bottles in the crate. Nine are plain milk bottles and the rest are chocolate milk bottles. How many are chocolate milk bottles?

- Ani adds some pink barrettes in her hair. She already had 7 blue barrettes in her hair. If Ani now has 11 barrettes in her hair, how many pink barrettes did she use?

- Laurie reads 5 books about frogs and then reads some books about toads. Laurie counts and realizes she has just read 13 books! How many books about toads did Laurie read?

Choose numbers and tasks differentiated for your learners. If students are having difficulty visualizing the story problems, use smaller numbers. For classes of students where they are very successful, they can use larger numbers within 20.

Have students project or draw their work on the board as the class shares and discusses each part of the RDW process. Ask students to find in the drawing where they can count on to find the solution, as well as where they can take away, or cover, a part as a method to finding the solution.

Problem Set (10 minutes)

Students should do their personal best to complete the Problem Set within the allotted 10 minutes. For some classes, it may be appropriate to modify the assignment by specifying which problems they work on first. Some problems do not specify a method for solving. Students solve these problems using the RDW approach used for Application Problems.

Student Debrief (10 minutes)

Lesson Objective: Solve *put together/take apart with addend unknown* word problems and relate counting on to the take from ten strategy.

The Student Debrief is intended to invite reflection and active processing of the total lesson experience.

Lesson 22:

Date:

Solve *put together/take apart with addend unknown* word problems and relate counting on to the take from ten strategy.

7/3/13

2.C.6

© 2013 Common Core, Inc. All rights reserved. commoncore.org

Invite students to review their solutions for the Problem Set. They should check work by comparing answers with a partner before going over answers as a class. Look for misconceptions or misunderstandings that can be addressed in the Debrief. Guide students in a conversation to debrief the Problem Set and process the lesson.

You may choose to use any combination of the questions below to lead the discussion.

- Look at Problems 1 and 2. Did you use the same or different strategy to solve? Explain why you chose to use the strategy (or strategies) you did.
- How did drawing the parts of the story help you solve the story problems?
- What new math strategy did we use today to communicate precisely how we solved the story problem (**RDW**.) Explain what it is and how we used it.

Exit Ticket (3 minutes)

After the Student Debrief, instruct students to complete the Exit Ticket. A review of their work will help you assess the students' understanding of the concepts that were presented in the lesson today and plan more effectively for future lessons. You may read the questions aloud to the students.

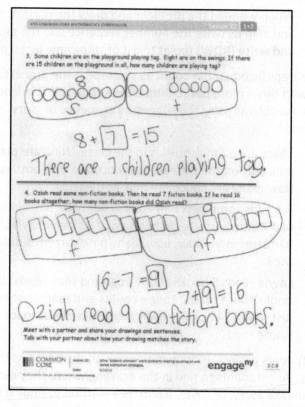

COMMON CORE | Lesson 22: | Solve *put together/take apart with addend unknown* word problems and relate counting on to the take from ten strategy.
| Date: | 7/3/13

2.C.7

A

Number correct:

Name _____   Date _____

*Write the missing number.

1	$2 + \square = 3$		16	$2 + \square = 8$	
2	$1 + \square = 3$		17	$4 + \square = 8$	
3	$\square + 1 = 3$		18	$8 = \square + 6$	
4	$\square + 2 = 4$		19	$8 = 3 + \square$	
5	$3 + \square = 4$		20	$\square + 3 = 9$	
6	$1 + \square = 4$		21	$2 + \square = 9$	
7	$1 + \square = 5$		22	$9 = \square + 1$	
8	$4 + \square = 5$		23	$9 = 4 + \square$	
9	$3 + \square = 5$		24	$2 + 2 + \square = 9$	
10	$3 + \square = 6$		25	$2 + 2 + \square = 8$	
11	$\square + 2 = 6$		26	$3 + \square + 3 = 9$	
12	$0 + \square = 6$		27	$3 + \square + 2 = 9$	
13	$1 + \square = 7$		28	$5 + 3 = \square + 4$	
14	$\square + 5 = 7$		29	$\square + 4 = 1 + 5$	
15	$\square + 4 = 7$		30	$3 + \square = 2 + 6$	

COMMON CORE

Lesson 22:

Date:

Solve *put together/take apart with addend unknown* word problems and relate counting on to the take from ten strategy.

7/3/13

2.C.8

B

Name _____   Date _____

Write the missing number.

1	$1 + \square = 3$		16	$3 + \square = 8$
2	$0 + \square = 3$		17	$2 + \square = 8$
3	$\square + 3 = 3$		18	$8 = \square + 1$
4	$\square + 2 = 4$		19	$8 = 4 + \square$
5	$3 + \square = 4$		20	$\square + 2 = 9$
6	$4 + \square = 4$		21	$4 + \square = 9$
7	$4 + \square = 5$		22	$9 = \square + 5$
8	$1 + \square = 5$		23	$9 = 6 + \square$
9	$2 + \square = 5$		24	$1 + 5 + \square = 9$
10	$4 + \square = 6$		25	$3 + 2 + \square = 8$
11	$\square + 2 = 6$		26	$2 + \square + 6 = 9$
12	$3 + \square = 6$		27	$3 + \square + 4 = 9$
13	$3 + \square = 7$		28	$5 + 4 = \square + 6$
14	$\square + 4 = 7$		29	$\square + 3 = 6 + 2$
15	$\square + 5 = 7$		30	$4 + \square = 2 + 7$

COMMON CORE   Lesson 22:   Solve *put together/take apart with addend unknown* word problems
and relate counting on to the take from ten strategy.

Date: 7/3/13   2.C.9

Name _____   Date _____

Read the word problem.
Draw and label.
Write a number sentence and a statement that matches the story.

1. This week, Maria ate 5 yellow plums and some red plums. If she ate 11 plums in all, how many red plums did Maria eat?

2. Tatyana counted 14 frogs. She counted 8 swimming in the pond and the rest sitting on lily pads. How many frogs did she count sitting on lily pads?

COMMON CORE   Lesson 22:   Solve *put together/take apart with addend unknown* word problems
and relate counting on to the take from ten strategy.

Date: 7/3/13

2.C.10

3. Some children are on the playground playing tag. Eight are on the swings. If there are 15 children on the playground in all, how many children are playing tag?

---

4. Oziah read some non-fiction books. Then he read 7 fiction books. If he read 16 books altogether, how many non-fiction books did Oziah read?

Meet with a partner and share your drawings and sentences.
Talk with your partner about how your drawing matches the story.

Lesson 22: Solve *put together/take apart with addend unknown* word problems
and relate counting on to the take from ten strategy.

Date: 7/3/13

2.C.11

Name _____   Date _____

Read the word problem.
Draw and label.
Write a number sentence and a statement that matches the story.

Remember to draw a box around your solution in the number sentence.

1. Some students in Mrs. See's class are walkers. There are 17 students in her class in all. If 8 students ride the bus, how many students are walkers?

2. I baked 13 loaves of bread for a party but some were burnt, so I threw them away. I brought 8 loaves of bread to the party. How many loaves of bread were burnt?

Lesson 22: Solve *put together/take apart with addend unknown* word problems
and relate counting on to the take from ten strategy.

Date: 7/3/13

2.C.12

Name _____   Date _____

Read the word problem.
Draw and label.
Write a number sentence and a statement that matches the story.

Remember to draw a box around your solution in the number sentence.

Strategies:

- Take from 10
- Make 10
- Count on
- I just knew

1. Michael and Anastasia pick 14 flowers for their mom. Michael picks 6 flowers. How many flowers does Anastasia pick?

2. Daquan buys 6 toy cars. He also buys some magazines. He buys 15 items in all. How many magazines does Daquan buy?

3. Henry and Millie baked some oatmeal cookies. If they baked 18 cookies altogether, and 9 were chocolate chip, how many cookies were oatmeal?

COMMON CORE

Lesson 22:   Solve *put together/take apart with addend unknown* word problems
              and relate counting on to the take from ten strategy.
Date: 7/3/13

2.C.13

4. Felix made 8 birthday invitations with hearts. He made some more with stars. He made 17 invitations in all. How many invitations had hearts?

5. Ben and Miguel are having a bowling contest. Ben wins 9 times. They play 17 games in all. There were no tied games. How many times did Miguel win?

6. Kenzie goes to soccer practice for 16 days this month. Only 9 of her practices were on a school day. How many times did she practice on a weekend?

COMMON CORE | Lesson 22: Solve *put together/take apart with addend unknown* word problems and relate counting on to the take from ten strategy.

Date: 7/3/13

2.C.14

Lesson 23

Objective: Solve *add to with change unknown* problems, relating varied addition and subtraction strategies.

Suggested Lesson Structure

■ Fluency Practice   (15 minutes)
■ Application Problem   (5 minutes)
■ Concept Development   (30 minutes)
■ Student Debrief   (10 minutes)
   Total Time   **(60 minutes)**

Fluency Practice (15 minutes)

▪ Subtraction with Partners **1.OA.6**   (5 minutes)
▪ Sprint: Missing Addended Within 10 **1.OA.6**   (10 minutes)

Subtraction with Partners (5 minutes)

Materials: (S) Personal white boards

Note: This fluency reviews subtracting 7, 8, and 9 from teen numbers. Allow students who still require pictorial representations to draw 5-groups to solve.

Assign partners of equal ability. Partners assign each other a number from 11 to 17 (e.g., 12). On their personal white boards, they write number sentences with 9, 8, and 7 as the subtrahend and solve them (e.g., $12 - 9 = 3$, $12 - 8 = 4$, $12 - 7 = 5$). Partners then exchange white boards and check each other's work.

Sprint: Missing Addend Within 10 (10 minutes)

Materials: (S) Missing Addended Within 10 Sprint

Note: This fluency activity is intended to strengthen students' ability to fluently add and subtract within 10, while preparing students for the problem types that will be presented in today's lesson.

Application Problem (5 minutes)

In the morning, there were 8 leaves on the floor under the ficus tree. During the day, more leaves fell on the floor. Now there are 13 leaves on the floor. How many leaves fell during the day?

Note: In today's lesson, students grapple with an *add to with change unknown* problem. By giving students time to try this problem type independently, teachers will have the opportunity to see how students are applying the RDW strategy without direct instruction on a specific method to solve.

$$8 + \boxed{5} = 13$$

5 leaves fell during the day.

Concept Development (30 minutes)

Materials: (S) Personal white boards and work from Application Problem

Students may sit next to their partners in the meeting area or at their seats with their materials.

T: (Project today's Application Problem.) Before we share our Application Problem with a partner, let's walk through the Read and Draw parts of the Read, Draw, Write strategy. We call this RDW. What does RDW stand for?

S: Read, draw, and write.

T: As I read the problem, find the part of your drawing that matches the story.

T: *In the morning, there were 8 leaves on the ground.* Point to where your drawing shows these 8 leaves on the ground. Do these leaves have a label so you can find them easily?

T: *During the day, more leaves fell on the ground.* Touch the part of your drawing that shows these leaves. Label this part if you haven't yet.

T: *Now there are 13 leaves on the ground.* Can you find these leaves in your drawing? Is this a part of your leaves or is this the total number of leaves?

S: It's the total number of leaves. (Touch their drawing to show.)

T: *How many leaves fell during the day?*

S: 5 leaves!

> **NOTES ON MULTIPLE MEANS OF ACTION AND EXPRESSION:**
>
> As students are using the RDW strategy, some may need some help with organizing their work. Not all students will use the blank, white space well, therefore drawing lines or a grid for these students to work within will help them be more spacially organized.

Lesson 23:   Solve add to with change unknown problems, relating varied addition and subtraction strategies.

Date: 7/3/13

2.C.16

T: Talk with your partner. How does your drawing help you see the story situation?

S: (Discuss.)

T: (Circulate and take note of students' language use, including terms such as *part, whole,* and *total.*)

T: What was missing, a part or the total number of leaves?

S: A part of the leaves.

T: Now that we know we are missing a part, how could we solve this problem?

S: We can start at 8 and then count on until we get to 13. That would be 5. → We can draw all 13 and then cover, or take away 8. We would have 5 left. → We can draw 13 as 10 and 3, so we can quickly cover the 8 without having to recount them. Then it's easy to see the 2 and 3 that are left. That's 5.

T: I saw many of you draw your 8 leaves first and use counting on. How can we use our friendly number 10 to count on in bigger amounts, instead of counting by ones?

S: We can think about how many more we need to get to 10, and then add the rest all at once.

T: Let's try that here. We have 8 leaves, so how many would we draw to get to 10 leaves?

S: 2 more leaves.

T: From 10 leaves, how many more to get to the total, 13 leaves?

S: 3 leaves!

T: So how many more leaves did we draw altogether?

S: 5 leaves!

T: Now that it's later in our Grade 1 year we can go a little faster by jumping from 8 to 10, and then jumping to the total. Counting on in this way is a little faster.

T: Once we solve the problem, we have to write our number sentence and our word sentence. Which number sentence best matches what happened in the story? Talk with your partner.

S: (Discuss.)

S: 8 + 5 = 13 matches the story best because there were 8 leaves in the morning, and then 5 leaves joined the pile. There were 13 leaves at the end of the story. The part we did not know was the 5.

T: Which number needs a rectangle around it to show it is our answer, or our solution?

S: 5.

T: What is our solution sentence?

S: 5 leaves fell during the day.

T: Let's try some more. Remember to think about which number sentence best matches the story.

**NOTES ON
MULTIPLE MEANS OF
REPRESENTATION:**

If students have trouble coming up with the answer sentence, have them re-read the question in the story problem. They can use the question to help write their answer sentence.

**COMMON
CORE**   Lesson 23:   Solve add to with change unknown problems, relating varied
                         addition and subtraction strategies.   2.C.17
             Date: 7/3/13

© 2013 Common Core, Inc. All rights reserved. **commoncore.org**

Present three more *add to with change unknown* story problems such as those below:

- Eight children were playing on the playground. More children came out to join them. Now there are 14 children on the playground. How many children came out to join them on the playground?
- Some new baby ducks hatched at the farm. There were 5 ducks on the farm, and now there are 12 ducks. How many new baby ducks were hatched?
- Thirteen cars are in the parking lot. Six were already there in the morning. The rest of the cars arrived after lunch. How many cars arrived after lunch?

For each story problem, project and read it aloud. Ask students, "Can you draw something? Listen again and ask yourself, what can I draw?" Read the problem again to allow students to think about what they can draw from the problem. Encourage the students to use the drawing to help them consider a strategy for solving by asking themselves, "What does my drawing show me?" Remind them to write a number sentence that matches the story and a word sentence, or solution statement, to answer the question. Give students approximately three minutes to work. Share one or two students' work by drawing it on the board or using a document camera. Have students explain their drawing, share their choices of labels, and explain how their number sentence matches the story.

Problem Set (10 minutes)

Students should do their personal best to complete the Problem Set within the allotted 10 minutes. For some classes, it may be appropriate to modify the assignment by specifying which problems they work on first.

Some problems do not specify a method for solving. Students solve these problems using the RDW approach used for Application Problems.

Student Debrief (10 minutes)

Lesson Objective: Solve *add to with change unknown* problems, relating varied addition and subtraction strategies.

The Student Debrief is intended to invite reflection and active processing of the total lesson experience.

Invite students to review their solutions for the Problem Set. They should check work by comparing answers with a partner before going over answers as a class. Look for misconceptions or misunderstandings that can be addressed in the Debrief. Guide students in a conversation to debrief the Problem Set and process the lesson. You may choose to use any combination of the questions below to lead the discussion.

| Lesson 23: | Solve add to with change unknown problems, relating varied addition and subtraction strategies. | 2.C.18 |
| Date: | 7/3/13 | |

© 2013 Common Core, Inc. All rights reserved. commoncore.org

- Compare the way you solved Problems 1 and 2. How are the strategies you used to solve the same or different?

- What do all of the story problems in the Problem Set have in common? (We always know the total and one of the parts. We had to look for the missing part.)

- Look at Problem 3. How did you use counting on? What did you do? How did that help you solve?

Exit Ticket (3 minutes)

After the Student Debrief, instruct students to complete the Exit Ticket. A review of their work will help you assess the students' understanding of the concepts that were presented in the lesson today and plan more effectively for future lessons. You may read the questions aloud to the students.

COMMON CORE™

Lesson 23:   Solve add to with change unknown problems, relating varied
Date: addition and subtraction strategies.
              7/3/13

2.C.19

A

Name _____   Date _____

*Write the missing number.

1	2 + □ = 3	16	2 + □ = 8
2	1 + □ = 3	17	4 + □ = 8
3	□ + 1 = 3	18	8 = □ + 6
4	□ + 2 = 4	19	8 = 3 + □
5	3 + □ = 4	20	□ + 3 = 9
6	1 + □ = 4	21	2 + □ = 9
7	1 + □ = 5	22	9 = □ + 1
8	4 + □ = 5	23	9 = 4 + □
9	3 + □ = 5	24	2 + 2 + □ = 9
10	3 + □ = 6	25	2 + 2 + □ = 8
11	□ + 2 = 6	26	3 + □ + 3 = 9
12	0 + □ = 6	27	3 + □ + 2 = 9
13	1 + □ = 7	28	5 + 3 = □ + 4
14	□ + 5 = 7	29	□ + 4 = 1 + 5
15	□ + 4 = 7	30	3 + □ = 2 + 6

B

Name _____ Date _____

*Write the missing number.

1	1 + ☐ = 3	16	3 + ☐ = 8
2	0 + ☐ = 3	17	2 + ☐ = 8
3	☐ + 3 = 3	18	8 = ☐ + 1
4	☐ + 2 = 4	19	8 = 4 + ☐
5	3 + ☐ = 4	20	☐ + 2 = 9
6	4 + ☐ = 4	21	4 + ☐ = 9
7	4 + ☐ = 5	22	9 = ☐ + 5
8	1 + ☐ = 5	23	9 = 6 + ☐
9	2 + ☐ = 5	24	1 + 5 + ☐ = 9
10	4 + ☐ = 6	25	3 + 2 + ☐ = 8
11	☐ + 2 = 6	26	2 + ☐ + 6 = 9
12	3 + ☐ = 6	27	3 + ☐ + 4 = 9
13	3 + ☐ = 7	28	5 + 4 = ☐ + 6
14	☐ + 4 = 7	29	☐ + 3 = 6 + 2
15	☐ + 5 = 7	30	4 + ☐ = 2 + 7

Name _____   Date _____

<u>R</u>ead the word problem.
<u>D</u>raw and label.
<u>W</u>rite a number sentence and a statement that matches the story.

1. Janet read 8 books during the week. She read some more books on the weekend.
   She read 12 books total. How many books did Janet read on the weekend?

2. Eric scored 13 goals this season! He scored 5 goals before the playoffs. How many
   goals did Eric score during the playoffs?

COMMON CORE™   Lesson 23:   Solve add to with change unknown problems, relating varied
                                   addition and subtraction strategies.

Date: 7/3/13

2.C.22

© 2013 Common Core, Inc. All rights reserved. commoncore.org

3. There were 8 ladybugs on a branch. Some more came. Then there were 15 ladybugs on the branch. How many ladybugs came?

4. Marco's friend gave him some baseball cards at school. If he was already given 9 baseball cards by his family, and he now has 19 cards in all, how many baseball cards did he get in school?

Meet with a partner and share your drawings and sentences. Talk with your partner about how your drawing matches the story.

COMMON CORE™

Lesson 23: Solve add to with change unknown problems, relating varied addition and subtraction strategies.
Date: 7/3/13

2.C.23

Name _____   Date _____

<u>R</u>ead the word problem.
<u>D</u>raw and label.
<u>W</u>rite a number sentence and a statement that matches the story.

Shanika ate 7 mini-pretzels in the morning. She ate the rest of her mini-pretzels in the afternoon. She ate 13 mini-pretzels altogether that day. How many mini-pretzels did Shanika eat in the afternoon?

![COMMON CORE] Lesson 23:   Solve add to with change unknown problems, relating varied
                            addition and subtraction strategies.
              Date: 7/3/13

2.C.24

Name _____ Date _____

<u>R</u>ead the word problem.

<u>D</u>raw and label.

<u>W</u>rite a number sentence and a statement that matches the story.

1. Micah collected 9 pinecones on Friday and some more on Saturday. Micah collected a total of 14 pinecones. How many pinecones did Micah collect on Saturday?

2. Giana bought 8 star stickers to add to her collection. Now she has 17 stickers in all. How many stickers did Giana have at first?

COMMON CORE

Lesson 23: Solve add to with change unknown problems, relating varied addition and subtraction strategies.

Date: 7/3/13

2.C.25

3. Samil counted 5 pigeons on the street. Some more pigeons came. There were 13 pigeons in all. How many pigeons came?

4. Claire had some eggs in the fridge. She bought a dozen more eggs. Now she has 18 eggs in all. How many eggs did Claire have in the fridge at first?

Lesson 24

Objective: Strategize to solve *take from with change unknown* problems.

Suggested Lesson Structure

■ Fluency Practice　　　　　(15 minutes)
■ Application Problem　　　　(5 minutes)
▢ Concept Development　　　 (30 minutes)
■ Student Debrief　　　　　 (10 minutes)
　 Total Time　　　　　　　**(60 minutes)**

Fluency Practice (15 minutes)

▪ Count by Fives **1.OA.5**　　　　　　　　　　　　(5 minutes)
▪ Sprint: Missing Subtrahends Within 10 **1.OA.6**　　(10 minutes)

Count by Fives (5 minutes)

Materials: (T) Rekenrek

Note: Counting by fives promotes fluency with adding and subtracting 5.

Use the Rekenrek to count by fives to 40 and back. Students say the numbers as you move the beads.
First, have students count the Say Ten way. Then do it again but have students count the regular way.

Sprint: Missing Subtrahends Within 10 (10 minutes)

Materials: (S) Missing Subtrahends Within 10 Sprint

Note: This review fluency is intended to strengthen students' ability to fluently add and subtract within 10,
while preparing students for the problem types that will be presented in today's lesson.

Application Problem (5 minutes)

Yesterday, I saw 11 birds on a branch. Then, 3 birds joined them on
the branch. How many birds were on the branch then?

Note: This problem is intentionally an *add to with result unknown*
problem. Having spent two days on *change* or *addend unknown*

situation types, students may be identifying a pattern in solving the problem type presented.

Misconceptions may arise through this Application Problem if students are overgeneralizing. Students will use the context of this problem to transition into today's lesson, where they will be working with *take from with change unknown* problem. While students are completing the Application Problem, circulate and select a student's work in which the drawings accurately represent the story situation and are simple, labeled, and aligned in a single row. Use this work as the sample for sharing during the lesson.

Concept Development (30 minutes)

Materials: (S) Personal white boards and work from Application Problem

Students may sit with their partners in the meeting area or at their seats with their materials.

T: (Project today's Application Problem.) We have been using the RDW process to solve problems. Before we share our Application Problem with a partner, what does RDW stand for again?

S: Read, draw, and write.

T: With your partner, share your solution, or answer. Be sure to discuss your drawings as you explain your idea. If you realize you forgot something or have to change something, you can do so.

T: (Project or redraw chosen student work.) This student's work uses simple shapes drawn in an organized line, which helps me see what we have. (See Application Problem image as an example.)

T: I need one volunteer to read the problem again for us, and another volunteer to explain how the picture shows each part. (Choose students other than the one whose solution is being shared.)

S1: Yesterday, I saw birds in a tree.

S2: Here are the birds. (Points to the full line of shapes.)

S1: There were 11 birds on a long branch, and then 3 birds joined them.

S2: These 11 birds are the ones on the branch first. I think that's why she wrote *f* under it. (Points to the first 11 birds.) Here are the 3 birds that joined in. That's why she wrote *j* under it. (Points to 3 birds at the end.)

S1: How many birds were in the tree?

S2: She wrote 11 + 3 = 14 and, "You saw 14 birds," because that matches the story and the question. There were 11, then 3 joined in, and now there are 14. (Points to the number sentence while explaining.)

T: You all did a great job reading, drawing, and writing to solve this problem. Let's try another problem.

T: (Project the following problem.) Today, I was passing the same tree. There were 11 birds in the tree when I first looked at it. I looked away, and when I looked back there were 5 birds. How many birds flew away?

S: (Begin to solve the problem.)

T: (Reread the question two more times to support struggling readers as students work.)

Lesson 24: Stategize to solve *take from with change unknown* problems.
Date: 7/3/13

2.C.28

T: (Remind students to think about these questions: *Can you draw something? What can you draw? What does your drawing show you?* Give students approximately three minutes to RDW. Invite two or more students to solve on the board or on chart paper in pairs.)

T: Let's look at the work these students did. They drew to show the 11 birds in the tree. Oh, and look at this, they drew a circle around 5 birds and wrote an *s* to show that these 5 birds that stayed were a part of all 11 birds that were in the tree. Let's draw another circle around these birds, the ones labeled *f*. These are the birds that flew away. (If neither group has a circle around them, draw a circle around each group.)

T: I'm going to use our lines from our number bonds to show that these two parts together make the total of 11 birds.

T: $11 - 6 = 5$. How many birds flew away? Let's put a rectangle around the solution.

S: Six birds flew away.

T: What strategies could you use to solve this?

S: I knew there were two parts, so I took away the 5 to find the other part. → I looked at the picture and counted them all. → I drew 11 like 5-group rows, so I put a box around the first 5 circles, and I could see 6 more very quickly. 5 and 1. → I thought of my doubles plus one fact. $5 + 5$ is 10, so I needed $5 + 6$ to make 11.

NOTES ON MULTIPLE MEANS OF ACTION AND EXPRESSION:

Direct students to analyze the work their classmates have completed. As their teacher, you should also analyze their ability to solve the problem type presented. Look for common misconceptions and the way in which students explain how they got their answer to tell you how your students are progressing.

Repeat the process above for three more *take from with change unknown* story problems such as those listed below:

- Mina had 13 ants in her ant farm. Some ants escaped. Now there are 9 ants in the ant farm. How many ants escaped?

- Jamal had 14 trains, but he only found 8 of his trains. How many of his trains are missing?

- June's baby brother hid some of her blocks. She has 7 blocks now. She used to have 15 blocks. How many blocks should June be looking for?

When sharing solutions and strategies, debrief quickly and move to the next problem. The goal is for students to love solving problems and to begin making connections between reading, drawing, and writing as a road to success as a problem solver!

Lesson 24: Stategize to solve *take from with change unknown* problems.
Date: 7/3/13

2.C.29

Problem Set (10 minutes)

Students should do their personal best to complete the Problem Set within the allotted 10 minutes. For some classes, it may be appropriate to modify the assignment by specifying which problems they work on first. Some problems do not specify a method for solving. Students solve these problems using the RDW approach used for Application Problems.

Student Debrief (10 minutes)

Lesson Objective: Strategize to solve *take from with change unknown* problems.

The Student Debrief is intended to invite reflection and active processing of the total lesson experience.

Invite students to review their solutions for the Problem Set. They should check work by comparing answers with a partner before going over answers as a class. Look for misconceptions or misunderstandings that can be addressed in the Debrief. Guide students in a conversation to debrief the Problem Set and process the lesson. You may choose to use any combination of the questions below to lead the discussion.

- Look at Problems 1 and 2. How are your drawings similar? How are they different?

- How was your drawing similar to or different from your partner's drawing?

- What did today's problems have in common? How were they the same or different from yesterday's problems? What was unknown in the problem, a part or the total? What strategies were easier for you to use when a part is missing instead of the total? (Note: Students might find Problem 2 tricky, since the first number given is the part that is left and the whole is given later in the problem.)

- Which problem was tricky for you? What did you draw? How can we add to the drawing with more information from the problem? What does the drawing show you? (Some students might find Problem 2 tricky, as it starts with an unknown amount but tells you what is left. Problems 1, 3, and 4 might prove tricky for students, as the

Lesson 24: Stategize to solve *take from with change unknown* problems.
Date: 7/3/13

2.C.30

quantity that is taken away is not known.)

▪ How did your drawings help you with the problems? Use a specific problem to explain your thinking.

Exit Ticket (3 minutes)

After the Student Debrief, instruct students to complete the Exit Ticket. A review of their work will help you assess the students' understanding of the concepts that were presented in the lesson today and plan more effectively for future lessons. You may read the questions aloud to the students.

A

Name _____ Ms. Emily _____ Date __9-18-18__

*Write the missing number.

1	$2 - \square = 1$		16	$6 - \square = 2$	
2	$2 - \square = 2$		17	$6 - \square = 3$	
3	$2 - \square = 0$		18	$6 - \square = 4$	
4	$3 - \square = 2$		19	$7 - \square = 3$	
5	$3 - \square = 1$		20	$7 - \square = 2$	
6	$3 - \square = 0$		21	$7 - \square = 1$	
7	$3 - \square = 3$		22	$8 - \square = 2$	
8	$4 - \square = 4$		23	$8 - \square = 3$	
9	$4 - \square = 3$		24	$4 = 8 - \square$	
10	$4 - \square = 2$		25	$2 = 9 - \square$	
11	$4 - \square = 1$		26	$3 = 9 - \square$	
12	$5 - \square = 0$		27	$4 = 9 - \square$	
13	$5 - \square = 1$		28	$10 - 3 = 9 - \square$	
14	$5 - \square = 2$		29	$9 - \square = 10 - 5$	
15	$5 - \square = 3$		30	$9 - \square = 10 - 6$	

B

Number correct:

Name _____   Date _____

*Write the missing number.

1	2 - ☐ = 2		16	6 - ☐ = 3	
2	2 - ☐ = 1		17	6 - ☐ = 4	
3	2 - ☐ = 0		18	6 - ☐ = 5	
4	3 - ☐ = 3		19	7 - ☐ = 4	
5	3 - ☐ = 2		20	7 - ☐ = 3	
6	3 - ☐ = 1		21	7 - ☐ = 2	
7	3 - ☐ = 0		22	8 - ☐ = 3	
8	4 - ☐ = 4		23	8 - ☐ = 4	
9	4 - ☐ = 3		24	5 = 8 - ☐	
10	4 - ☐ = 2		25	3 = 9 - ☐	
11	4 - ☐ = 1		26	4 = 9 - ☐	
12	5 - ☐ = 5		27	5 = 9 - ☐	
13	5 - ☐ = 4		28	10 - 4 = 9 - ☐	
14	5 - ☐ = 3		29	9 - ☐ = 10 - 6	
15	5 - ☐ = 2		30	9 - ☐ = 10 - 5	

Name _____ Date _____

<u>R</u>ead the word problem.
<u>D</u>raw and label.
<u>W</u>rite a number sentence and a statement that match the story. ⬭Circle⬯ the number
sentence and the statement.

1. Jose sees 11 frogs on the shore. Some of the frogs hop into the water. Now there
   are 8 frogs on the shore. How many frogs hopped into the water?

2. Cameron gives some of his apples to his sister. He still has 9 apples left. If he had
   15 apples at first, how many apples did he give to his sister?

Lesson 24:   Stategize to solve *take from with change unknown* problems.
Date: 7/3/13

2.C.34

3. Molly had 16 books. She loaned some to Gia. How many books did Gia borrow if Molly has 8 books left?

---

4. 18 baby goats were playing outside. Some went into the barn. 9 stayed outside to play. How many baby goats went inside?

Meet with a partner and share your drawings and sentences. Talk with your partner about how your drawing tells the story.

Lesson 24: Stategize to solve *take from with change unknown* problems.
Date: 7/3/13

2.C.35

Name _____ Date _____

<u>R</u>ead the word problem.
<u>D</u>raw and label.
<u>W</u>rite a number sentence and a statement that matches the story. (Circle) the number sentence and the statement.

There were 18 dogs splashing in a puddle. Some dogs left. There are 9 dogs still splashing in the puddle. How many dogs left?

Name _____ Date _____

Read the word problem.
Draw and label.
Write a number sentence and a statement that matches the story. (Circle) the number sentence and the statement.

1. Toby dropped 12 crayons on the classroom floor. Toby picked up 9 crayons. Marnie picked up the rest. How many crayons did Marnie pick up?

2. Of the students on the playground, 7 went back into the classroom. If 11 students stayed outside, how many were on the playground at first?

3. At the play, 8 students from Room 24 got a seat. If there were 17 children from Room 24, how many children did not get a seat?

4. Simone had a dozen bagels. She shared some with friends. Now she has 9 bagels left. How many did she share with friends?

COMMON CORE

Lesson 24:   Stategize to solve *take from with change unknown* problems.
Date: 7/3/13

2.C.38

Lesson 25

Objective: Strategize and apply understanding of the equal sign to solve equivalent expressions.

Suggested Lesson Structure

■ Fluency Practice   (15 minutes)
■ Application Problem   (7 minutes)
▢ Concept Development   (28 minutes)
■ Student Debrief   (10 minutes)

  Total Time   **(60 minutes)**

Fluency Practice (15 minutes)

- Make it Equal: Addition Expressions **1.OA.6**   (5 minutes)
- Sprint: Make it Equal **1.OA.6**   (10 minutes)

Make it Equal: Addition Expressions (5 minutes)

Materials: (S) Personal white boards, counters

Note: This activity builds fluency with the make ten addition strategy and reinforces the meaning of the equal sign, which prepares students for today's lesson.

Write or project 9 + ☐ = 8 + ☐ Students find different numbers that make the equation true and check their answers with a partner. If necessary, students can use counters in addition to drawings that they can make on their white boards. In the last minute, ask for volunteers to share the equations they found. Write them on the board and ask if anyone notices a pattern (that the numbers are always consecutive).

Sprint: Make it Equal (10 minutes)

Materials: (S) Make it Equal Sprint

Note: This Sprint uses review addition facts to strengthen students' understanding of the equal sign.

COMMON CORE™

Lesson 25:   Strategize and apply understanding of the equal sign to solve
Date: equivalent expressions.
            7/3/13

2.C.39

Application Problem (7 minutes)

Micah had 16 trucks and lost 9 of them. Charles had 1 truck and received 6 more trucks from his mother. Who has more trucks, Micah or Charles?

Note: Students apply their prior understanding of *take from with result unknown* and *add to with result unknown* problems as they solve this two-part problem. This provides a context for exploring today's objective of further understanding the meaning of the equal sign by pairing equivalent expressions and constructing true number sentences.

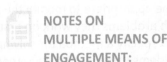

Concept Development (28 minutes)

Materials: (T) Expression cards (S) Personal white boards and work from Application Problem

Students may sit in the meeting area or at their seats, next to a partner, with all materials.

- T: Who has more trucks, Micah or Charles? (Write Micah on the left side of the board and Charles on the right side of the board.)
- S: Neither, they both have the same number of trucks!
- T: Talk with a partner. Use your drawings to help you prove to your partner that Micah and Charles have the same number of trucks.
- S: (Share using their drawings to explain.)
- T: (Circulate and listen to ensure that all students see that Micah and Charles have the same amount of trucks.) What number sentence did you write to match Micah's part of the story?
- S: $16 - 9 = 7$. (Write $16 - 9 = 7$ below Micah.)
- T: What number sentence did you write to match Charles' part of the story?
- S: $1 + 6 = 7$. (Write $1 + 6 = 7$ below Charles.)
- T: So Micah and Charles have an equal number of trucks?
- S: Yes!
- T: (Write $16 - 9$ under the Micah section and $1 + 6$ under the Charles section.) We can say, then, that $16 - 9$ is equal to $1 + 6$. (Draw equal sign in between expressions.)
- T: How does our story help us see that $16 - 9 = 1 + 6$? (Point to each part while reading them the number sentence.) Talk with your partner. (Listen as students explain their thinking to their partner.)

MP.2

- S: Since $16 - 9$ is 7 and $1 + 6$ is 7, they are equal. $16 - 9$ equals $1 + 6$. → Once I took the 9 from 10, Micah and Charles both show 1 and 6. They both have 7.

NOTES ON MULTIPLE MEANS OF ENGAGEMENT:

For those students who are able to quickly repeat the process, cultivate excitement by connecting on-level math to higher math, presenting numbers to 40.

Lesson 25: Strategize and apply understanding of the equal sign to solve equivalent expressions.
Date: 7/3/13

2.C.40

T: Let's try to make some more cool number sentences like this.

T: Work with your partner to make at least two expressions that equal 12.

S: (Work with partners.) We found 10 + 2 and 11 + 1.

T: Great. I'll use 10 + 2. Who has another?

S: We found 6 + 6.

T: True or false, 10 + 2 = 6 + 6?

S: True!

T: Let's all write this cool number sentence on our personal white boards and read it together.

S: (Write number sentence.) 10 + 2 = 6 + 6.

After having generated several similar number sentences, start erasing some addends.

T: If I erase this 6 (erase the 6 after the equal sign), what number goes here to make this equation true?

S: 6! You would need to have two sixes to equal 12.

T: (Distribute an expression card to each student. Odd numbered classes will need to pair two students together.) Solve the expression. You may use linking cubes or another strategy. If you're using linking cubes, you may need to borrow extras from a neighbor. After you solve it, make a linking cube stick to show your final amount.

T: There is someone in the room who has the same answer. Find that person and create a number sentence together to show that your two expressions make equal amounts.

T: What true number sentences did we make?

Problem Set (10 minutes)

Students should do their personal best to complete the Problem Set within the allotted 10 minutes. For some classes, it may be appropriate to modify the assignment by specifying which problems they work on first. Some problems do not specify a method for solving. Students solve these problems using the RDW approach used for Application Problems.

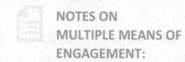

NOTES ON MULTIPLE MEANS OF ENGAGEMENT:

Remember to challenge your advanced learners. An extension activity can be given where number sentences are false and students have to make them true. If they are given a false statement such as 3 + 5 = 7 + 2, they could make the 5 a 6 or the 2 a 1.

Lesson 25:   Strategize and apply understanding of the equal sign to solve
              equivalent expressions.
Date: 7/3/13

2.C.41

Student Debrief (10 minutes)

Lesson Objective: Strategize and apply understanding of the equal sign to solve equivalent expressions.

The Student Debrief is intended to invite reflection and active processing of the total lesson experience.

Invite students to review their solutions for the Problem Set. They should check work by comparing answers with a partner before going over answers as a class. Look for misconceptions or misunderstandings that can be addressed in the Debrief. Guide students in a conversation to debrief the Problem Set and process the lesson. You may choose to use any combination of the questions below to lead the discussion.

- (Write 14 + 2 = 10 + 6 on the board.) Show how you know these are equal expressions. What do you notice about the numbers when you break apart 14?

- (Point to the number sentence written on the board.) Which of the parts of the number sentence are the expression? What does it mean to use = between the two expressions? Explain the meaning of equal.

- Look at your Problem Set. Which expressions can you solve in your head? How can they help you solve other expressions that might be harder for you?

- Look at the true number sentences we made during today's partner activity. What did you notice about the expressions that made these number sentences true?

- Which expressions were missing a part? Which expressions were missing the total?

- How did the Application Problem connect to today's lesson?

Exit Ticket (3 minutes)

After the Student Debrief, instruct students to complete the Exit Ticket. A review of their work will help you assess the students' understanding of the concepts that were presented in the lesson today and plan more effectively for future lessons. You may read the questions aloud to the students.

COMMON CORE | Lesson 25: | Strategize and apply understanding of the equal sign to solve | 2.C.42
| Date: | equivalent expressions.
| | 7/3/13

A

Number correct: _____

Name _____

Date _____

*Write the missing number.

1	$\square = 4 + 1$		16	$7 + 3 = 4 + \square$	
2	$\square = 4 + 2$		17	$6 + 4 = 5 + \square$	
3	$\square = 4 + 3$		18	$5 + 5 = 6 + \square$	
4	$\square = 5 + 1$		19	$5 + 3 = \square + 1$	
5	$\square = 5 + 2$		20	$5 + 4 = \square + 5$	
6	$\square = 5 + 3$		21	$4 + 5 = \square + 5$	
7	$\square = 6 + 1$		22	$2 + \square = 6 + 2$	
8	$8 = 7 + \square$		23	$4 + \square = 5 + 3$	
9	$9 = 8 + \square$		24	$\square + 4 = 5 + 2$	
10	$9 = \square + 1$		25	$\square + 6 = 4 + 3$	
11	$9 = \square + 9$		26	$4 + 2 = 1 + \square$	
12	$8 = \square + 1$		27	$3 + 4 = \square + 2$	
13	$\square = 7 + 1$		28	$4 + 4 = 2 + \square$	
14	$10 = 8 + \square$		29	$3 + \square = 2 + 7$	
15	$10 = \square + 8$		30	$\square + 2 = 2 + 6$	

COMMON CORE™

Lesson 25: Strategize and apply understanding of the equal sign to solve
equivalent expressions.
Date: 7/3/13

2.C.43

B

Number correct: _____

Name _____

Date _____

*Write the missing number.

1	$\square = 3 + 1$		16	$5 + 5 = 4 + \square$	
2	$\square = 3 + 2$		17	$6 + 4 = 7 + \square$	
3	$\square = 3 + 3$		18	$3 + 7 = 8 + \square$	
4	$\square = 4 + 1$		19	$5 + 2 = \square + 1$	
5	$\square = 4 + 2$		20	$5 + 3 = \square + 5$	
6	$\square = 4 + 3$		21	$4 + 4 = \square + 4$	
7	$\square = 5 + 1$		22	$3 + \square = 6 + 3$	
8	$8 = 1 + \square$		23	$4 + \square = 5 + 4$	
9	$9 = 1 + \square$		24	$\square + 4 = 2 + 5$	
10	$8 = \square + 7$		25	$\square + 6 = 3 + 4$	
11	$8 = \square + 8$		26	$4 + 3 = 1 + \square$	
12	$7 = \square + 1$		27	$4 + 4 = \square + 2$	
13	$\square = 6 + 1$		28	$4 + 5 = 2 + \square$	
14	$10 = 9 + \square$		29	$3 + \square = 2 + 6$	
15	$10 = \square + 9$		30	$\square + 2 = 2 + 7$	

COMMON CORE™ | Lesson 25: | Strategize and apply understanding of the equal sign to solve equivalent expressions.
| Date: | 7/3/13

2.C.44

COMMON CORE MATHEMATICS CURRICULUM

Lesson 25 Problem Set 1•2

Name _____ Date _____

Use the expression cards to play Memory. Write the matching expressions to make true number sentences.

1.

[ ] = [ ]

2.

[ ] = [ ]

3.

[ ] = [ ]

4.

[ ] = [ ]

5.

[ ] = [ ]

COMMON CORE

Lesson 25: Strategize and apply understanding of the equal sign to solve equivalent expressions.

Date: 7/3/13

2.C.45

6. Write a true number sentence using the expressions that you have left over. Use pictures and words to show how you know that both expressions have the same unknown numbers.

7. Use other facts you know to write at least two true number sentences similar to the type above.

8. The following addition number sentences are FALSE. Change one number in each problem to make a TRUE number sentence and rewrite the number sentence.

    8 + 5 = 10 + 2   _____

    9 + 3 = 8 + 5   _____

    10 + 3 = 7 + 5   _____

9. The following subtraction number sentences are FALSE. Change one number in each problem to make a TRUE number sentence and rewrite the number sentence.

    12 - 8 = 1 + 2   _____

    13 - 9 = 1 + 4   _____

    1 + 3 = 14 - 9   _____

Name _____   Date _____

You are given these new expression cards. Write matching expressions to make true number sentences.

| 8 + 9 | | 12 - 7 | | 19 - 2 | | 2 + 15 |

| 3 + 2 | | 10 + 7 | | 14 - 9 | | 1 + 4 |

| | = | |

| | = | |

| | = | |

COMMON CORE

Lesson 25:   Strategize and apply understanding of the equal sign to solve equivalent expressions.

Date: 7/3/13

2.C.47

© 2013 Common Core, Inc. All rights reserved. commoncore.org

Name _____ Date _____

1. Circle "true" or "false."

Equation	True or False?
a. 2 + 3 = 5 + 1	True / False
b. 7 + 9 = 6 + 10	True / False
c. 11 – 8 = 12 – 9	True / False
d. 15 – 4 = 14 – 5	True / False
e. 18 – 6 = 2 + 10	True / False
f. 15 - 8 = 2 + 5	True / False

2. Lola and Charlie are using expression cards to make true number sentences. Use pictures and words to show who is right.

   a. Lola picked 4 + 8 and Charlie picked 9 + 3. Lola says these expressions are equal but Charlie disagrees. Who is right? Explain your thinking.

COMMON CORE Lesson 25: Strategize and apply understanding of the equal sign to solve equivalent expressions.

Date: 7/3/13

2.C.48

b. Charlie picked 11 – 4 and Lola picked 6 + 1. Charlie says these expressions are not equal, but Lola disagrees. Who is right? Use a picture to explain your thinking.

c. Lola picked 9 + 7 and Charlie picked 15 – 8. Lola says these expressions are equal but Charlie disagrees. Who is right? Use a picture to explain your thinking.

3. For each set of cards, circle the two that are equal.

a.

| 14 + 5 | 7 + 11 | 11 + 8 |

b.

| 19 - 7 | 15 - 3 | 16 - 7 |

c.

| 5 + 14 | 11 - 7 | 10 - 6 |

d.

| 17 + 2 | 2 + 17 | 9 + 8 |

COMMON CORE   Lesson 25:   Strategize and apply understanding of the equal sign to solve
                    equivalent expressions.
                Date: 7/3/13

2.C.49

12 - 7	3 + 2
7 + 8	10 + 5

15 - 9	1 + 5
6 + 8	10 + 4

15 - 8	2 + 5
17 - 9	1 + 7

COMMON CORE

Lesson 25:   Strategize and apply understanding of the equal sign to solve
                    equivalent expressions.

Date: 7/3/13

2.C.50

11 - 7	3 + 1
6 + 7	10 + 3

17 - 8	2 + 7
4 + 8	10 + 2
11 - 9	1 + 1

8 + 9	10 + 7

COMMON CORE™   **Lesson 25:**   Strategize and apply understanding of the equal sign to solve equivalent expressions.

Date: 7/3/13

2.C.51

$9 + 9$	$10 + 8$
$7 + 9$	$10 + 6$
$11 - 8$	$2 + 1$
$4 + 8$	$10 + 2$
$17 - 5$	$9 + 3$
$15 - 8$	$13 - 6$
$11 - 4$	$16 - 9$

COMMON CORE

Lesson 25:   Strategize and apply understanding of the equal sign to solve equivalent expressions.

Date: 7/3/13

2.C.52

12 + 4	10 + 6
14 + 2	9 + 7

COMMON CORE™

Lesson 25: Strategize and apply understanding of the equal sign to solve equivalent expressions.

Date: 7/3/13

© 2013 Common Core, Inc. All rights reserved. commoncore.org

2.C.53

Topic D

Varied Problems with Decompositions of Teen Numbers as 1 Ten and Some Ones

1.OA.1, 1.NBT.2a, 1.NBT.2b, 1.NBT.5

Focus Standard:	1.OA.1	Use addition and subtraction within 20 to solve word problems involving situations of adding to, taking from, putting together, taking apart, and comparing, with unknowns in all positions, e.g., by using objects, drawings, and equations with a symbol for the unknown number to represent the problem.
	1.NBT.2ab	Understand that the two digits of a two-digit number represent amounts of tens and ones. Understand the following as special cases:
		a. 10 can be thought of as a bundle of ten ones—called a "ten."
		b. The numbers from 11 to 19 are composed of a ten and one, two, three, four, five, six, seven, eight, or nine ones.
Instructional Days:	4	
Coherence -Links from:	GK–M4	Number Pairs, Addition and Subtraction to 10
-Links to:	G2–M3	Place Value, Counting, and Comparison of Numbers to 1000
	G2–M5	Addition and Subtraction Within 1000 with Word Problems to 100

Topic D closes the module with students renaming ten as a unit: *a ten* (**1.NBT.2a**). This is the very first time students are introduced to this language of ten as a unit, so this is exciting! The unit of ten is the foundation for our whole number system, wherein all units are comprised of ten of the adjacent unit on the place value chart.

In Lesson 26, students take a walk down memory lane to revisit representations of 10 ones worked with in the past. They rename their Rekenrek bracelet, the ten-frame, the fingers on two hands, and two 5-groups as 1 ten. They connect teen numbers to the unit form, e.g., 1 ten and 1 one, 1 ten and 2 ones, and represent the numbers with Hide Zero cards. They now analyze the digit 1 in the tens place as representing both 10 ones and 1 unit of ten, further setting the foundation for later work with place value in Module 4 and beyond. Students use their very own Magic Counting Sticks (their fingers) to help them bundle 1 ten. By bundling 1 ten, students realize that some ones are left over, which clarifies the meaning of the ones unit (**1.NBT.2b**).

In Lesson 27, students solve both abstract and contextualized *result unknown* problems (**1.OA.1**). The lesson takes them through a progression from problems with teens decomposed or composed using 1 ten and some ones to problems wherein they find the hidden ten, e.g., 8 + 6 or 12 − 5.

In Lesson 28 students solve familiar problems such as, "Maria had 8 snowballs on the ground and 5 in her arms. How many snowballs did Maria have?" As students write their solutions, they break apart an addend to make a ten with another addend, and write two equations leading to the solution (see the bond and equations to the right). This movement forward in their ability to record the two steps allows them to own the structure of the ten they have been using for the entire module, on a new level (MP.7).

$$9 + 6 =$$
$$\wedge$$
$$1 \quad 5$$

$$9 + 1 = 10$$
$$10 + 5 = 15$$

Topic D closes with Lesson 29, where students solve *add to with change unknown* and *take apart/put together with addend unknown* problems. Similarly to Lesson 28, students write both equations leading to solution, as they take from the ten (see bond and equation to the right).

$$13 - 8$$
$$\wedge$$
$$10 \quad 3$$

$$10 - 8 = 2$$
$$2 + 3 = 5$$

A Teaching Sequence Towards Mastery of Solving Varied Word Problems with Decompositions of Teen Number as 1 Ten and Some Ones
Objective 1: Identify 1 ten as a unit by renaming representations of 10. (Lesson 26)
Objective 2: Solve addition and subtraction problems decomposing and composing teen numbers as 1 ten and some ones. (Lesson 27)
Objective 3: Solve addition problems using ten as a unit, and write two-step solutions. (Lesson 28)
Objective 4: Solve subtraction problems using ten as a unit, and write two-step solutions. (Lesson 29)

Lesson 26

Objective: Identify 1 ten as a unit by renaming representations of 10.

Suggested Lesson Structure

■ Fluency Practice   (11 minutes)
■ Application Problem   (4 minutes)
■ Concept Development   (35 minutes)
■ Student Debrief   (10 minutes)
  Total Time   **(60 minutes)**

Fluency Practice (11 minutes)

- Addition with Partners **1.OA.6**   (6 minutes)
- Happy Counting by Fives **1.OA.5**   (2 minutes)
- 10 More/10 Less **1.NBT.5**   (3 minutes)

Addition with Partners (6 minutes)

Materials: (S) Personal white boards

Note: This fluency reviews the make ten addition strategy, with addends of 7, 8, and 9. Allow students to draw 5-groups if they still need pictorial representations to solve.

Assign partners of equal ability. Partners assign each other a number from 1 to 10 (e.g., 5). On their personal boards, they write number sentences with 9, 8, and 7 as the other addend and solve them (e.g., 9 + 5 = 14, 8 + 5 = 13, 7 + 5 = 12). Partners then exchange boards and check each other's work.

Happy Counting by Fives (2 minutes)

Note: This maintenance fluency reviews adding and subtracting 5.

Do the Happy Counting activity from G1–M2–Lesson 4, counting by fives from 0 to 40 and back. First count the Say Ten way, and then count the regular way.

10 More/10 Less (3 minutes)

Materials: (T) 20-bead Rekenrek

Note: This activity addresses the grade level standard of finding 10 more than a number without having to count and prepares students to see ten as a unit.

COMMON CORE | Lesson 26: | Identify 1 ten as a unit by renaming representations of 10.
Date: | 7/3/13

2.D.3

Practice identifying 10 more and 10 less on the Rekenrek.

    T: (Show a number within 3 on the Rekenrek.) Say the number.

    S: 3.

    T: (Slide over 10 from the next row). What's 10 more than 3, the Say Ten way?

    S: Ten 3.

    T: What is it the regular way?

    S: 13.

Repeat a few times to practice 10 more. Next show a teen number and have students practice identifying 10 less. Then put the Rekenrek away and play Cold Call.

    T: 10 more than 5? Boys.

    S: (Boys only.) 15.

    T: 10 less than 14? Girls.

    S: (Girls only.) 4.

Continue playing, varying the sentences (e.g., take 10 out of 16. Add 10 to 2. 12 is 10 more than…?).

Application Problem (4 minutes)

Ruben has 18 toy cars. His car carrier holds 10 toy cars. If Ruben's carrier is full, how many cars are in the carrier and how many cars are outside of the carrier?

Note: This problem enables students to continue considering situations with missing parts where the context presents a grouping of 10. This grouping of 10 will lead into today's lesson, during which students will be focusing on ten as a unit.

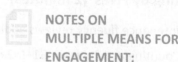

$$18 - 10 = 8$$

10 cars are in the carrier.

8 cars are out.

Concept Development (35 minutes)

Materials: (T) Rekenrek bracelet stretched into a straight line (first used in G1–M1–Lesson 8), 5-group cards, Hide Zero cards (from G1–M1–Lesson 38), 9 Rekenrek beads (separated from pipe cleaner), images to project (template)

Students sit in a semi-circle in the meeting area, next to their partner.

    T: (Lay materials in front of class.) We have used many different tools during math this year. Can you name each of these models?

NOTES ON MULTIPLE MEANS FOR ENGAGEMENT:

Students demonstrate an understanding of math concepts when they can apply them in a variety of situations. It is important for students to recognize the relationship between 1 ten and the tools used in this lesson. They are seeing that no matter the tool used, they still think about 1 ten.

Lesson 26:   Identify 1 ten as a unit by renaming representations of 10.
Date: 7/3/13

2.D.4

S: The Rekenrek bracelet! → A 5-group card of 10! → A ten-frame!

T: Talk with a partner. What do these models have in common?

S: (Discuss.) They all show ten!

T: We have another math tool that we carry around with us everywhere we go. Show me the math tools you carry everywhere.

S: (Wave hands.)

T: (Wiggle your fingers.) These fingers can help us with our math in so many ways. How many fingers do we carry around with us?

S: Ten!

T: (Pick up the Rekenrek.) We can carry around loose beads to count, but instead we use Rekenrek bracelets. Why do we like using the bracelet?

S: It keeps the beads together. → They're organized and we can count them quickly. → We can look at it and see the amount right away.

T: Right! Instead of having 10 loose beads to count one by one, we can pick up this Rekenrek bracelet and count all 10 at once. When I pick up this one bracelet, I know that I have 10 beads altogether. I can call this 1 group of...

S: Ten!

T: We call this **1 ten**.

T: Why do we frame the 10 circles when we use 5-group rows?

S: It's easier to see ten. → We don't have to recount them, because we know there are ten. → Then we can just count on the extras and know how many there are quickly.

T: Just like we called our Rekenrek bracelet 1 ten, when we frame 10 circles in the 5-group rows, we have 1 frame of ten, or...

S: 1 ten!

T: Let's see if we can make 1 ten with our fingers. Let's bundle them up into a set of 10. First, show me all 10 of your fingers.

S: (Raise hands, palms out.)

T: Count with me.

S/T: (Count on fingers from left to right, starting with the pinky) 1, 2, 3, 4, 5, 6, 7, 8, 9, 10. (As you say 10, clasp two hands together.)

T: With our hands bundled like this, we've taken our 10 fingers, and put them together to show 1 set of ten, or 1 ten.

T: Let's make 12 with real and imaginary fingers now. Put out all of your fingers. How many imaginary ones can you see to make 12?

S: 2!

T: Let's bundle the 10 fingers on our hands. 1, 2, 3, 4, 5, 6, 7, 8, 9, 10. (Clasp hands.) We have 1 ten, and, hmm, how many more fingers?

S: 2 more fingers!

T: Let's make more with a partner. (Show the number 19 with Hide Zero cards.) Use your fingers to show the number 19.

S: (Students show 10 on one partner's hands and 9 on the other partner's hands.)

T: (Pull apart Hide Zero cards.) Right now, you are showing 10 fingers (hold up the 10 card) and 9 fingers (hold up the 9 card).

T: If you are showing 10 fingers, bundle them together to make 1 ten.

S: (One student in partnership bundles to form clasped hands, illustrating 1 ten.)

T: Do you still have 19 fingers?

S: Yes!

T: How many tens do you have?

S: 1 ten.

T: How many extra ones do you have out?

S: 9!

T: We call these 9 ones, since they are all apart and we can count them one by one. (Touch each extended finger of a student's hand who is holding out 9 fingers.)

T: So our 10 fingers and our 9 fingers become how many tens and how many ones? (Hold up the 10 and 9 Hide Zero cards.)

S: 1 ten and 9 ones!

T: (Slip the Hide Zero cards together to show 19.)

> **NOTES ON MULTIPLE MEANS OF REPRESENTATION:**
>
> When using the new format of drawing 5-groups as a stick and some circles, it is important to be sure that students grasp the meaning and are able to connect this new representation to ways of drawing they already know. Allow for some time to transition from drawing them horizontally to vertically.

Repeat the process with the following numbers: 18, 15, 14.

T: (Place 1 Rekenrek bracelet and 4 separate beads in front of the class.) How many beads are here?

S: 14!

T: How did you know that so quickly?

S: There are 10 on the Rekenrek and I can see 4 more.

T: So I have how many tens and how many ones?

S: 1 ten and 4 ones!

T: When we draw our 5-groups, let's draw a stick through our circles, like the beads, whenever it is 1 ten. (Draw a vertical line, add 10 circles to it. Then, draw 4 circles in a vertical formation without the line.) We can call this a **5-group column**. Can you pick out the ten from the ones? Draw 14 in 5-group columns like mine.

S: (Draw the same picture.)

T: Put your finger on your 1 ten.

S: (Touch 1 ten in 5-group column.)

T: Put your finger on your 4 ones.

S: (Touch 4 ones in 5-group drawing.)

5-group column

Project images, one at a time. Have students draw 5-group columns as above and state the number of tens and ones for each picture. The teacher should use the Hide Zero cards to show students the ten and ones separated as well as together.

Problem Set (10 minutes)

Students should do their personal best to complete the Problem Set within the allotted 10 minutes. For some classes, it may be appropriate to modify the assignment by specifying which problems they work on first. Some problems do not specify a method for solving. Students solve these problems using the RDW approach used for Application Problems.

Student Debrief (10 minutes)

Lesson Objective: Identify 1 ten as a unit by renaming representations of 10.

The Student Debrief is intended to invite reflection and active processing of the total lesson experience.

Invite students to review their solutions for the Problem Set. They should check work by comparing answers with a partner before going over answers as a class. Look for misconceptions or misunderstandings that can be addressed in the Debrief. Guide students in a conversation to debrief the Problem Set and process the lesson. You may choose to use any combination of the questions below to lead the discussion.

- Look at Problems 1–5. Which were you able to answer most quickly? Why?

- The cards we used today are called Hide Zero cards. Why do you think they have that name? Explain how they work.

- Look at Problems 7 and 8. What is the same about them? What is different?

- Talk with a partner. How do you know 9 ones and 1 **ten** is the same as 1 ten and 9 ones? How is this like other addition rules we have learned?

- (Hold up a 5-group row next to a **5-group column**.) How are these different? How are they the same? How can the 5-group column help us *see* the ten better than with the 5-group row?

- Today we talked about 1 ten. How is 1 ten the same as having 10 ones? How is it different?

- How did the Application Problem connect to today's lesson?

Exit Ticket (3 minutes)

After the Student Debrief, instruct students to complete the Exit Ticket. A review of their work will help you assess the students' understanding of the concepts that were presented in the lesson today and plan more effectively for future lessons. You may read the questions aloud to the students.

Name _____   Date _____

Circle **ten**.   How many **tens** and **ones**?

1.

is the same as

____ ten and ____ ones.

2.

is the same as

____ ten and ____ ones.

3.

is the same as

____ one and ____ tens.

4.

is the same as

____ ten and ____ ones.

5.

Crayons 10

is the same as

____ ten and ____ ones.

Show the total, tens and ones with Hide Zero cards. Write how many **tens** and **ones**.

6.

is the same as

_____ ten and _____ ones.

7.

is the same as

_____ ten and _____ ones.

8.

is the same as

_____ ones and _____ ten.

Draw the circles/beads in the ten and the extra ones. How many **tens** and **ones**?

9.

is the same as

_____ ten and _____ ones.

10.

_____ ten and _____ ones

_____ ten and _____ ones

COMMON CORE | **Lesson 26:** | Identify 1 ten as a unit by renaming representations of 10.
| **Date:** | 7/3/13

2.D.10

Name _____   Date _____

Match the pictures of tens and ones to hide zero cards. Complete the sentence frame.

is the same as

____ ten and ____ ones.

is the same as

____ ten and ____ ones.

    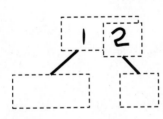

is the same as

____ ten and ____ ones.

Name _____   Date _____

1-2. Circle **ten**.   How many **tens** and **ones**?

is the same as

_____ ten and _____ ones.

is the same as

_____ ones and _____ ten.

3-4. Use the hide zero pictures to draw the ten and ones shown on the cards.

_____ ten and _____ ones   _____ ten and _____ ones

2.D.12

5-6. Draw using 5-groups columns to show the tens and ones.

_____ ten and _____ ones

_____ ten and _____ ones

7-8. Draw your own examples using 5-groups columns to show the tens and ones.

16

is the same as

____ ones and _____ ten.

19

is the same as

_____ ten and _____ ones.

Lesson 26:   Identify 1 ten as a unit by renaming representations of 10.
Date: 7/3/13

2.D.13

How many pineapples?

How many beads?

How many animals?

How many lunches?

How many pieces of fruit?

How many cupcakes?

10 cupcakes

Lesson 27

Objective: Solve addition and subtraction problems decomposing and composing teen numbers as 1 ten and some ones.

Suggested Lesson Structure

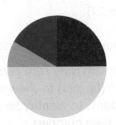

■ Fluency Practice   (15 minutes)
■ Application Problem   (5 minutes)
■ Concept Development   (30 minutes)
■ Student Debrief   (10 minutes)
  Total Time   **(60 minutes)**

Fluency Practice (15 minutes)

- Say Ten: 5-Group Column **1.NBT.2**   (2 minutes)
- Sprint: 10 More and 10 Less **1.NBT.5**   (10 minutes)
- Magic Counting Sticks **1.NBT.2**   (3 minutes)

Say Ten: 5-Group Columns (2 minutes)

Materials: (T) 5-group column cards (from G1–M2–Lesson 27)

Note: This fluency activity reviews the unit of 1 ten as a 5-group column, which was introduced in yesterday's lesson.

> T: (Hold up the card showing 14.) Tell me how many, the Say Ten way.
> S: Ten 4.
> T: How many tens?
> S: 1 ten.
> T: How many ones?
> S: 4 ones.

Repeat this process and alternate between requesting that students respond the Say Ten way and saying the number of tens and ones.

Lesson 27:	Solve addition subtraction problems decomposing and composing teen numbers as 1 ten and some ones.
Date:	7/3/13

2.D.15

Sprint: 10 More and 10 Less (10 minutes)

Materials: (S) 10 More and 10 Less Sprint

Note: This activity addresses the grade level standard of mentally finding 10 more and 10 less than a number.

Magic Counting Sticks (3 minutes)

Materials: (T) Hide Zero cards (from G1–M2–Lesson 27)

Note: This activity reviews the concept of ten as a unit, and prepares students for today's lesson.

Divide students into partners. Show a teen number with Hide Zero cards (e.g., 15). Partner A uses his "magic counting sticks" (fingers) to show a bundle of ten and Partner B shows 5 ones. Ask students to identify how many tens and ones they made. Repeat with other teen numbers, alternating the roles of Partner A and B. Extend the game by calling out a teen number and letting one partner choose whether to show the ten or the ones. Then ask the other partner to show the missing part.

Application Problem (5 minutes)

Ruben was putting away his 14 toy cars. He filled his car carrier and had 4 cars left that could not fit. How many cars fit in his car carrier?

Note: This problem continues to consider contexts where 10 is grouped together within a unit. During the debrief, the unitization of ten will be within the problem being discussed.

Concept Development (30 minutes)

Materials: (T) Hide Zero cards (S) Personal white boards, Hide Zero cards

Students sit in a semi-cirlce in the meeting area with their personal boards next to their partner.

  T: Get out your magic counting sticks! With your partner, show 13.
  S: (One student bundles 10 fingers by clasping their hands together; the other student shows 3 fingers.)
  T: Good! Now make 13 with your Hide Zero cards. You can talk with your partner if you're stuck.
  S: (Layer 3 on top of 10 to make 13.)
  T: How many tens do you have in 13?
  S: 1 ten!
  T: (Hold up the 10 Hide Zero card.) How many extra ones do you have in 13?

Lesson 27: Solve addition subtraction problems decomposing and composing teen numbers as 1 ten and some ones.
Date: 7/3/13

2.D.16

S: 3 ones!

T: (Hold up the 3 Hide Zero card.) Yes, 13 is made of 1 ten (hold the 10 card out), and 3 ones (hold the 3 card out). (Layer the Hide Zero cards again to show 13.)

T: (Project 13 – 3.) How can you use your Hide Zero cards to solve this?

S: Just take away 3.

T: And how many are left?

S: Ten!

T: We can also call that...

S: 1 ten.

Repeat this process as needed with the following suggested sequence: 15 – 5, 16 – 4 (asking, "How many tens and ones are left?"), 18 – 7.

T: Work with your partner to show 14 with your magic counting sticks and your Hide Zero cards.

S: (One student bundles 10 fingers by clasping hands together; the other student shows 4 fingers. They put 14 in front of them.)

T: (Project 14 + 2.) How can you do this? Will you add to the ten or the ones?

S: Just add more to the ones! → Count 2 more! → Use your fingers to count 2 more!

T: So we don't have to add to the ten in order to figure this out, we can just add to the ones?

S: Yes! It's 16!

T: How many tens and ones make up 16?

S: 1 ten and 6 extra ones.

14 + 2

10 + 4 + 2

Project 14 + 2 and ask students to model it with their Hide Zero cards. As they take apart the 4 from 14, they add 4 ones and 2 ones together first to make 6. Now with a ten and a 6, they layer these to make their total. Discuss the tens and ones that comprise the total each time. Repeat this process as needed with the following suggested sequence: 15 + 3, 17 + 2, 13 + 7 (be sure to discuss the significance of 2 tens).

T: (Project 8 + 5.) Work with your partner. Partner A, use your personal board to show how to make 1 ten. Partner B, when she's done, use your Hide Zero cards to show the solution.

S: (Partner A models the addition with the number sentence and number bond. Partner B shows 13 with Hide Zero cards.)

T: Point to the card that tells how many tens are in your answer, and say the number of tens. If you're not sure, you can check!

S: (Point to the 1 in 13.) 1 ten.

NOTES ON MULTIPLE MEANS OF REPRESENTATION:

While some students are experts at solving these number sentences, others may need more support with their Hide Zero cards. Students should use the Hide Zero cards as much as you see fit. Remove the scaffold for students who are able to do more mental calculations. Others can use the cards to help develop their mental calculations.

Lesson 27: Solve addition subtraction problems decomposing and composing
teen numbers as 1 ten and some ones.
Date: 7/3/13

2.D.17

T: Point to the card on your Hide Zero cards that tells how many ones are in your answer, and say how many ones.

S: 3 ones.

If students need more practice with this process, switch the partners, and repeat the same process with the following suggested sequence: 8 + 6, 7 + 5, 6 + 9.

T: Hmmm…I wonder how we can use our Hide Zero cards and white boards to help us solve 13 – 4?

S: Take from the ten! → Count back! → Count on!

T: Let's try taking from the ten, just like [Student 1] said. Let's make our total of 13 with our cards.

S: (Make 13 with their Hide Zero cards.)

T: How can we take from the ten here?

S: Take apart the 10 and take 4 away from the ten!

T: (Draw a matching illustration on the board, showing 10 and 3 separated. Touch the 10.) And how many are left?

MP.7

S: 6.

T: (Write on the board 10 – 4 = 6.) How many do we have altogether? (Touch the 6 and the remaining 3.)

S: 9. (Write 6 + 3 = 9 on the board when students answer.)

T: 9 tens or 9 ones?

S: 9 ones!

T: How many tens are left?

S: 0 tens!

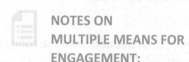

NOTES ON
MULTIPLE MEANS FOR
ENGAGEMENT:

Remember to challenge your advanced learners. Students enjoy working with larger numbers so extend their knowledge of place value. Give them a larger two digit number and they can tell you how many ones and tens are in that number. You can also find many interactive games online when searching 'place value games.' These games can be played with numbers appropriate for the students you are working with.

Repeat this process as needed with the following suggested sequence: 12 – 5, 14 – 8, 15 – 7.

Problem Set (10 minutes)

Students should do their personal best to complete the Problem Set within the allotted 10 minutes. For some classes, it may be appropriate to modify the assignment by specifying which problems they work on first. Some problems do not specify a method for solving. Students solve these problems using the RDW approach used for Application Problems.

COMMON
CORE

Lesson 27:   Solve addition subtraction problems decomposing and composing
               teen numbers as 1 ten and some ones.
Date: 7/3/13

2.D.18

Student Debrief (10 minutes)

Lesson Objective: Solve addition and subtraction problems decomposing and composing teen numbers as 1 ten and some ones.

The Student Debrief is intended to invite reflection and active processing of the total lesson experience.

Invite students to review their solutions for the Problem Set. They should check work by comparing answers with a partner before going over answers as a class.
Look for misconceptions or misunderstandings that can be addressed in the Debrief. Guide students in a conversation to debrief the Problem Set and process the lesson. You may choose to use any combination of the questions below to lead the discussion.

- How did you use what we learned during the lesson to help you solve the word problems in the Problem Set?

- How was Problem 3 helpful in solving Problem 4?

- Look at Problem 4. How many tens are there altogether? Explain how you solved this.

- What do you notice about the problems that have 0 tens in the answer? What is similar about them?

- What do you notice about the problems that have 1 ten in the answer? How are they similar and different?

- Look at your work from the Application Problem. What's another way to say the answer using tens and ones? If Ruben and his friend played with a total of 6 cars, how many tens and ones would be left in the carrier?

Exit Ticket (3 minutes)

After the Student Debrief, instruct students to complete the Exit Ticket. A review of their work will help you assess the students' understanding of the concepts that were presented in the lesson today and plan more effectively for future lessons. You may read the questions aloud to the students.

Lesson 27:

Date:

Solve addition subtraction problems decomposing and composing teen numbers as 1 ten and some ones.

7/3/13

2.D.19

© 2013 Common Core, Inc. All rights reserved. commoncore.org

A

Number correct:

Name _____ Date _____

*Write the missing number.

1	10 + 3 = ☐		16	10 + ☐ = 11
2	10 + 2 = ☐		17	10 + ☐ = 12
3	10 + 1 = ☐		18	5 + ☐ = 15
4	1 + 10 = ☐		19	4 + ☐ = 14
5	4 + 10 = ☐		20	☐ + 10 = 17
6	6 + 10 = ☐		21	17 - ☐ = 7
7	10 + 7 = ☐		22	16 - ☐ = 6
8	8 + 10 = ☐		23	18 - ☐ = 8
9	12 - 10 = ☐		24	☐ - 10 = 8
10	11 - 10 = ☐		25	☐ - 10 = 9
11	10 - 10 = ☐		26	1 + 1 + 10 = ☐
12	13 - 10 = ☐		27	2 + 2 + 10 = ☐
13	14 - 10 = ☐		28	2 + 3 + 10 = ☐
14	15 - 10 = ☐		29	4 + ☐ + 3 = 17
15	18 - 10 = ☐		30	☐ + 5 + 10 = 18

COMMON CORE

Lesson 27: Solve addition subtraction problems decomposing and composing teen numbers as 1 ten and some ones.

Date: 7/3/13

2.D.20

B

Number correct: ⭐

Name _____   Date _____

*Write the missing number.

1	$10 + 1 = \square$		16	$10 + \square = 10$	
2	$10 + 2 = \square$		17	$10 + \square = 11$	
3	$10 + 3 = \square$		18	$2 + \square = 12$	
4	$4 + 10 = \square$		19	$3 + \square = 13$	
5	$5 + 10 = \square$		20	$\square + 10 = 13$	
6	$6 + 10 = \square$		21	$13 - \square = 3$	
7	$10 + 8 = \square$		22	$14 - \square = 4$	
8	$8 + 10 = \square$		23	$16 - \square = 6$	
9	$10 - 10 = \square$		24	$\square - 10 = 6$	
10	$11 - 10 = \square$		25	$\square - 10 = 8$	
11	$12 - 10 = \square$		26	$2 + 1 + 10 = \square$	
12	$13 - 10 = \square$		27	$3 + 2 + 10 = \square$	
13	$15 - 10 = \square$		28	$2 + 3 + 10 = \square$	
14	$17 - 10 = \square$		29	$4 + \square + 4 = 18$	
15	$19 - 10 = \square$		30	$\square + 6 + 10 = 19$	

Lesson 27: Solve addition subtraction problems decomposing and composing
teen numbers as 1 ten and some ones.

Date: 7/3/13

Name _____   Date _____

Solve the problems. Write your answers to show how many **tens** and **ones**. If there is only 1 ten, cross off the "s."

Add.

1.

$12 + 6 =$ ▢▢

____ tens and ____ ones

2.

$5 + 13 =$ ▢▢

____ tens and ____ ones

3.

$8 + 7 =$ ▢▢

____ tens and ____ ones

4.

▢▢ $= 8 + 12$

____ tens and ____ ones

Subtract.

5.

$17 - 4 =$ ▢▢

____ tens and ____ ones

6.

$17 - 5 =$ ▢▢

____ tens and ____ ones

7.

$14 - 6 =$ ▢▢

____ tens and ____ ones

8.

▢▢ $= 16 - 7$

____ tens and ____ ones

Read the word problem. Draw and label. Write a number sentence and statement. Rewrite your answer to show its tens and ones.

9. Frankie and Maya made 4 big sandcastles at the beach. If they made 10 small sandcastles, how many total sandcastles did they make?

_____ tens and _____ ones

10. Ronnie has 8 stickers that are stars. Her friend, Sina gives her 7 more. How many stickers does Ronnie have now?

_____ tens and _____ ones

11. We tied 14 balloons to the tables for a party, but 3 floated away! How many balloons were still tied to the tables?

_____ tens and _____ ones

12. I ate 5 of the 16 strawberries that I picked. How many did I have left over?

_____ tens and _____ ones

COMMON CORE

Lesson 27: Solve addition subtraction problems decomposing and composing teen numbers as 1 ten and some ones.

Date: 7/3/13

2.D.23

Name _____   Date _____

Solve the problems. Write the answers to show how many tens and ones. If there is only one, ten cross off the "s".

1.

13 + 6 = ☐ ☐

_____ tens and _____ ones

2.

7 + 6 = ☐ ☐

_____ tens and _____ ones

<u>R</u>ead the word problem. <u>D</u>raw and label. <u>W</u>rite a number sentence and statement that matches the story. Rewrite your answer to show its tens and ones.

3. Kendrick went bowling. He knocked down 16 pins in the first two frames. If he knocked down 9 in the first frame, how many pins did he knock down in the 2nd frame?

_____ tens and _____ ones

Lesson 27:   Solve addition subtraction problems decomposing and composing
              teen numbers as 1 ten and some ones.
Date: 7/3/13

2.D.24

Name _____ Date _____

Solve the problems. Write the answers to show how many tens and ones. If there is only one, ten cross off the "s".

1.

$8 + 5 =$

____ tens and ____ ones

2.

$12 - 4 =$

____ tens and ____ ones

3.

$15 - 6 =$

____ tens and ____ ones

4.

$14 + 5 =$

____ tens and ____ ones

5.

$13 + 5 =$

____ tens and ____ ones

6.

$17 - 8 =$

____ tens and ____ ones

COMMON CORE™

Lesson 27:   Solve addition subtraction problems decomposing Lend composing teen numbers as 1 ten and some ones.

Date: 7/3/13

2.D.25

Read the word problem. **D**raw and label. **W**rite a number sentence and statement that matches the story. Rewrite your answer to show its tens and ones.

---

9. Mike has some red cars and 8 blue cars. If Mike has 9 red cars, how many cars does he have in all?

_____ tens and _____ ones

---

10. Yani and Han had 14 golf balls. They lost some balls when they hit them over the fence. They had 8 golf balls left. How many balls did they hit over the fence?

_____ tens and _____ ones

---

11. Michai rides his bike for 6 miles over the weekend. He rides 15 miles during the week. How many total miles does Michai ride?

_____ tens and _____ ones

Lesson 27:   Solve addition subtraction problems decomposing land composing
teen numbers as 1 ten and some ones.

Date: 7/3/13

2.D.26

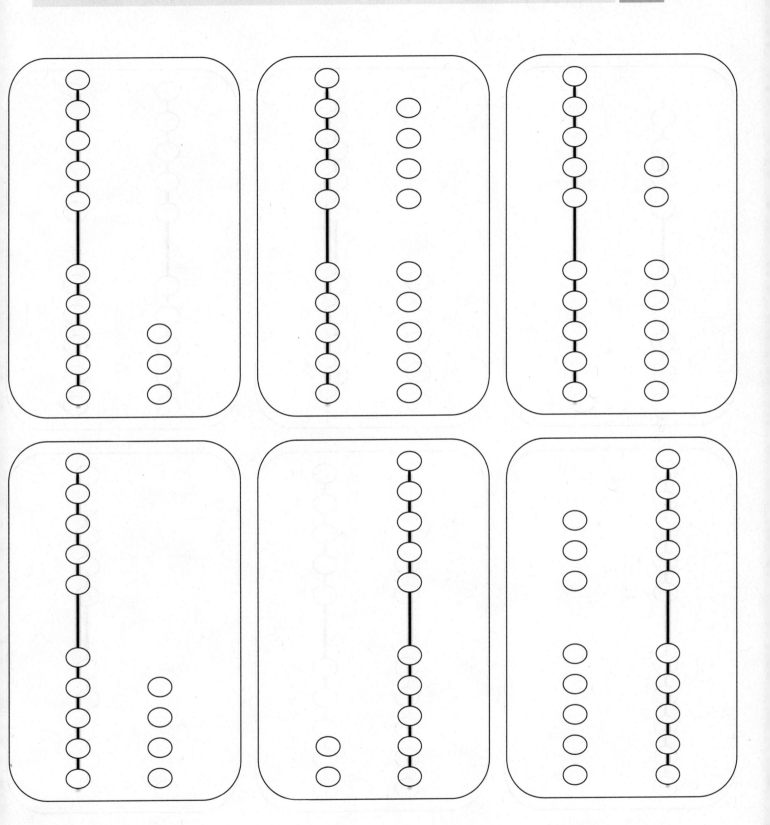

COMMON CORE™

Lesson 27: Solve addition subtraction problems decomposing and composing teen numbers as 1 ten and some ones.

Date: 7/3/13

2.D.27

COMMON CORE™

Lesson 27: Solve addition subtraction problems decomposing and composing
teen numbers as 1 ten and some ones.
Date: 7/3/13

2.D.28

Lesson 28

Objective: Solve addition problems using ten as a unit, and write two-step solutions.

Suggested Lesson Structure

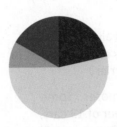

■ Fluency Practice   (13 minutes)
■ Application Problem   (5 minutes)
□ Concept Development   (32 minutes)
■ Student Debrief   (10 minutes)

   Total Time   **(60 minutes)**

Fluency Practice (13 minutes)

- Magic Counting Sticks **1.NBT.2**   (3 minutes)
- Sprint: Adding by Decomposing Teen Numbers **1.OA.6**   (10 minutes)

Magic Counting Sticks (3 minutes)

Materials: (T) Hide Zero cards (from G1–M1–Lesson 38)

Note: This activity reviews the concept of ten as a unit, and prepares students for today's lesson.

   T: (Divide students into partners. Show 13 with Hide Zero cards.) Partner A, show the ones. Partner B, show the tens. How many tens are in 13?

   S: 1.

   T: How many ones?

   S: 3.

   T: If I wanted to add 2, which partner could do it?

   S: Partner A.

   T: Yes. Add 2 to 13. What number do you see?

   S: 15.

Alternate partners and continue with the suggested sequence: 12 + 2, 14 + 1, 15 + 3, 14 + 2, 15 + 3, 16 + 3, etc. All sums should be between 11 and 19.

Lesson 28:   Solve addition problems using ten as a unit, and write two-step
             solutions.
Date: 7/3/13

2.D.29

Sprint: Adding by Decomposing Teen Numbers (10 minutes)

Materials: (S) Adding with Ten as a Unit Sprint

Note: This Sprint addresses the Grade 1 core fluency objective of adding and subtracting within 20.

Application Problem (5 minutes)

Ruben has 7 blue cars and 6 red cars. If Ruben puts all of the blue cars in his car carrier that carries 10 cars, how many red cars will fit in the carrier, and how many will be left out of the carrier?

Note: This Application Problem serves multiple purposes. Some students may respond to the problem with an answer of 13 cars, anticipating the question as, "How many cars does Ruben have?" Look for such misinterpretations as an opportunity to reinforce the importance of reading the question carefully. In addition, the problem gives students a chance to focus on the decomposition of the second addend when creating a unit of ten. This leads into today's lesson, where students will be writing number sentences to show the two steps in the Level 3 strategy of making ten.

Concept Development (32 minutes)

Materials: (T) Hide Zero cards (from G1–M1–Lesson 38) (S) Personal white boards

Students gather in a semi-circle in the meeting area with their personal white boards.

- T: (Project 8 + 4.) Solve this problem with a partner.
- S: (Partners discuss.)
- T: How many is 8 + 4?
- S: 12!
- T: In the number 12, do we have any tens? How many tens do we have?
- S: Yes! 1 ten!
- T: Along with 1 ten, do we have any extra ones? How many?
- S: Yes! 2 ones!
- T: (Hold up the number 12 with Hide Zero cards.) Right, the number 12 is made of 1 ten and 2 ones. (Pull apart the two cards to show 10 card and 2 card separately.)
- T: How many tens in the number 8?
- S: None!
- T: How many tens in the number 4?
- S: None!
- T: Then how did we take 8 and 4, which didn't have any tens, and make a number that has 1 ten and 2 ones? Talk with your partner.

Lesson 28: Solve addition problems using ten as a unit, and write two-step solutions.
Date: 7/3/13

2.D.30

S: (Partners discuss.)

T: (Listen for students to articulate the making of 1 ten and extra ones when adding 8 and 4.)

T: How did we add 8 and 4 to make 12, which has 1 ten and 2 ones?

As students share, the goal is to create two number sentences: the first shows the addition that makes ten and the second shows the addition of the ten and extra ones to make the final total as pictured to the right.

S: Break apart 4 into 2 and 2, and add 8 and 2 to make 1 ten, and then add 2 more ones. → If you start at 8 and count on, you get to ten after 2 counts. That's 1 ten. Then you still have 2 more, that makes 12. 1 ten and 2 ones.

$$8 + 2 = 10$$
$$10 + 2 = 12$$

T: While you were sharing, I wrote your explanations as number sentences. You said to solve 8 + 4, you started with 8 and added 2 out of the 4. That made 1 ten. (Point to 8 + 2 = 10 in the first number sentence.)

T: Then, we have 2 more left from the 4, so you added your 1 ten and 2 ones to make 12. (Point to 10 + 2 = 12 in the second number sentence.) Did I explain that correctly?

S: Yes!

T: Write down the two number sentences I have on the board, and talk with your partner to explain how it shows the way we made 1 ten and 2 ones when adding 8 + 4.

S: (Partners discuss.)

T: (Listen for students who are using accurate language. If students are not explaining *1 ten,* emphasize the creation of *1 ten* in upcoming examples.)

T: Today, let's write two number sentences each time we solve a problem like this, so we can see how we made 1 ten first, and then added the ones.

Repeat the process, having students write two number sentences to show making 1 ten and adding the extra ones, using the following sequence: 8 + 5, 8 + 6, 9 + 6, 7 + 5, 7 + 9. If students appear to require more support at the onset, complete the first problem or two as a class.

Problem Set (10 minutes)

Students should do their personal best to complete the Problem Set within the allotted 10 minutes. For some classes, it may be appropriate to modify the assignment by specifying which problems they work on first. Some problems do not specify a method for solving. Students solve these problems using the RDW approach used for Application Problems.

NOTES ON MULTIPLE MEANS FOR ACTION AND EXPRESSION:

In the beginning, students may get confused about which numbers go where when writing their two number sentences. Emphasize the importance of the addition of the ten for the first number sentence. Some students may need number sentences more concretely framed out. Have an example of a completed problem where they can easily see it to reference if they get confused.

NOTES ON MULTIPLE MEANS OF REPRESENTATION:

For those students who have difficulty writing, provide the sentence frame when doing word problems. This will help these students focus on their math and not worry about the writing being their challenge.

Student Debrief (10 minutes)

Lesson Objective: Solve addition problems using ten as a unit, and write two-step solutions.

The Student Debrief is intended to invite reflection and active processing of the total lesson experience.

Invite students to review their solutions for the Problem Set. They should check work by comparing answers with a partner before going over answers as a class. Look for misconceptions or misunderstandings that can be addressed in the Debrief. Guide students in a conversation to debrief the Problem Set and process the lesson. You may choose to use any combination of the questions below to lead the discussion.

- Look at Problem 1. How many tens and how many ones are there? Use a yellow crayon and find all of the places 1 ten is hiding within the Problem Set. (Color the 1 in all numbers from 10 through 19 within the Problem Set. They may also color the two-digit representation of 10.)

- Look at Problems 1 and 3. What do the number sentences have in common? (The first number sentence is the same.) Do you have any other problems on the set that have 9 + 1 = 10 as the first number sentence? What is similar about the problems that caused them to have the same number sentence as part of the solution?

- Look at Problems 1 and 2. How are they the same and how are they different?

- Look at the Application Problem. Ruben has a carrier that fits 10 cars. How is Ruben's 1 carrier like 1 ten?

- How many cars does Ruben have? Use two number sentences to show how we can make 1 ten and then add the extra ones.

COMMON CORE

Lesson 28: Solve addition problems using ten as a unit, and write two-step solutions.

Date: 7/3/13

2.D.32

© 2013 Common Core, Inc. All rights reserved. commoncore.org

Exit Ticket (3 minutes)

After the Student Debrief, instruct students to complete the Exit Ticket. A review of their work will help you assess the students' understanding of the concepts that were presented in the lesson today and plan more effectively for future lessons. You may read the questions aloud to the students.

Lesson 28: Solve addition problems using ten as a unit, and write two-step solutions.

Date: 7/3/13

2.D.33

© 2013 Common Core, Inc. All rights reserved. commoncore.org

A

Name _____   Date _____

*Write the missing number.

1	10 + 2 = ☐		16	12 + 3 = ☐
2	2 + 1 = ☐		17	13 + 3 = ☐
3	10 + 3 = ☐		18	14 + 3 = ☐
4	4 + 10 = ☐		19	13 + 5 = ☐
5	4 + 2 = ☐		20	14 + 5 = ☐
6	6 + 10 = ☐		21	15 + 5 = ☐
7	10 + 3 = ☐		22	4 + 14 = ☐
8	3 + 3 = ☐		23	4 + 15 = ☐
9	10 + 6 = ☐		24	12 + ☐ = 14
10	2 + 1 = ☐		25	12 + ☐ = 15
11	12 + 1 = ☐		26	12 + ☐ = 16
12	2 + 2 = ☐		27	☐ + 4 = 16
13	12 + 2 = ☐		28	5 + ☐ = 16
14	3 + 3 = ☐		29	5 + ☐ = 26
15	13 + 3 = ☐		30	5 + ☐ = 26

COMMON CORE™   Lesson 28:   Solve addition problems using ten as a unit, and write two-step solutions.

Date: 7/3/13

2.D.34

B

Number correct:

Name _____   Date _____

*Write the missing number.

1	10 + 1 = ☐		16	12 + 2 = ☐
2	1 + 1 = ☐		17	13 + 2 = ☐
3	10 + 2 = ☐		18	14 + 2 = ☐
4	3 + 10 = ☐		19	13 + 4 = ☐
5	3 + 2 = ☐		20	14 + 4 = ☐
6	5 + 10 = ☐		21	15 + 4 = ☐
7	10 + 2 = ☐		22	5 + 14 = ☐
8	2 + 2 = ☐		23	5 + 15 = ☐
9	10 + 4 = ☐		24	11 + ☐ = 12
10	2 + 1 = ☐		25	11 + ☐ = 13
11	12 + 1 = ☐		26	11 + ☐ = 14
12	1 + 1 = ☐		27	☐ + 3 = 14
13	11 + 1 = ☐		28	6 + ☐ = 19
14	3 + 2 = ☐		29	6 + ☐ = 29
15	13 + 2 = ☐		30	5 + ☐ = 39

Name _____

Date _____

Solve the problems. Show your solution in two steps:

Step 1: Write one number sentence to make ten.

Step 2: Write one number sentence to add to ten.

$9 + 4 = \boxed{1}\ \boxed{3}$

$9 + 1 = 10$

$10 + 3 = 13$

1. $9 + 5 = \boxed{}$

_____ + _____ = _____

_____ + _____ = _____

2. $8 + 6 = \boxed{}$

_____ + _____ = _____

_____ + _____ = _____

Write a statement to show your answer.

3. Su-Hean put together a collage with 9 pictures. Adele put together another collage with 6 pictures. How many pictures did they use?

$\underline{9} + \underline{6} = \underline{}$

_____ + _____ = _____

_____ + _____ = _____

4. Imran has 8 crayons in his pencil case and 7 crayons in his desk. How many crayons does Imran have altogether?

_____ + _____ = _____

_____ + _____ = _____

COMMON CORE

Lesson 28: Solve addition problems using ten as a unit, and write two-step solutions.

Date: 7/3/13

2.D.36

5. At the park, there were 4 ducks swimming in the pond. If there were 9 ducks resting on the grass, how many ducks were at the park in all?

_____ + _____ = _____

_____ + _____ = _____

6. Cece made 7 frosted cookies and 8 cookies with sprinkles. How many cookies did Cece make?

7. Payton read 8 books about dolphins and whales. She read 9 books about dogs and cats. How many books did she read about animals altogether?

COMMON CORE | Lesson 28: | Solve addition problems using ten as a unit, and write two-step solutions. | 2.D.37
Date: | 7/3/13

© 2013 Common Core, Inc. All rights reserved. commoncore.org

Name _____   Date _____

Solve the problems. Write your answers to show how many **tens** and **ones**.

$9 + 7 =$ ☐1☐ ☐6☐

$9 + 1 = 10$

$10 + 6 = 16$

1. $8 + 7 =$ ☐ ☐

_____ + _____ = _____

_____ + _____ = _____

2. $9 + 4 =$ ☐ ☐

_____ + _____ = _____

_____ + _____ = _____

COMMON CORE™

Lesson 28:   Solve addition problems using ten as a unit, and write two-step solutions.
Date: 7/3/13

2.D.38

Name _____   Date _____

Solve the problems. Write your answers to show how many **tens** and **ones**.

> 9 + 3 = | 1 | 2 |
>
> 9 + 1 = 10
>
> 10 + 2 = 12

1.   9 + 7 = [ ][ ]

2.   8 + 5 = [ ][ ]

____ + ____ = ____   ____ + ____ = ____

____ + ____ = ____   ____ + ____ = ____

Solve. Write the two number sentences for each step to show how you make **a ten**.

3. Boris has 9 board games on his shelf and 8 board games in his closet. How many
    board games does Boris have altogether?

____ + ____ = ____

____ + ____ = ____

4. Sabra built a tower with 8 blocks. Yuri put together another tower with 7 blocks.
    How many blocks did they use?

5. Camden solved 6 addition word problems. She also solved 9 subtraction word problems. How many word problems did she solve altogether?

_____

6. Minna made 4 bracelets and 8 necklaces with her beads. How many pieces of jewelry did Minna make?

_____

7. I put 5 peaches into my bag at the farmer's market. If I already had 7 apples in my bag, how many pieces of fruit did I have in all?

COMMON CORE | Lesson 28: Solve addition problems using ten as a unit, and write two-step solutions.
Date: 7/3/13

2.D.40

Lesson 29

Objective: Solve subtraction problems using ten as a unit, and write two-step solutions.

Suggested Lesson Structure

■ Fluency Practice   (15 minutes)
■ Application Problem   (5 minutes)
□ Concept Development   (30 minutes)
■ Student Debrief   (10 minutes)
   Total Time   **(60 minutes)**

Fluency Practice (15 minutes)

- Say Ten: 5-group Column **1.NBT.2**   (3 minutes)
- Magic Counting Sticks **1.OA.6**   (4 minutes)
- Happy Counting by Fives **1.OA.5**   (3 minutes)
- Take from Ten Subtraction **1.OA.6**   (5 minutes)

Say Ten: 5-group Columns (3 minutes)

Materials: (T) 5-group column cards from G1–M2–Lesson 27

Note: This fluency activity reviews the unit of 1 ten as a 5-group column, which was introduced in yesterday's lesson.

   T: (Hold up the card showing 13.) Tell me how many, the Say Ten way.
   S: Ten 3.
   T: How many tens?
   S: 1 ten.
   T: How many ones?
   S: 3 ones.

Repeat this process and alternate between requesting that students respond the Say Ten way and saying the number of tens and ones.

COMMON CORE   Lesson 29:   Solve subtraction problems using ten as a unit, and write   2.D.41
                                       two-step solutions.
                         Date: 7/3/13

© 2013 Common Core, Inc. All rights reserved. commoncore.org

Magic Counting Sticks (4 minutes)

Materials: (T) Hide Zero cards

Note: This activity reviews decomposing teen numbers in order to subtract.

> T: (Divide students into partners. Show 15 with Hide Zero cards.) Partner A, show the ones. Partner B, show the tens. How many ones are in 15?
>
> S: 5.
>
> T: How many tens?
>
> S: 1.
>
> T: If I wanted to subtract 2, which partner should do it?
>
> S: Partner A.
>
> T: Yes. Subtract 2 from 15. What number do you see?
>
> S: 13.

Alternate partners and continue with the suggested sequence: $12 - 2$, $13 - 1$, $14 - 2$, $14 - 3$, $15 - 3$, $16 - 4$, etc. Differences should be between 10 and 19.

Happy Counting: by Fives (3 minutes)

Note: This maintenance fluency reviews adding and subtracting 5.

Do the Happy Counting activity from G1–M2–Lesson 4, counting by fives from 0 to 40 and back. First count the Say Ten way, and then count the regular way.

Take from Ten Subtraction (5 minutes)

Materials: (T) Subtract 9 (G1–M2–Lesson 17), Subtract 8 (G1–M2–Lesson 20), and Subtract 7 and 6 flashcards

Note: This activity reviews the take from ten subtraction strategy.

Show a flashcard (e.g., $12 - 8 =$ _____). Play Cold Call, where you flash a card and cold call a student or group of students to answer. If students need additional help subtracting 8, use the following paradigm.

> T: Say 12 the Say Ten way.
>
> S: Ten 2.
>
> T: $10 - 8 =$ _____. (Snap.)
>
> S: 2.
>
> T: $2 + 2 =$ _____. (Point to the 2 on the flashcard, and snap.)
>
> S: 4.
>
> T: So $12 - 8 =$ _____. (Snap.)
>
> S: 4.

Application Problem (5 minutes)

Hae Jung had 13 markers and she gave some to Lily. If Hae Jung then had 5 markers, how many markers did she give to Lily?

Note: Students continue to consider *take apart with addend unknown* problem types in this problem. During the Debrief, students will have the opportunity to apply today's objective to the problem, writing number sentences to show the two steps in the Level 3 strategy of taking from ten.

$$13 - 5 = \boxed{8}$$

She gave Lily 8 markers.

Concept Development (30 minutes)

Materials: (T) Hide Zero cards (from G1–M1–Lesson 38) (S) Personal white boards

Students gather in a semi-circle in the meeting area with their personal white boards.

- T: (Project and read.) Suhani has some presents left to open. If she received 13 presents and already opened 8 of them, how many presents does Suhani still need to open? Solve this problem with your partner.

- T: I see that many of you used a subtraction sentence, 13 – 8, to solve this problem. What is 13 – 8? How many presents does Suhani need to open?

- S: 5 presents!

- T: In the number 13, do we have any tens? How many tens do we have?

- S: Yes! 1 ten!

- T: Along with 1 ten, do we have any extra ones? How many?

- S: Yes! 3 ones!

- T: (Hold up the number 13 with Hide Zero cards.) The number 13 is made of 1 ten and 3 ones. (Pull apart the two cards to show the 10 card and the 3 card separately.)

- T: Where should I take 8 from? The 1 ten or the 3 ones?

- S: From the ten.

 T: How many ones are left over when we take 8 from the ten?

 S: 2 ones.

- T: Write down the number sentence to show how we just subtracted 8.

NOTES ON MULTIPLE MEANS OF REPRESENTATION:

Some students may benefit from connecting the abstract number bonds and equations with concrete materials. Linking cubes in sticks of 10 and separated ones, or Rekenreks can be used along with the numbers. Using concrete and abstract representations simultaneously develops stronger mental images. Moving to using the abstract while visualizing the concrete materials can increase students' confidence and math fluency.

MP.7

COMMON CORE

Lesson 29: Solve subtraction problems using ten as a unit, and write two-step solutions.

Date: 7/3/13

2.D.43

MP.7

S: 10 − 8 = 2.

T: (Put down the 10 card and hold up 2 fingers next to the 3 card.)

T: Did we have any extra ones from the starting number?

S: Yes. We had 3 ones.

T: Let's put the ones together. (Continue to hold up 2 fingers and the 3 card.) Write down the number sentence that tells how many ones we have altogether.

S: 2 ones + 3 ones = 5 ones.

T: So when we solve 13 − 8 and got 5, we started with 1 ten and 3 ones. We ended with no tens and 5 ones. Where did the ten go? Turn and talk to your partner. Point to the number sentence that shows how we ended with 0 tens.

S: We don't have a ten anymore because we used it to take away 8. (Point to 10 − 8.)

T: Explain to your partner how we then ended with 5 ones. (Point to 2 + 3 = 5.)

S: We had 2 ones left from 10 − 8 and we still had 3 extra ones, so we added 2 and 3 to get 5.

T: Today, let's write two number sentences each time we solve a problem like this, so we can see how we took away from the ten first, and then added the extra ones.

$$10 - 8 = 2$$
$$2 + 3 = 5$$

NOTES ON MULTIPLE MEANS OF EXPRESSION:

As students explain their thinking, the teacher can support them by recording their strategies, using mathematical number sentences. This helps students make the connection between abstract equations and their oral language.

Repeat the process, having students write two number sentences to show taking way from the ten and adding the extra ones, using the following sequence with *add to with change unknown* and *take apart/put together with addend unknown* problem types: 11 − 5, 12 − 9, 14 − 6, 17 − 8, 16 − 7. If students appear to require more support at the onset, complete the first problem or two as a class.

Note: Some students may find it easier to count back when subtracting. When solving 13 − 8, students may subtract 3 first to make a ten, then subtract 5 more, writing 13 − 3 = 10, 10 − 5 = 5 as their number sentences. This is another efficient Level 3 stratey that uses two steps. However, today you are asking students to record the problems taking from ten first.

Problem Set (10 minutes)

Students should do their personal best to complete the Problem Set within the allotted 10 minutes. For some classes, it may be appropriate to modify the assignment by specifying which problems they work on first. Some problems do not specify a method for solving. Students solve these problems using the RDW approach used for Application Problems.

Lesson 29:   Solve subtraction problems using ten as a unit, and write
              two-step solutions.
Date: 7/3/13   2.D.44

Student Debrief (10 minutes)

Lesson Objective: Solve subtraction problems using ten as a unit, and write two-step solutions.

The Student Debrief is intended to invite reflection and active processing of the total lesson experience.

Invite students to review their solutions for the Problem Set. They should check work by comparing answers with a partner before going over answers as a class. Look for misconceptions or misunderstandings that can be addressed in the Debrief. Guide students in a conversation to debrief the Problem Set and process the lesson.

You may choose to use any combination of the questions below to lead the discussion.

- Look at Problem 7 in your Problem Set. How many tens do you have left? Explain how we started with 1 ten and some ones and ended with 0 tens and some ones.

- How is Problem 6 different from the rest of the problems in your Problem Set? How did you solve Problem 6 using two number sentences? Explain why we still have 1 ten as a part of your answer.

- In what new way did we solve subtraction problems today?

- How can you solve today's Application Problem using two number sentences so we can see how we took away from the ten first, and then added the extra ones?

Exit Ticket (3 minutes)

After the Student Debrief, instruct students to complete the Exit Ticket. A review of their work will help you assess the students' understanding of the concepts that were presented in the lesson today and plan more effectively for future lessons. You may read the questions aloud to the students.

Lesson 29: Solve subtraction problems using ten as a unit, and write two-step solutions.

Date: 7/3/13

2.D.45

© 2013 Common Core, Inc. All rights reserved. **commoncore.org**

Name _____ Date _____

Solve the problems. Write your answers to show how many **tens** and **ones**.

Show your solution in two steps:

Step 1: Write one number sentence to subtract from ten.

Step 2: Write one number sentence to add the remaining parts.

```
┌─────┬─────┐
│  1  │  2  │  - 4 = 8
└─────┴─────┘
  10 - 4 = 6
   6 + 2 = 8
```

1.
```
┌─────┬─────┐
│  1  │  4  │  - 5 = _____
└─────┴─────┘
```

____ - ____ = ____

____ + ____ = ____

2.
```
┌─────┬─────┐
│  1  │  3  │  - 8 = _____
└─────┴─────┘
```

____ - ____ = ____

____ + ____ = ____

3. Tatyana counted 14 frogs. She counted 8 swimming in the pond and the rest sitting on lily pads. How many frogs did she count sitting on lily pads?

```
┌─────────────────────────────┐
│  14  -  8  = ____            │
└─────────────────────────────┘
```

____ - ____ = ____

____ + ____ = ____

4. This week, Maria ate 5 yellow plums and some red plums. If she ate 11 plums in all, how many red plums did Maria eat?

```
┌─────────────────────────────┐
│                             │
│                             │
│                             │
└─────────────────────────────┘
```

____ - ____ = ____

____ + ____ = ____

COMMON CORE™   Lesson 29:   Solve subtraction problems using ten as a unit, and write
                   two-step solutions.
         Date: 7/3/13

2.D.46

5. Some children are on the playground playing tag. Eight are on the swings. If there are 16 children on the playground in all, how many children are playing tag?

____ - ____ = ____

____ + ____ = ____

6. Oziah read some nonfiction books. Then he read 6 fiction books. If he read 18 books altogether, how many nonfiction books did Oziah read?

7. Hadley has 9 buttons on her jacket. She has some more buttons on her shirt. Hadley has a total of 17 buttons on her jacket and shirt. How many buttons does she have on her shirt?

Name _____   Date _____

Solve the problems. Write your answers to show how many **tens** and **ones**.

```
 ┌───┬───┐
 │ 1 │ 2 │  - 5 = 7
 └───┴───┘
   10 - 5 = 5
   5 + 2 = 7
```

1.

```
 ┌───┬───┐
 │ 1 │ 5 │  - 6 = _____
 └───┴───┘
```

____ - ____ = ____

____ + ____ = ____

2.

```
 ┌───┬───┐
 │ 1 │ 4 │  - 8 = _____
 └───┴───┘
```

____ - ____ = ____

____ + ____ = ____

COMMON CORE

Lesson 29:   Solve subtraction problems using ten as a unit, and write
             two-step solutions.
Date: 7/3/13

2.D.48

Name _____ Date _____

Solve the problems. Write your answers to show how many **tens** and **ones**.

1.

$\boxed{1 \; 7} - 8 =$ _____

_____ - _____ = _____

_____ + _____ = _____

2.

$\boxed{1 \; 6} - 7 =$ _____

_____ - _____ = _____

_____ + _____ = _____

Solve. Write the two number sentences for each step to show how you take from **ten**. Remember to put a box around your solution and write a statement.

3. Yvette counted 12 kids at the park. She counted 3 on the playground and the rest playing in the sand. How many kids did she count playing in the sand?

$\boxed{12 - 3 =}$ ___

_____ - _____ = _____

_____ + _____ = _____

4. Eli read some science magazines. Then he read 9 sports magazines. If he read 18 magazines altogether, how many science magazines did Eli read?

COMMON CORE

Lesson 29: Solve subtraction problems using ten as a unit, and write two-step solutions.

Date: 7/3/13

2.D.49

5. On Monday, Paulina checked out 6 whale books and some turtle books from the library. If she checked out 13 books in all, how many turtle books did Paulina check out?

6. Some children are at the park playing soccer. Seven are wearing white shirts. If there are 14 children playing soccer in all, how many children are wearing shirts that are another color?

7. Dante has 9 stuffed animals in his room. The rest of his stuffed animals are in the TV room. Dante has 15 stuffed animals. How many of Dante's stuffed animals are in the TV room?

COMMON CORE | Lesson 29: | Solve subtraction problems using ten as a unit, and write two-step solutions. | 2.D.50
Date: | 7/3/13

© 2013 Common Core, Inc. All rights reserved. commoncore.org

10 - 7	11 - 7
12 - 7	13 - 7
14 - 7	15 - 7
16 - 7	17 - 7
10 – 6	11 – 6

COMMON CORE™

Lesson 29: Solve subtraction problems using ten as a unit, and write two-step solutions.

Date: 7/3/13

12 - 6	13 - 6
14 - 6	15 - 6
16 - 6	

Lesson 29: Solve subtraction problems using ten as a unit, and write two-step solutions.

Date: 7/3/13

2.D.52

Name _____   Date _____

1. Pedro has 8 pennies. Anita has 4 pennies. Olga has 2.

   a. Whose pennies together make ten?

   b. How many pennies do they have in all? Explain your thinking using a math drawing and a number sentence. Complete the statement.

   Pedro, Anita, and Olga have _____ pennies in all.

2. Circle the pairs of numbers that make ten in each problem. Then write the numbers that make the number sentences true. The first one is done for you.

   a. (9) + 5 + (1) = 15   2 + 6 + 8 = ____   4 + 3 + 7 = _____

   b. 8 + 2 + ___ = 15   9 + ____ + 1 = 16   1 + 7 + 9 = 10 + ____

3. Hakop has 6 pennies in a bowl. 9 pennies are in his drawer. How many pennies does Hakop have in all? Explain how you know with a labeled math drawing and number sentence. Complete the statement.

Hakop has _____ pennies in all.

4. Write a number bond in each number sentence to show how to make ten.

   a. 9 + 5 = 14

   b. 8 + 5 = 13

   c. 6 + 9 = 15

   d. 17 = 8 + 9

5. Eva has 6 marbles in her hand and 8 in her pocket.

a. Two students drew the pictures below to show how they found out how many pennies Eva has. Label their drawings with P and H for Pocket and Hand. Write a number sentence to go with each drawing.

b. True or false: You have to start with 6 marbles and then add the 8 marbles. (Circle one.)   **True   False**
Use pictures or words to explain how you know.

c. Draw and label two other ways to find the number of Eva's marbles that show how to make ten. Write a number sentence for each.

d. Jerry has 4 pennies in his pocket and 10 in his hand. Explain how it is that Jerry and Eva have the same number of pennies. Use words, math drawings, and numbers.

Mid-Module Assessment Task Standards Addressed	Topic A

Represent and solve problems involving addition and subtraction.

1.OA.1   Use addition and subtraction within 20 to solve word problems involving situations of adding to, taking from, putting together, taking apart, and comparing, with unknowns in all positions, e.g., by using objects, drawings, and equations with a symbol for the unknown number to represent the problem.

1.OA.2   Solve word problems that call for addition of three whole numbers whose sum is less than or equal to 20, e.g., by using objects, drawings, and equations with a symbol for the unknown number to represent the problem.

Understand and apply properties of operations and the relationship between addition and subtraction.

1.OA.3   Apply properties of operations as strategies to add and subtract. (Students need not use formal terms for these properties.) *Examples: If 8 + 3 = 11 is known, then 3 + 8 = 11 is also known. (Commutative property of addition.) To add 2 + 6 + 4, the second two numbers can be added to make a ten, so 2 + 6 + 4 = 2 + 10 = 12. (Associative property of addition.)*

Add and subtract within 20.

1.OA.6   Add and subtract within 20, demonstrating fluency for addition and subtraction within 10. Use strategies such as counting on; making ten (e.g., 8 + 6 = 8 + 2 + 4 = 10 + 4 = 14); decomposing a number leading to a ten (e.g., 13 − 4 = 13 − 3 − 1 = 10 − 1 = 9); using the relationship between addition and subtraction (e.g., knowing that 8 + 4 = 12, one knows 12 − 8 = 4); and creating equivalent but easier or known sums (e.g., adding 6 + 7 by creating the known equivalent 6 + 6 + 1 = 12 + 1 = 13).

Evaluating Student Learning Outcomes

A Progression Toward Mastery is provided to describe steps that illuminate the gradually increasing understandings that students develop *on their way to proficiency.* In this chart, this progress is presented from left (Step 1) to right (Step 4). The learning goal for each student is to achieve Step 4 mastery. These steps are meant to help teachers and students identify and celebrate what the student CAN do now, and what they need to work on next.

A Progression Toward Mastery				
Assessment Task Item	STEP 1 Little evidence of reasoning without a correct answer. (1 Point)	STEP 2 Evidence of some reasoning without a correct answer. (2 Points)	STEP 3 Evidence of some reasoning with a correct answer or evidence of solid reasoning with an incorrect answer. (3 Points)	STEP 4 Evidence of solid reasoning with a correct answer. (4 Points)
1 1.OA.1 1.OA.2	The student is unable to complete either question accurately.	The student correctly answers one question, but may not explain his thinking adequately.	The student correctly answers both questions but fails to explain using a math drawing, number sentence, and complete statement. Or, the student explains his thinking using a math drawing, number sentence, and complete statement, but answers one or both questions incorrectly.	The student correctly: • Identifies that Olga and Pedro's pennies together make ten. • Finds the total number of pennies. • Explains his thinking using a math drawing, number sentence and complete statement.
2 1.OA.3 1.OA.6	The student solves for one unknown correctly or is unable to complete the task.	The student solves for up to four of the unknowns incorrectly but circles the pairs of ten.	The student may solve for the unknown in each equation, but fails to circle the pairs that make ten or solves for one unknown incorrectly.	The student correctly: • Solves for the unknown in each equation. • Circles the pairs that make ten.
3 1.OA.1	The student's answer is incorrect and there is no evidence of reasoning.	The student's answer is incorrect but there is evidence of reasoning. For example, the student is able to write a number sentence or draw 5-groups.	The student's answers are correct but his response is incomplete, possibly missing labels for the drawing or an addition sentence, but the work is essentially strong.	The student correctly: • Finds there are 15. • Correctly draws and labels. • Writes a corresponding number sentence.

A Progression Toward Mastery

4 **1.OA.3** **1.OA.6**	The student is unable to draw number bonds that demonstrate the make ten strategy.	The student draws one or two of the number bonds correctly, showing how to make ten.	The student draws three out of the four number bonds correctly, showing how to make ten.	The student correctly: • Draws a number bond for each of the four problems, showing how to make ten.
5 **1.OA.1** **1.OA.2** **1.OA.3** **1.OA.6**	The student's answers are incorrect and there is no evidence of reasoning.	The student's answers are incorrect but there is evidence of reasoning. For example, the student is able to write a number sentence.	The student's answers are correct but the responses are incomplete (e.g., may be missing labels for the drawing, an addition sentence, or may lack explanation). The student's work is essentially strong.	The student correctly: • Labels the student drawings and writes a number sentence for each. • Identifies the statement as false, and explains why citing the commutative property with pictures or words (no formal terms necessary). • Draws to show how to make ten to solve the problem. • Explains how they have the same number of pennies.

Name **Maria**   Date _____

1. Pedro has 8 pennies. Anita has 4 pennies. Olga has 2.

   a. Whose pennies together make ten?

   Pedro   **Olga**

   b. How many pennies do they have in all? Explain your thinking using a math drawing and a number sentence. Complete the statement.

   $10 + 4 = 14$

   Pedro, Anita and Olga have __14__ pennies in all.

2. Circle the pairs of numbers that make ten in each problem. Then write the numbers that make the number sentences true. The first one is done for you.

   a.   ⑨+ 5 +① = __15__   ②+ 6 +⑧ = __16__   4 +③+⑦ = __14__

   b.   ⑧+②+ __5__ = 15   ⑨+ __6__ +① = 16   ①+ 7 +⑨ = 10 + __7__

3. Hakop has 6 pennies in a bowl. 9 pennies are in his drawer. How many pennies does Hakop have in all? Explain how you know with a labeled math drawing and number sentence. Complete the statement.

$9 + 6 = 15$

Hakop has _15_ pennies in all.

4. Write a number bond in each number sentence to show how to make ten.

    a.   9 + 5 = 14

          1   4

    b.   8 + 5 = 13

          2   3

    c.   6 + 9 = 15

          5   1

    d.   17 = 8 + 9

          7   1

5. Eva has 6 marbles in her hand and 8 in her pocket.

  a. Two students drew the pictures below to show how they found out how many
     pennies Eva has. Label their drawings with P and H for Pocket and Hand. Write
     a number sentence to go with each drawing.

$8 + 6 = 14$

$6 + 8 = 14$

  b. True or false: You have to start with 6 marbles and then add the 8 marbles.
     (Circle one.)   True   (False)
     Use pictures or words to explain how you know.

You can start with eether as long
as you add them all.

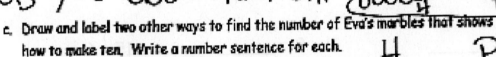

  c. Draw and label two other ways to find the number of Eva's marbles that shows
     how to make ten. Write a number sentence for each.

$10 + 4 = 14$

$10 + 4 = 14$

  d. Jerry has 4 pennies in his pocket and 10 in his hand. Explain how it is that Jerry
     and Eva have the same number of pennies. Use words, math drawings, and
     numbers.

$4 + 10 = 14$ $14 = 14$

$8 + 6 = 14$

Name _____   Date _____

1. Mr. Baggy owns a pet store.

   He counted 10 goldfish in a big tank and 5 goldfish in a small tank. He sold 8 goldfish out of the big tank. How many goldfish did he have left in all? Explain your answer using a labeled math drawing and a number sentence.

   Mr. Baggy had _____ goldfish.

2. Write the numbers that make the number sentences true.

   a.   12 – 9 = _____   11 – 8 = _____   15 – 6 = _____

   b.   9 + _____ = 13   8 + _____ = 12   12 = _____ + 7

   c. Write a related subtraction fact for each of the three problems in the last row in the spaces below.

   _____   _____   _____

3. Write a number bond in each number sentence to show how to use ten to subtract.
   Draw 5-groups and some ones to show each subtraction sentence.

   a. 13 – 9 = 4

   b. 12 – 8 = 4

   c. Use your pictures and numbers to explain how both subtraction problems equal 4.

4. Mr. Baggy also has 9 birds, 15 snakes and 12 turtles.

   a. Show the number of snakes as a ten and some ones with a number bond, a 5-group drawing, and a number sentence.

b. Mr. Baggy sold some snakes. Now he has 5. How many snakes did he sell? Explain your solution using a number bond or a math drawing. Write a number sentence. Complete the statement.

Mr. Baggy sold _____ snakes.

c. Mr. Baggy sold 8 turtles. How many turtles does he have left? Explain your solution using a number bond or a math drawing. Write a number sentence. Complete the statement.

Mr. Baggy has _____ turtles left.

d. Mr. Baggy's daughter says she can find the number of turtles Mr. Baggy has left using subtraction or addition. Show 2 ways Mr. Baggy's daughter can solve this problem.

e. As Mr. Baggy gets ready to close his pet store for the day, he needs to know how many animals he has altogether. How many birds, snakes, and turtles does Mr. Baggy have left in his store altogether? Explain your solution using number bonds or math drawings. Write a number sentence. Complete the statement.

Mr. Baggy has _____ animals left.

f. True or false: You will get a different answer if you add 9 and 5 first, then add 4, than if you add 9 and 4 first, then add 5. (Circle one.)   **True**   **False**

Use pictures or words to show how you know.

End-of-Module Assessment Task
Standards Addressed

Topics A–D

Represent and solve problems involving addition and subtraction.

1.OA.1   Use addition and subtraction within 20 to solve word problems involving situations of adding to, taking from, putting together, taking apart, and comparing, with unknowns in all positions, e.g., by using objects, drawings, and equations with a symbol for the unknown number to represent the problem.

1.OA.2   Solve word problems that call for addition of three whole numbers whose sum is less than or equal to 20, e.g., by using objects, drawings, and equations with a symbol for the unknown number to represent the problem.

Understand and apply properties of operations and the relationship between addition and subtraction.

1.OA.3   Apply properties of operations as strategies to add and subtract. (Students need not use formal terms for these properties.) *Examples: If 8 + 3 = 11 is known, then 3 + 8 = 11 is also known. (Commutative property of addition.) To add 2 + 6 + 4, the second two numbers can be added to make a ten, so 2 + 6 + 4 = 2 + 10 = 12. (Associative property of addition.)*

1.OA.4   Understand subtraction as an unknown-addend problem. *For example, subtract 10 − 8 by finding the number that makes 10 when added to 8.*

Add and subtract within 20.

1.OA.6   Add and subtract within 20, demonstrating fluency for addition and subtraction within 10. Use strategies such as counting on; making ten (e.g., 8 + 6 = 8 + 2 + 4 = 10 + 4 = 14); decomposing a number leading to a ten (e.g., 13 − 4 = 13 − 3 − 1 = 10 − 1 = 9); using the relationship between addition and subtraction (e.g., knowing that 8 + 4 = 12, one knows 12 − 8 = 4); and creating equivalent but easier or known sums (e.g., adding 6 + 7 by creating the known equivalent 6 + 6 + 1 = 12 + 1 = 13).

Understand place value.

1.NBT.2   Understand that the two digits of a two-digit number represent amounts of tens and ones. Understand the following as special cases:

     a.   10 can be thought of as a bundle of ten ones—called a "ten."

     b.   The numbers from 11 to 19 are composed of a ten and one, two, three, four, five, six, seven, eight, or nine ones.

Evaluating Student Learning Outcomes

A Progression Toward Mastery is provided to describe steps that illuminate the gradually increasing understandings that students develop *on their way to proficiency.* In this chart, this progress is presented from left (Step 1) to right (Step 4). The learning goal for each student is to achieve Step 4 mastery. These steps are meant to help teachers and students identify and celebrate what the student CAN do now, and what they need to work on next.

A Progression Toward Mastery

Assessment Task Item	STEP 1 Little evidence of reasoning without a correct answer. (1 Point)	STEP 2 Evidence of some reasoning without a correct answer. (2 Points)	STEP 3 Evidence of some reasoning with a correct answer or evidence of solid reasoning with an incorrect answer. (3 Points)	STEP 4 Evidence of solid reasoning with a correct answer. (4 Points)
1 **1.OA.1**	The student's drawing and number sentence are completely unrelated to the problem, showing no understanding of the problem.	The student has the incorrect answer but shows some understanding through drawings or number sentences.	The student answers correctly (7), but is missing the drawing or the number sentence. Or the student draws a picture or number sentences to show her thinking, but has an incorrect answer.	The student correctly: • Answers 7. • Explains using a drawing and a number sentence (i.e., 2 + 5 = 7 or 10 − 8 = 2).
2 **1.OA.3** **1.OA.4** **1.OA.6**	The student answers one to two answers problems correctly, demonstrating a limited understanding of the problems.	For each problem, the student: • Subtracts from a teen number, • Finds the missing addend, • Writes the corresponding subtraction sentences, with three or four calculation errors.	For each problem, the student: • Subtracts from a teen number, • Finds the missing addend, • Writes the corresponding subtraction sentences, with one or two calculation errors.	For each problem, the student correctly: • Subtracts from a teen number. • Finds the missing addend. • Writes the corresponding subtraction sentences.
3 **1.OA.3** **1.OA.6**	The student is not able to correctly accomplish any component of the task, demonstrating a lack of understanding of the problems.	The student may show some understanding and skill with 5-group drawings but is unable to execute the bonds or explain his thinking. Or, the student is able to show the bonds, but is unable to draw the 5-groups or explain appropriately.	The student draws the bonds and 5-groups but is unable to explain how both have an answer of 4. Or the student explains well, and draws 5-groups well, but does not execute the bonds accurately.	The student correctly: • Models the number bonds and 5-group drawings. • Explains how both problems equal 4 using pictures or numbers (i.e., 1 + 3 = 2 + 2).

A Progression Toward Mastery

| 4

1.OA.1
1.OA.2
1.OA.3
1.OA.4
1.OA.6
1.NBT.2a
1.NBT.2b | Answers one or fewer questions correctly, and is unable to show work, thus demonstrating a lack of understanding of the concepts. | Answers two of the questions correctly with all accompanying models, but demonstrates inconsistent understanding of the take from ten strategy, the connection between addition and subtraction, or the associative property. | Answers three of the four questions correctly and with all requested models and number sentences.

Computes and explains the final question, but may have errors in previous computations that impact accuracy (i.e., 1 or 2 off). | The student correctly:

• Represents 15 with a number bond, 5-group drawing, and number sentence.

• Explains that 10 birds were sold.

• Explains that 4 turtles are left.

• Writes both an addition and subtraction equation $12 - 8 = 4$ and $8 + 4 = 12$.

• Explains that 18 animals are left altogether. Identifies the statement as false, and explains why citing the associative property with pictures or words (no formal terms necessary). |

1. Mr. Baggy owns a pet store.
   He counted 10 goldfish in a big tank and 5 goldfish in a small tank. He sold 8
   goldfish out of the big tank. How many goldfish did he have left in all? Explain your
   answer using a labeled math drawing and a number sentence.

$$2 + 5 = 7$$

Mr. Baggy had ____7____ goldfish.

2. Write the numbers that make the number sentences true.

   a. $12 - 9 =$ __3__ $11 - 8 =$ __3__ $15 - 6 =$ __9__

        10 ∧ 2 $1 + 2$ 10 ∧ 1 $2 + 1$ 10 ∧ 5 $4 + 5$

   b. $9 +$ __4__ $= 13$ $8 +$ __4__ $= 12$ $12 =$ __5__ $+ 7$

   c. Write a related subtraction fact for each of the three problems in the last row
   in the spaces below.

   __$13 - 9 = 4$__   __$12 - 8 = 4$__   __$12 - 7 = 5$__

3. Write a number bond in each number sentence to show how to use ten to subtract. Draw 5-groups and some ones to show each subtraction sentence.

c. Use your pictures and numbers to explain how both subtraction problems equal 4.

$$ 1 + 3 = 2 + 2 $$

$$ 10-9 \qquad\qquad 10-8 $$

$$ 4 = 4 $$

4. Mr. Baggy also has 9 birds, 15 snakes and 12 turtles.

a. Show the number of snakes as a ten and some ones with a number bond, a 5-group drawing and a number sentence.

$$ 15 = 10 + 5 $$

15 number bond: 10 and 5

OOOOO OOOOO OOOOO → 15

b. Mr. Baggy sold some snakes. Now he has 5. How many snakes did he sell? Explain your solution using a number bond or a math drawing. Write a number sentence. Complete the statement.

$15 - \boxed{} = 5$

$15 - 5 = \boxed{10}$

Mr. Baggy sold __10__ snakes.

c. Mr. Baggy sold 8 turtles. How many turtles does he have left? Explain your solution using a number bond or a math drawing. Write a number sentence. Complete the statement.

$12 - 8 = 4$

10   2   2 + 2

OO ~~OOO~~ ~~OOOO~~ OO

Mr. Baggy has __4__ turtles left.

d. Mr. Baggy's daughter says she can find the number of turtles Mr. Baggy has left using subtraction or addition. Show 2 ways Mr. Baggy's daughter can solve this problem.

$8 + \boxed{} = 12$ $12 - 8 = \boxed{}$

e. As Mr. Baggy gets ready to close his pet store for the day, he needs to know how many animals he has altogether. How many birds, snakes and turtles does Mr. Baggy have left in his store altogether? Explain your solution using number bonds or math drawings. Write a number sentence. Complete the statement.

$$10 + 8 = 18$$ Mr. Baggy has __18__ animals left.

f. True or false: You will get a different answer if you add 9 and 5 first, then add 4, than if you add 9 and 4 first, then add 5. (Circle one.)   True   (False)
Use pictures or words to show how you know.

ooooooooo• •••••o ooo
$$9 + 5 = 14$$ $$14 + 4 = \text{(18)}$$

oooooooooo• •••oo ooo
$$9 + 4 = 13$$ $$13 + 5 = \text{(18)}$$

Your just starting with a difrent number, but your adding them all.